PRAISE F

"Jennifer Barclay takes the rea~~der on a delightful meander~~ ~~, journey~~ along paths less well trodden in the Dodecanese. She is an engaging travelling companion whose knowledge of and affection for the islands she holds dear shines through. *Wild Abandon* is a must read for anyone who loves the Greek Islands."

**Richard Clark, author of *The Lost Lyra*
and *The Greek Islands Notebook***

"I loved it, it's a magical book; and so great to be taken beyond the tourist enclaves by someone who knows these islands and their history so well. Barclay travels and writes with wonderful energy, affection and honesty and I was transported to the dusty tracks and into the cool waves with her and her dog Lisa. She travels with a brave freedom that so many of us will envy – a three-day journey to one island turning into a year and a half – and this allows her to dig beneath the surface and tell us the stories, the real stories, of these out-of-the-way places that take time to emerge. Highly recommended."

Iain Campbell, author *From the Lion's Mouth*

"I devoured it – a truly gorgeous book, full of abandoned buildings, hidden trails and precious ways of life in remote places."

Greek Island Dreaming

"Part travel memoir, part history book, part ode to a lost way of living. Her poignant prose is at once an education in the history of these islands, but also makes you reconsider how you travel. There's much to see and do in well-known places, but there's also something magical, sad, yet delightful in discovering an almost forgotten, faraway place. One that rescues us – even for a little while – away from the rat race and into a simpler, more meaningful, unrestricted life."

Maria Karamitsos, *Windy City Greek* magazine

AUTHOR BIOGRAPHY

Jennifer Barclay grew up in a village in the north of England; she lived for a year in Athens and has travelled widely in the Greek islands. She worked in Canada, France and England as a literary agent and editor before going freelance and settling on Tilos, a small island in the Dodecanese. She has written a book about Korea, *Meeting Mr Kim*, and two books about Greek island life, *Falling in Honey* and *An Octopus in my Ouzo*. A contributor to publications including the Bradt travel anthologies *The Irresponsible Traveller* and *Roam Alone* as well as *The Times*, *Metro*, *The Guardian*, *Daily Mail*, *Food* and *Travel* and *Psychologies*, she has also appeared on BBC Radio 4, Australian national radio and Korean and Greek television. For more information including a link to photographs of places in *Wild Abandon*, please visit: www.octopus-in-my-ouzo.blogspot.com.

ACKNOWLEDGEMENTS

It's an honour to be published by Bradt, and a pleasure to work with such a great team. I'm extremely grateful to Samantha Cook for making this a much better book and for being the nicest editor I could wish for. Big thanks to Caroline Hardman for the initial encouragement, to all the people who appear in the book, and to the friends who helped me with the journey, including Ian, David, Yiannis, Anna, Charlie and Minas. For your love and support, thanks to my mum, dad and brother, the rest of my family, the lovely Lisa and Mark. And thanks to you, reader, for picking up this book. I hope you like it.

Wild ABANDON

A JOURNEY TO THE DESERTED PLACES OF THE DODECANESE

JENNIFER BARCLAY

Bradt

First published in the UK in July 2020 by
Bradt Travel Guides Ltd
31a High Street, Chesham, HP5 1BW, England
www.bradtguides.com

Print edition published in the USA by The Globe Pequot Press Inc,
PO Box 480, Guilford, Connecticut 06437-0480

Text copyright © 2020 Jennifer Barclay
Edited by Samantha Cook
Cover illustration by Neil Gower
Layout and typesetting by Ian Spick
Map by David McCutcheon FBCart.S
With thanks to Sarah Dickinson
Production managed by Sue Cooper, Bradt & Jellyfish Print Solutions

ISBN: 978 1 78477 696 1

British Library Cataloguing in Publication Data
A catalogue record for this book is available from the British Library
Digital conversion by www.dataworks.co.in
Printed in the UK

If you pull Greece apart, at the end you'll see that what
is left is an olive tree, a vine and a boat. Which means
with these, you can rebuild.

Odysseus Elytis, winner of the
Nobel Prize for Literature 1979

NOTE ON USE OF GREEK

Because the Greek alphabet is different to the Roman, there's no standard or perfect system of spelling Greek words with English letters. In general, I spell words more or less as they sound (Ayios rather than Agios, Halki rather than Chalki), except where it would look too unusual. As there is no 'c' in Greek, the letters 'c' and 'k' are generally interchangeable in transliteration, so Kastellorizo can also be spelled Castellorizo.

Male Greek names frequently end in -s when they're the subject of a sentence (Michalis) but drop the -s in the vocative form, ie: when you are addressing a person ('Michali!'), and in other forms. For simplicity, when I'm writing in English I use the -s form, except in speech.

I've used the English Rhodes rather than Rodhos and omitted any accents on island names.

I've used 'America' to translate the Greek Ameriki, although technically it's referring to North America.

CONTENTS

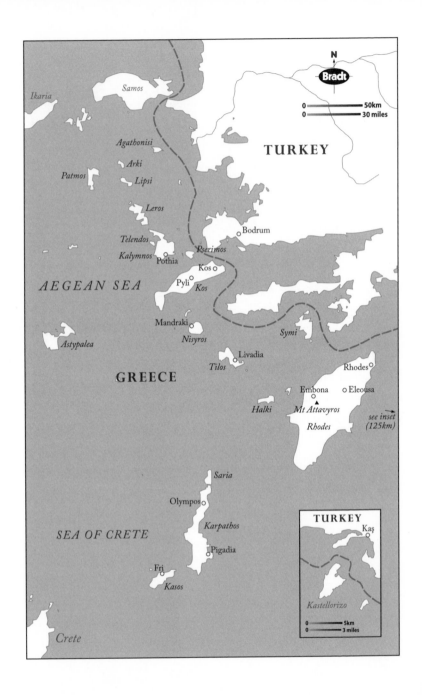

INTRODUCTION

At the end of my trip back to Britain, my mum and I learn the radio news off by heart as we listen repeatedly to how traffic on our part of the motorway is moving very slowly due to accidents and weather. Then we drive around and around an almost-full multi-storey car park at the airport, paying to look for space. We finally laugh about it over coffee, testing one another on the news items. I'm on my way home.

After a flight to Rhodes at the eastern reaches of the Greek archipelago, the edge of Europe, I'll take a ferry between Greek islands and Turkish promontories to a small island called Tilos, with a winter population of around three hundred. Once the ferry departs, there will be little noise except the waves. I'll listen to the silence.

If you can hear traffic or air traffic now, erase it. Turn off any television or radio, any devices that hum or beep. Replace them with the rhythmic stroke of sea on pebbles, or with the cry of a goat or the hoot of an owl.

Tilos, where I first moved ten years ago and have come to call home, is in the middle of a group of islands in the South Aegean known as the Dodecanese. The name, *Dodecanisa* in Greek, means 'Twelve Islands', but in fact there are closer to twenty inhabited islands, and maybe a hundred more uninhabited islets, stretching over an area of two thousand six hundred and sixty-three square kilometres: north to Agathonisi, south to Kasos, east to Kastellorizo and west to Astypalea. The largest is Rhodes, followed by Kos and Karpathos.

The rocky landscape is more Middle Eastern than European, and long, dry summers are followed by lush, green winters. This region, where Greece almost touches Turkey, the lands virtually intertwined (and often disputed), was historically a pivotal point in

the Mediterranean, a link between Europe and Asia. It is still busy
with ships plying distant routes, but they no longer have much reason
to stop here except to shelter during rough weather.

The oldest ruins and written accounts show the islands we now
call the Dodecanese were significant in the Ancient Greek world.
Christianity arrived with saints Paul and John in the first century and,
after the Roman Empire split in 395AD, the islands gradually became
part of the Byzantine Empire. Temples devoted to Ancient Greek
gods were rebuilt to become churches.

In 1309 Rhodes was captured by the Knights Hospitaller, or
Knights of St John. The crusaders found this group of islands a useful
base on the route to the Holy Land, and left their mark by building
castles and communication towers.

The Knights were ousted in 1522 by the Ottoman Turks under
Suleiman the Magnificent. Under Ottoman rule, all the islands in
the group except Rhodes and Kos were granted privileges pertaining
to taxation and self-government: the Greek inhabitants of these so-
called 'Privileged Islands' were largely allowed to continue their way of
life so long as they paid their taxes to the Turkish overlords.

Many of the islands fought in the Greek War of Independence
in 1822, expecting to become part of the new kingdom of Greece.
However, when Britain, France and Russia formulated the London
Protocol in 1830, which recognised Greece as an independent state,
the Dodecanese were excluded and remained part of the Ottoman
Empire. It was a terrible blow. Slowly, people began to leave.

Following the 'Young Turk' revolution of 1908, Greeks under
Turkish rule optimistically hoped for greater justice, freedom and

religious tolerance. A wave of patriotism surged, people painting their houses the blue of the Greek flag in anticipation of independence. In the event, the new government instead stripped away the islands' privileges and enforced military service, requiring Greek villagers to join the Turkish army. Those who refused, hiding in the mountains and forests, were hunted down and captured. The only escape was to leave secretly for overseas. Thus began another wave of migration, chiefly to the USA and Australia.

In 1911, war was declared between Italy and Turkey. The following year, Italy took over administration of 'Rhodes and the Dodecanese', which at that point did not include Kastellorizo. Their occupation was initially intended merely to curb Turkey's activities in Libya; they found the Dodecanese strategically useful but were generally benevolent and seen as liberators, planning eventually to cede the islands to Greece.

The islands declared their autonomy as the 'State of the Aegean', with the goal of uniting with Greece, but to no avail. Reacting to various developments in the region, Italy annexed the Dodecanese and, after the 1923 Treaty of Lausanne, set about the policy of 'Italianisation', suppressing Greek culture and language. By 1936, under the Fascist regime, 16,700 Italians had been resettled in the Dodecanese, most of them on Rhodes and Leros. Mussolini initiated grand construction projects, sometimes using enforced Greek labour. The Greek language and history were forbidden in school from 1938 onwards; today many older residents are still fluent in Italian.

During World War II, the islands became battlegrounds. After Italy eventually surrendered to the Allies and Germany assumed control of the islands, the local people resisted however they could. At the end of the war, Germany handed the Dodecanese over to the

British, who officially recognised them as inhabited by Greeks. After seven centuries of occupation, they were granted independence by the international powers in 1947.

The Dodecanese had throughout their history been a meeting point of cultures; economically important, bustling and, if not always thriving, mostly self-sufficient. But between the eighteenth and nineteenth centuries, the effects of brutal wars, natural disasters and oppression by occupiers, combined with cultural change and economic opportunities arising elsewhere, led the islanders to start leaving. As Titsa Pipinou writes in *The Women of the Dodecanese*, 'There is no family without migrants.' Homes, villages, entire islands were deserted.

This dereliction has created the havens of peace and calm we know and love today. Far from the Greek mainland, most people get by here on farming, fishing and tourism, and the smallest islands are sparsely inhabited except in the summer. The landscape is dotted with ruined stone buildings where no-one has lived for decades, offering stories of the past, of ambition and hope and abandonment.

In rural places, there's little obvious difference between buildings from the fifteenth century and those from a hundred years ago. I've always been drawn to the beautiful things left behind from earlier times. Many are gradually reclaimed by nature, which, in the lovely words of Gustave Flaubert in a letter of 1846, comes 'swiftly to bury the work of man the moment his hand is no longer there to defend it'.

By contrast, I'm scared of what we've left behind in the last few decades. There's something about seeing a plastic toilet brush, toothbrush, clothes peg or drinking straw washed up on a beach that makes you question things you use every day. Sometimes what washes up is plastic confetti: multi-coloured scraps from objects no longer identifiable. Today's detritus is often detrimental to the landscape; when it starts to blend with the wild, it's terrifying.

In this journey I am seeking the goodness and beauty of the abandoned ways of living, connecting with the past. I'm finding a refuge from the noise of contemporary life and, in these small and seemingly insignificant places, potential for renewal and regeneration.

Exploring abandoned places often means immersing myself in the wild: pulling myself up a near-vertical hillside to find ruins, walking across an island bathed in silver moonlight, standing on a volcanic crater breathing in the sulphurous heat of the earth's pores. I've learned that I'd rather get a few scratches and scrapes than be complacent and bored.

From the age of five, I lived in a village in Saddleworth on the edge of the moors in northern England's Pennine hills. I could walk out of our house straight into the countryside. In the nineteenth century the area had been home to a thriving cotton-weaving industry; it was now a place of empty mills and disused canals, stone barns and drystone walls, space and solitude. When we moved to southern England, when I was seventeen, I missed those hills. My dad grew up in Scotland and I recall family holidays on sheep farms in the Highlands, swimming in the river, staying in a stone cottage far from the nearest road. Later we started travelling to Greece as a family, and I spent a year after university working in Athens where I would take the elevator up to the top floor of my apartment building to see the hills and the sea, and ships going places. I took ferries to islands for weekends and holidays, plunging into the sea all year round on windswept beaches, hitchhiking and roaming alone in mountains.

I spent the best part of two decades travelling and living in different countries. And whenever I've stayed long in a city, I've needed to escape into rugged, empty country. Returning to England, I settled for work in a town between the chalk ridge of the South Downs and the English Channel. I walked and cycled up to an Iron Age hill fort or to areas of woodland where I encountered deer. I woke to the sound of traffic but could cross the ring road and wander through fields. One winter, walking a long-distance footpath and discovering new landscapes, I realised that spending time outdoors was more important to me than anything else. Soon after, I came to live on Tilos. Now, no longer restrained by office hours, walking in the hills stimulates my brain when it feels dull. And my Rhodes-born dog Lisa, part golden retriever, part local hunting dog, loves a new walk as much as I do.

This project of exploring the abandoned places of the Dodecanese started with a thought I had while on Nisyros in spring 2015, when I first saw its almost deserted villages on the rim of the volcano, and the churches built by islanders who had emigrated to America. I began thinking about how much changed, and how dramatically, over the course of a century in most cases. I set out to learn more by exploring different islands, and revisiting places I already knew to look deeper. As I travelled, I started to see patterns emerging, to recognise what I was looking at and to observe the details local to each place. My interest reached the point of obsession as I searched out ruined and deserted places to poke my nose into. Even as I finally tried to pull the book together in 2019, casually looking inside some abandoned houses at the edge of my own village, I found elements of these buildings that I'd never noticed before although they had been right under my nose. I knew I was only scratching the surface.

Lisa, who came into my life when she was two months old, has helped to shape this journey. With her silky, strawberry blonde hair and dark brown, kohl-rimmed eyes, floppy ears and tail like a pale feather boa, she's a beauty. And she loves attention. Travelling is often trickier with a dog, but Lisa helps me meet people and sometimes takes me further than I'd otherwise go.

As this Dodecanese journey took place over several years, Lisa and I were often joined by different companions; in these pages I refer to most fellow travellers simply as 'my friend' to keep the focus on what we found along the way.

The discoveries I've described here are incomplete – I could have continued forever – and my conclusions surely flawed in places, but it's an authentic journey and a labour of love, a simple tale of my travels in some deserted places of the Dodecanese. I'm glad there are more still to explore.

GHOSTS AND GOATS
TILOS

The empty shells of ruined stone houses cling to the hillside above. Lisa half-pulls me up the road and then the footpath, rose-and-grey slabs worn smooth with age. It's a winter day and dark clouds augur rain but there are patches of blue sky. I pick my way carefully up an overgrown, rubble-strewn path while Lisa sniffs excitedly at animal tracks.

Plaster is cracked and falling away from grey and flesh-coloured walls. Roofs are missing, as if the village had been bombed. Doorways and windows are empty gaps, the wood taken to be used elsewhere, and trees grow within stone walls. Many houses have a name or initials spray-painted on their exterior, an island way of asserting ownership. Mikro Horio, 'Small Village', was once home to 2,500 people, built inland many centuries ago to be largely hidden from the sea and from pirates. It was abandoned half a century ago.

Passing long-neglected olive and wild pear trees, I stop to look at a massive carved rock, the size of a dining table, smoothed flat on top for crushing grain or olives; after lying on the ground for generations, it would function just as well today. Here and there is a domed outdoor oven, or a channel to direct rainwater from the roof to a cistern in the ground; Mikro Horio never had much water. At the top of the village, among stone field enclosures I find a threshing circle: a couple of metres in diameter, these flat areas encircled by slabs of rock were used most likely from antiquity until the nineteenth century for threshing wheat, drying fruit, slaughtering animals, perhaps even dancing – the traditional circular dances still enjoyed today. I climb further and reach the ridge, the spine of the island which drops away steeply on the other side. From up here, the view of terraced fields spreading down the hillside is magnificent, bulging contours describing the shape of the land, stone walls brought into relief by the green of winter.

Though a cold wind blows from the northwest, howling through bare trees, sunlight suddenly picks out the round tower built in the fifteenth century by the crusading Knights of St John. Despite the island's long periods of occupation by foreign powers, there are few other signs here of the overseers' influence. During the Italian administration of the early twentieth century, some Tilos residents moved to Rhodes where Greek school was taught secretly in the churches, but there were still close to two thousand people living in Mikro Horio before World War II.

During that war, however, life became harder than ever. 'Look for the bullet holes,' a friend tells me, adding that people don't like to talk about it. Taking hostages to ensure the islanders' compliance, the German army ate through the livestock and imposed curfews and other curbs on freedom that prevented people from looking after their animals and land – their sole means of survival. People suffered severe hunger, their livelihood stripped away. Supply boats were often targeted by enemy attacks. By the time Tilos was liberated and, along with other Dodecanese islands, reunited with Greece (1947–48), the islanders had begun to leave in force. Some, as before, went to Rhodes, others to a district of Athens called Marousi, and some travelled to the USA and Australia as economic refugees. Others simply moved down to the coast, where the area around the port called Livadia, or 'Meadows', expanded.

A young woman called Nikoleta, who I met by chance one day in a shop in Rhodes, told me her family had lived in Livadia and kept their animals in Mikro Horio. Her mother, born in 1945, sang her lullabies in Italian; she remembered her father wore traditional baggy trousers. 'They had no fridge, just kept food in a mesh bag hanging from the rafters. The first time my mother saw a truck, she didn't know what it was.'

In his heartfelt and lyrical account *Tilos in the Past*, Vangelis Papadopoulos, born in Mikro Horio in 1953, recalls a time when the land behind Livadia was fields, tamarisks on the shore protecting crops from the wind, while Mikro Horio still resounded with the voices of children playing after school. The adults brought home the animals at night to feed and water them and keep them away from the crops; they brought wood for the fireplace for cooking, and the houses were lit by oil lamps. There would always be plenty of eggs, milk and cheese. Pork meat was preserved in jars; almonds and carob seeds were collected from the trees, dried and stored for winter. As children, he writes, they helped with the threshing of barley, wheat and peas. It was hard work in the heat of summer. 'But it was work that we had to do. Our life depended on it.' When they made their beds under the stars, they would see aeroplanes passing and hear stories of when bombs dropped during the war. Many people had gone to find work in America or Australia, and those remaining waited for letters to come by boat.

But gradually, people locked up their houses in Mikro Horio and went away, finding life easier elsewhere, until only old people remained. Vangelis's grandparents were among them. It was where they were born and where they wanted to die. His grandfather had helped to build many of the houses in the village, 'And his heart was breaking when they were abandoned.'

The last two remaining inhabitants left in 1964. In his memoir, Iakovos Kypriotis, a teacher who had recently arrived on the island, recalls that the school at Livadia then had 120 students, its numbers boosted by the exodus from Mikro Horio. From then on, he writes, Mikro Horio was 'wrapped in eternal silence'. Livadia, meanwhile, grew around the bay and would become the main settlement when the first few tourists started arriving in the 1970s.

But Mikro Horio was not entirely doomed to eternal silence, although it remained uninhabited. Many visitors would take the footpath up to wander among its ruins. In the middle of August, the church hosts a festival of the Virgin Mary with traditional music and food, a continuation of the rituals that always punctuated the village year. Moreover, one of the houses has been converted into a music bar that opens late at night throughout the summer, with a terrace where people gather and dance under the stars surrounded by the blackness of empty hills and valleys. To complete the ambiance, some of the empty houses are dimly lit inside as if by lamplight (in fact by generator), conjuring an illusion of how the village would once have been.

I open the gate to the walled compound of the restored and well-kept eighteenth-century church of the Dormition of the Virgin to find the grave of a priest who died in 1941, rows of other unmarked graves and a couple of old goat carcasses. Lisa rejoices as she's convinced we're hunting for goats, not deserted places. Maybe it's the same thing; the ghosts and goats are all that's left. A little further down the hill is a small chapel built into the rock; a brass plaque says it's dedicated to Christ the Saviour and dates from 1430. Through the grille in the locked door I see frescoes all around the walls and the ceiling, intricate artwork showing rows of haloed saints and biblical scenes. I walk down the footpath between houses where families lived through so much across the centuries.

Lisa and I continue down into the valley, stopping at the spring that flows through pink rocks, the area covered with wild pink and white cyclamen. The deep-red trail winds over the hill until it overlooks the sea. Down below, the land opens out into old fields below slopes faintly ridged with traces of terraces. A beach of multi-coloured pebbles faces a ridge of mountains across the sea. It looks like another island but is in fact a long finger of Turkey, reaching out into the midst of the Dodecanese.

Summer on Tilos means endless days of limpid sea and cloudless deep blue skies, tavernas filled with holidaymakers, bays busy with sailboats. But winter makes you aware of nature's cycles and the power of the wild. Storms last for days, lightning takes out the electricity, waves thunder in and the ferries that link us to the outside world cannot come so supplies in shops dwindle, post gets delayed. We are at the mercy of the elements.

And after each storm, sunshine returns and streams flow, new wildflowers appearing in the fields and bursting through the footpaths. The temperature is cool enough to walk anywhere, and the island is thrillingly empty. Winds blow away the cobwebs in my mind and even if it looks bleak and desolate I feel alive, renewed by the sense of space.

Islands like this can be tricky to reach; Greece having so many islands, there aren't the resources to run daily ferries all year. This allows for the survival of little outposts of eccentricity and nonconformity; places that haven't been built over and built up but are still endowed with the spirit of the past. The population of Tilos is officially about eight hundred; in reality, only a few hundred live here year-round. The island is known for tranquillity. It's a place where children play football in the square after school and sheep come down to the fields at dusk. Rugged but fertile, it has mostly escaped development by a combination of luck and management. In 1989 the mayor at the time went against the Greek Constitution by imposing a total ban on hunting, establishing a Special Protection Area for wildlife such as Bonelli's eagle and Eleonora's falcon. It's an important stopover for migrating birds such as bee-eaters, and a safe habitat for endangered monk seals and sea turtles.

Approaching or leaving by boat, Tilos can appear to be all sharply triangular hills and jagged, forbidding cliffs; a gnarled land, brown and beige rock, mostly empty, no signs of life. These sixty-four square kilometres of land twist and turn amid steep, rocky inclines concealing places that are rarely frequented these days when people mostly get around by car or truck. If you look closely, there are signs of desertion almost everywhere: broken stone buildings, drystone walls. On the ridge above Livadia are the Pano Meri, the 'Upper Places' or 'High Places', where the ruins of farms left behind decades ago, though still solid with fitted stones and wooden lintels, are fading back into the landscape. Behind many deserted beaches are the overgrown remains of fields from when the island was intensively farmed, when people got around by boat and mule and the paths were well trodden. Tilos thrived agriculturally, having the climate, soil and springs, and was blessed with large bays. From the flat valleys ascending in stepped terraces to the sheer hilltops, every scrap of land was used. The freedom and solitude that drew me to live here would not have been possible even half a century ago. This fascinates me.

On a cold, bright day with waves crashing loudly on to shore, I put on shorts and thermal top and walking boots. Optimistically stuffing a towel in my backpack as well as gloves and a woolly hat, I set off with Lisa along a high coast path to a beach that might be slightly sheltered from the north wind. I undo the ropes and wires securing the gate that keeps the goats out of the village. The first section of path has been repaired unnervingly in places after weather damage and dramatic rockslides. A well-built stone track winds its way up a hillside covered in euphorbia and sage bushes, with expanding views over the deep blue bay, until a small cairn of rocks marks the start of a thin track that leads steeply down among stones and thorny scrub to a striking red cove. I have it to myself at this time of year unless a fishing boat happens to come by.

Out to sea the wind is whipping up whitecaps, but the water doesn't feel too cold. I swim out to the mouth of the bay and then back and forth, enjoying the stretch of muscles, the sensation of being immersed in the cool winter sea while watching afternoon sun on the fresh green of the land. When I get out, the breeze helps me dry. I pull on warm clothes and have such a burst of energy that I run half the way back, letting Lisa pull me up the steep slope. I catch sight of an eagle above, pause to watch the gentle lift of its wingtips and powerful wingspan as it dips and wheels, looking for prey. Home again, I crawl under the duvet for a sleep, before cooking chard with olive oil and lemon from the farmer, fish from the fisherman this morning. At night, I watch the moonlight on the bay and listen to the waves.

At the southern end of Livadia bay, above the little medieval harbour of Ayios Stefanos, the road turns abruptly up to a chapel and a few fields. When I walked here in 2008, I saw intricate wood stacks. Vangelis, who wrote *Tilos in the Past*, was then in his sixties and living in Livadia. He told me he used to make charcoal here in the winter, having learned the skill from his father. 'On an island like this, you must make money where you can. And it's peaceful on the hillside, looking out to sea.' He worked with goats and sheep in the winter, and in the summer helped his children run businesses catering to tourists, happy to meet people who were bringing life back to Tilos. He died in 2012 and today the field is empty, only memories remaining along with grazing goats.

A well-built path winds higher while the sea glints clear and blue and inaccessible far below down sheer slopes. There's a lush gully where a branch of the path heads steeply uphill past an old spring towards Pano Meri, but I continue. Among almond and wild pear and olive trees a handful of old stone houses are crumbling from the roof down. The hillsides are fragrant with sage and thyme. I jump when a handful of partridges, hidden in a bush, rise in a flapping panic before gliding away. In many other places they've disappeared through overhunting.

Around a jutting point a softer landscape suddenly appears, gentle terraces leading down a slope to the former settlement of Gera, where hundreds of people from Mikro Horio would stay while looking after their summer crops – grapes and figs, wheat and barley. Overlooked by the huge limestone crag of Koutsoumbas, around two dozen stone houses stand huddled together with just narrow alleys between them, as if the space was too valuable to be wasted. Even on the forbidding grey rock face opposite, you can just make out narrow ridges of terracing where once every bit of earth was used for cultivation. The houses, deserted for more than half a century, have straight walls, the stones so deftly packed that they needed nothing to bind them, it seems. Large round rocks are carefully arranged around the top to hold the roof in place – though only wooden beams, a chimney and some packed earth remain. A special kind of clay was found here that helped waterproof the houses.

In among them are the occasional fig tree, hardy euphorbia bushes and a prolific, pungent green bush with long, thin leaves. Entering one ruin I realise the roof is still packed with branches of the shrub; I am told later that it's called *glastros* and that even the goats don't eat it – a good choice for a roof. I walk up past a threshing circle to a palm tree where a spring was fed through a pipe, now rusted and no longer flowing, into the tub inscribed '1954'. I continue and see fields, dry yellow grasses golden in the late afternoon light, shaggy sheep grazing wild.

Vangelis's father had a café near the spring, with stones for chairs, where men would gather to enjoy coffee, mastic and wine. This would still have been happening in the 1950s, the era of Coca-Cola, television and rock and roll. Perhaps they'd talk of such things – having heard about them from relatives living far away – as they sat there on a moonlit night.

I've always liked scrabbling around in old stones. I was about eight years old when director John Schlesinger came to shoot part of the World War II film *Yanks*, starring Richard Gere and Vanessa Redgrave, in our village. Schoolchildren were invited to audition as extras and I dutifully joined the queue but returned home filthy at the end of the day, my mother livid as I'd been missing for hours. Instead of waiting, I'd gone to a local quarry with a friend to hunt in the earth for interesting bits of broken pottery.

Thanks to family holidays in Greece and an enthusiastic teacher of Ancient Greek at grammar school, my love of old artefacts grew. While studying English Literature and Language at university, I opted for courses on archaeology and Old English, sifting through fragments of ancient texts. When, aged twenty-one, I moved to

Athens for a year, I spent Sundays at museums or wandering around islands. Pinned to my bedroom walls were postcards of ancient art and photos of sculptures torn from the museum guides. It gave me the shivers when a few years ago, on Tilos, I was allowed to watch an archaeologist unearth a cache of pottery from around 1600BC.

But in this landscape shaped by the things left behind, I also feel drawn to things more recently deserted. There's beauty in the craftsmanship, as well as the stories they tell about the way life was lived for centuries. Change here came abruptly and completely, and so much has been abandoned, even within my lifetime. In busier places, it might have been built over or fenced in, but here it lies exposed to the elements, slowly reclaimed by nature and hidden amid the tough scrub.

There is an island culture of leaving things where they fall, sometimes because they might be used again, sometimes because there's nowhere for them to go. Barbecues are made from discarded boilers and tomato plants protected from birds by torn fishing nets. Where I lived in my first years on Tilos, down a lovely rough track in the dry riverbed, the turn-off was marked (and still is) by a rusted and long-stationary cement mixer. Up the track, below aromatic Mediterranean pines that make a soothing sound in the wind, are the remains of a café-bar, the benches and tables all given up to the elements, as if the owner always thought about opening again but never did. Under a tree in Livadia, a boxy black Mercedes is given up for dead and mysteriously filled to the roof with plastic bottles, like an art installation.

Meanwhile, plastic rubbish from the dump blows across a hillside; unwanted fridges and truck tyres litter an old way through a riverbed. A derelict reservoir lined with a black synthetic material, faulty from the start, mars a valley of farms and olive groves, a waste not only of the money spent but of the land seconded to build it. In the north of the island the water is drinkable year-round, but the summer influx of people in Livadia drains the supply and makes it salty, and most people buy plastic bottles – even in winter. Recycling systems are only just filtering through to the smaller islands.

Winter storms and currents wash things ashore: tar from ships, plastic bottles and bottle caps and 'disposable' coffee cups, all sorts of shoes; plastic sheeting, broken plastic buckets and crates, plastic containers often printed with Turkish lettering. The island designates clean-up days on the main beaches before the start of the summer, so most visitors don't see it.

Yet the things left behind from two thousand years ago, two hundred years ago, even fifty years ago, are often precious, beautiful; they do no harm and exist in harmony with the wild. These artefacts have grace, the simplicity of painstakingly worked stone and wood held together with earth, or shards of terracotta pottery.

One overcast winter day, I find myself on an unfamiliar uphill track in the north of the island which promises great things but degenerates into a barely perceptible path overgrown with *phrygana*, the spiny shrub that thrives in craggy limestone ground, adapted to drought, wind and grazing. Lisa pants and surges forward, leaping over thorny bushes and pulling me through stands of dead trees. I'm not really enjoying it but then I spot some ruined buildings and an old chapel.

Crouching under the heavy rock lintel – the doorway now half-sunk under rubble – I tiptoe over a carpet of goat dung. The walls seem bare but when I look closely into an arched recess, I make out very faint colours of frescoes, the top of a saint's head with a tiny forelock of hair, probably painted several hundred years ago. The fallen, simple altar is made from a column and a slab of marble, a couple of thousand years old. The whole thing will one day crumble into the hillside.

When I emerge, the pale grey day is dappled with sunshine and the green grass liberally dotted with purple, lilac, pink and white anemones. By the time we make it down to the shore at Ayios Antonis, the sun is winning over the clouds. I see a head above water, someone swimming – no, it's a seal. Usually they keep to themselves, unseen in caves and on remote beaches, but they love to find a fisherman's net full of food. It flips, showing its tail, and dives down; surfaces, flips and dives down again as it heads out to sea.

After my first couple of years on Tilos, I moved into the heart of Megalo Horio ('Big Village') when a house with a lemon tree and views of mountains and sea was offered for a small rent. To one side was a home owned by a potter from Crete, who had bought a ruin and restored it but visited only a few weeks a year. The neighbour on the other side had died years ago and the house was slowly disintegrating, the garden overgrown and the shutters hanging askew.

If I looked up I could see the ruins of the castle that hovers above Megalo Horio on a sheer outcrop of rock. The walls were constructed by the Knights of St John, while its tall, solid gateway and a few large blocks of marble date from an earlier temple to Apollo and Athena. Below it, blending into the rocky, scrub-covered hillside, were the broken walls of buildings and enclosures from the village's older incarnations. Houses were built into the mountain for protection from the north winds and potential invaders, benefitting from being naturally cooler in summer and warmer in winter.

These days every third or fourth house, many with a Christian cross carved into the stone lintel, sports a handwritten 'For Sale' sign; for every one that's inhabited, there's a ruin with gaping walls and roof, wooden cupboards still intact, trees still dropping fruit in the courtyard. The village with its narrow, twisting alleys is half-empty, more than half-empty in winter, shutters closed. Many people don't have the money to fix up the hundred-year-old house built by their forebears. The edges of Megalo Horio are scattered with abandoned dwellings built long and low into the gently descending terraces, earth packed into double-skinned stone walls and roofs of rough-cut logs, now covered with grass and flowers.

My village house had rusty metal railings and broken door handles, and a frequently blocked kitchen drain that couldn't be fixed without breaking a stone wall half a metre thick. There were occasionally cockroaches, and slugs at night from the disused well. But I loved the space, the empty rooms, the rambling, ramshackle building with additions from different eras: a heavy old wooden trapdoor divided upstairs from downstairs; outside, modern concrete steps leading to the terrace were haphazardly built over the stone archway of the original front door, which had '1868' carved into it – a century before my birth. In the summer I slept on the terrace, rigging up a shelter to block the streetlight so I could see the stars. Scops owls made their high-pitched calls in the evening.

The low rent allowed me a different kind of life, less dominated by regular work, yet I marvelled every morning that I could sit in my office overlooking the arched roof of a tiny medieval chapel, and across the valley to Harkadio Cave, where the last elephants in Europe died four thousand years ago. To the left on top of the mountain stood the observatory, dating from the Italian occupation, the shell of a building with no roof and gaping windows. The sun gradually lit and defined the terraces on the hill below it, where people once grew everything they needed, when the island was yellow with wheat fields, perhaps when the house was built for a newly married couple.

In the 1880s, the British couple Theodore and Mabel Bent came to Megalo Horio – albeit on a very brief visit – and their diaries record what they saw. They were on a longer trip around the Dodecanese, aiming to excavate and remove items of archaeological interest, usually without permission or with Ottoman officials turning a blind eye in return for baksheesh. In Tilos they stayed with the priest, who also cured hides for making shoes. The houses were dark, they wrote, and women sat spinning on their roofs. Tilos was 'thinly populated, and as remote a spot as well could be found from any centre of civilisation', rarely visited by steamer or even sailing boats. The only communication with the outside world in winter was when one Mr Kammas went to Rhodes to sell grain. Women wore coats of homespun material, white shirts edged with embroidery, and pointed leather shoes; they had wild, gypsy looks and wore earrings so big they deformed their ears. There was no doctor; the local people would 'live and die as birds of the air'.

The Bents were shocked by the islanders' 'ignorance and superstition'. But could Theodore and Mabel, I wonder, have built a house or made their own clothes and sustenance, survived in such a rugged, isolated place on what they could find and grow?

It was around this time, towards the end of the Turkish rule (*Tourkokratia*), that the first big wave of emigration from the Dodecanese to the United States began. Greeks had established communities in the USA in the eighteenth and nineteenth centuries, but almost half a million emigrated there between 1890 and 1917, looking for opportunities. Many worked as labourers on the railroads and in mines, then set up their own businesses.

An American woman called Chris wrote to me telling the story of her grandfather, who was born in Megalo Horio in 1894. Stamatios Psychogios was coming of age in 1909 when a flyer arrived on the island inviting young men to Athens to apply to become king's guards. Stamatios went, but presumably didn't qualify, as his family then sent him on a steamer to New York City with the name of a relative in Harrisburg, Pennsylvania. Arriving at Ellis Island, he was given an Americanised name, Samuel, and settled in Harrisburg, learning to be a cook. After army service during World War I, he returned to America and cooked for different restaurants over the years, marrying and having five children. He sent money back home to his family in Tilos until he died in 1946, when his wife continued to send care packages of food and clothes. His granddaughter said, 'I know he always dreamed of returning, as back in the 1920s or 1930s he had been buying a piece of land but never was able to live that dream of coming home.'

There was another big wave of emigration in the 1960s. After years of increasingly harsh occupation and then the deprivation of World War II, people had little left and farming was still the only means of survival. A softly spoken man called Antonis Kammas – a common name in the north of the island – left Megalo Horio in 1963 when his family moved to Athens, and spent his working life in Rhodes, but on retirement moved back to live nearby. His children now have professional lives abroad. He remembers growing up on one of the steeply stepped alleyways near the old bakery, and says, 'Back then, all the houses had local families living in them.' I strain to imagine the quiet village fully occupied. 'I was sad to leave all my friends, and no longer spend my summers by the sea. But those were difficult years for the people.'

One day in the municipality offices, in what was once the village school, Maria Koumpaniou shows me a photograph on the wall from when she was a child in the 1960s. 'There were twenty-five children just in my class,' she says. 'And there were six classes, so you can imagine!' Her father ran the kafeneio. Like Antonis, she remembers the village as a busy place, before people began to leave en masse. Megalo Horio had between five hundred and a thousand people in the 1960s but declined to fewer than a hundred over the following half century. She knows I like it especially in winter because it's quiet, not too many people. 'For us, though, we like it when there are people, *kosmo*.' Some people today leave because they need *kosmo*.

Panayiotis Ikonomou is an ineffably cheery man born around 1950. He can often be found sitting at the roadside opposite his mini-market in Livadia, picking the buds and leaves from branches of thyme or oregano, or curing pilchards and octopus. He'll usually shout a greeting and ask me where I'm going or where I've been. Ikonomou is another important family name on the island, and Panayiotis grew up in Megalo Horio where his father ran a shop selling dry goods such as rice and sugar between the church and kafeneio. He recalls his siblings carrying water up to the village from the spring in the Skafi valley in baskets on their shoulders. His sisters moved away but Panayiotis and his brothers stayed, working as fishermen on a traditional wooden caique. With little prompting all three give impassioned monologues on why life on the island is enough for them and how they see no reason to travel; typically, as fishermen, they love their traditional dances. But the family house in Megalo Horio has been sold to a foreigner, and their father's shop is for sale.

So many calamities have left their mark. The Greek government-debt crisis that began in 2009 and endured for close to a decade led to more people moving abroad for work, although some returned to the island, unable to find work in the cities. The increase in property taxes as Greece tries to pull itself out of the crisis has made it even harder for people to rebuild and restore, however. Foreigners and outsiders have bought many houses in Megalo Horio and restored them; 'thankfully,' says Antonis, 'otherwise most of the village would be in ruins.'

Tilos began to welcome independent travellers in the 1970s. A man who came to do restoration work on the monastery in those years tells me there were still no hotels or restaurants, so he slept in the school and ate with the teacher and the priest. But over the following decades the first hotels were built, one in the 1970s, the next in the 1980s, and in the 1990s a couple of stone barns on the rocky water's edge were converted into café-bars. The pedestrian path with streetlights along the shore came in the decade after that. It changed the look of the waterfront, but it's used by everyone from dog-walkers to mothers with pushchairs and children walking home from school.

Some of us would prefer as little development as possible. I'm no fan of bright electric signs, others say roads have changed the island – but without the road, perhaps Megalo Horio would have been completely abandoned. High-speed internet is necessary for businesses and the municipality (notices about doctors visiting are posted on the Facebook page), for checking how late the ferry is or keeping in touch with distant relatives – all crucial if the island wants young local families to stay. Without a local population, Tilos would turn into one big playground for tourists.

It's still a place where people pull nets out of the sea, keep bees and goats and harvest olives. It's a refuge from the crime and hectic pace of cities, from modern commercialism; a refuge for artists and outsiders, for people who want a life with fewer rules and regulations.

It's also a refuge for refugees.

The young woman said they arrived in the middle of night and were told the boat had a problem and they must get out, taking nothing with them. They jumped ashore in the dark and saw no houses, no road. They lit a fire on the beach. They'd paid to get to Italy. In the morning they saw a path and the young men walked to see where it led. Deserted places are convenient for people-smugglers.

It was summer 2014 when I first came across brand-new lifejackets, several for small children, strewn, along with clothing and shoes, on Skafi beach, half an hour's walk from Megalo Horio. At first I thought they had been lost from a charter yacht; then I learned there had been a new arrival overnight of Syrian refugees. They were given clothes and food and a place to stay in a seldom-used monastery.

For now they were safe, and it was sad to think that these were probably the best days they'd have for a while, before being shipped off to a holding centre on the mainland. When my mother and I visited them in the monastery above Livadia, several of the young children – shy, wide-eyed – gleefully stroked Lisa while we spoke to the young woman. A man held a baby only a few months old. Later we went back, taking books and toys for the children. A young man greeted us cautiously and asked what we wanted. We showed him our picture books and finger puppets and he smiled. 'You have one more for me?'

They began to arrive regularly over the next months and I would gather up lifejackets and food wrappers. The farmer Menelaos and his sons helped people as they struggled up the path without water or any idea where they were. In the peaceful village it became a familiar sound as I sat at my desk with my first morning coffee, the murmuring of voices as they waited for the police to come and process them.

As the migrants passed through the island, each group staying for a few days at a time, they were welcomed. Many Greek families were refugees once. Years before, a few boys from the Middle East had arrived on a refugee boat and been allowed to stay; they integrated, finding work and learning the language. The wooden boat was left to sink in the harbour until a storm broke it up a few years ago, and people salvaged the wood.

One day, I swam with a mask and snorkel and watched the fish: *skaros* or parrotfish, purple-brown, with big scales like armour and anxious yellow eyes, gnawing at the rocks; the tiny ones with forked black tails and white bellies, curious and bold. On the walk home, I noticed more lifejackets in the bushes behind the beach, and empty water bottles on the path. Back in Megalo Horio, Marios told me proudly that he had been up all the night before. He'd been working on his car when he heard a voice in the dark say, 'My friend, I want water.' He helped them find their way. 'I like Syrians,' he said. 'Good people.'

At midnight, I saw Maria who lived at the end of the alleyway whispering over the wall to him. 'More refugees!' she told me. 'They arrived just now.' The police had gone to find them. We joked that Tilos would become Syrian if the refugees kept coming. 'We give them Mikro Horio,' said Marios, grinning.

Bees are buzzing on a calm day, the winter sky is a bright blue and the sun warm as Lisa and I set off. Putting Megalo Horio behind us, we descend through a valley that's vivid green with thyme and oleander. Across the flat sapphire sea, mountains are clear; I turn off my phone before it switches to a Turkish network. Crystalline water glints invitingly over colourful pebbles. Diving in takes willpower – no question, the water is cold – but after the first few minutes of fast swimming it feels good, sharp and clean, and I relax. The pay-off in exhilaration is immense.

I've been to this bay when a summer wind was blowing so hard I could barely stand, waves crashing on the cliffs, sea spray blown horizontally across the green valley. Careful not to be knocked over as I waded in, I dived through waves and was carried up and down by the swell. I've always loved swimming – it was the one sport I was decent at. I remember being tossed around in big waves on an Atlantic beach with my brother when we were children, emerging bruised but laughing, our swimsuits filled with pebbles.

Swimming in the sea year-round restores my equilibrium, and I believe it must make you stronger. One morning in 2010, while travelling on Korea's wild, windy and volcanic Jeju island, I happened upon a group of women divers in black wetsuits stitched and repaired many times. They were lithe and strong as seals, hauling sacks of shellfish and octopus from the water on to the rocks. In the nineteenth and twentieth centuries, while the men were away for months in fishing boats, these *haenyo* went diving to feed their families. They would free-dive to a depth of ten metres, even in winter, wearing just cotton suits with buttons for adjusting when pregnant. It was humbling to meet a woman in her eighties who had dived since she was a teenager, slipping money into her mask as she lithely squatted down to slice fish, making me overcome my squeamishness about eating raw sea slug. Nowadays the *haenyo* sell the seafood and send their daughters to university. The skills will soon be lost.

In the bay where I'm swimming now are underwater piles of rocks that I've been told were ballast from ships that once loaded up here with cargo. Where the fields meet the beach are shards of old pottery gradually being washed away by the sea, and a dilapidated stone chapel I've been told is dedicated to St Nicholas, the patron saint of fishermen. Feeling the chill of the water again, I speed up my strokes and head to shore, get out and pile clothes back on, then full of energy, I decide to walk up the hill that overlooks the bay from the north.

The ascent is gentle and dune-like at first, soon becoming steeper and rockier. Lisa leaps over the spikiest bushes with grace. Below me, the valley that from ground level seems impenetrable, thick with hardy shrubs, reveals itself as deserted fields, the disused track that winds through the valley still marked by stone walls but clogged with oleander. I've found square stone walls down there going several metres deep into the ground, probably a well, beside the remains of a shallow cistern sealed by plaster.

Once this land was full of crops. The island had to be self-sufficient. In the hills were hundreds of oaks, used for dyes and tanning, and *gramithia* or turpentine trees, whose tiny, hard berries were eaten as nuts or ground to make oil. The goats would have been herded and used for their milk, hair and hides; moved from pasture to pasture, not left to their own devices. Many bushes were used medicinally. It's all still there. Though trees such as almonds are now neglected and unproductive, and few goats herded or milked, there is small-scale farming and the island is rich with wild foods: fish, salt, herbs, capers, wild asparagus.

Lisa and I follow the ridge back towards the village, sometimes along the terraces, sometimes pulling ourselves up rocks. There are purple blooms on the sage bushes, and endless tiny blossoms in blue and yellow, white and pink. On a flattish high area I find a threshing circle; after a tough scramble up a steep slope we approach a semicircular tower with tiny windows looking out to sea in all directions and steps up to the top. I watch the silver, rippling sea and clouds casting their shadows.

After a couple of hours, my legs are covered in scratches and tired enough that I must be careful not to fall. We get a little fractious at times like this; Lisa has no patience with my stopping to take photos of flowers, and I have no patience with her making detours to scare partridges. I'm glad there's no-one around to hear me talking to my dog: 'Well, this was your idea…' We happen upon a newborn goat, peer into a chapel filled with snail shells, then clamber up rocks to enter the castle. To the west, the sun gleams brilliantly on the sea, while two eagles wheel in the sky. Far below, waves sweep into the shore. On every slope in every direction are terraces that were full of crops and herds years ago, now abandoned to wild goats and spiny garrigue.

The path from the castle down to the village feels easy. At home, I've left bread dough to rise and, ravenous, can barely wait for it to finish baking before I am tearing chunks off and eating. In the evening, at the taverna with its enclosed terrace warmed by a wood-burning stove, Michalis gives me shellfish he's plucked from the water that day. They are a pure taste of the sea, dressed with the fruits of the land, olive oil and lemon.

At the small harbour of Ayios Antonis the waves are thundering in, roaring and glittering, and date palms and tamarisks shake in the breeze. In a rubble-strewn field, goats scavenge from the mastic bushes.

This large bay was important once to Megalo Horio. The surrounding land was productive all the way from here to the monastery, with its continually flowing spring, several kilometres around the other side of the mountain Profitis Ilias. There was no road then; people travelled by donkey, taking their produce to sell at a little market near the church in Megalo Horio. Ayios Antonis is now one of the smallest settlements on the island, with a scruffy abandon that I love. The remains of an old petrol station, modern concrete protected by ugly tiles, the shell of a boat, unfinished buildings.

Stone walls still stand, their use long forgotten. Theodore and Mabel Bent were disappointed here to unearth 'nothing but bones, and two little earthen tear-bottles, one broken, and a lamp – all coarse'. But while digging foundations for a new home in recent years, my Swedish friends found part of a Roman house. By the shore was a cemetery, perhaps early Christian; there used to be skeletons in the eroding cliffs, and at low tide you still see stone circles in the reef.

Often half-built things get abandoned when the money runs out. But maybe it's good sometimes for the money to run out. I read in the news a couple of years ago that a multi-billion-euro plan backed by Chinese and Gulf investment to convert a 'wasteland' outside Athens into a complex of luxury accommodation, yachting marina and casinos was stalled because critics believed it would damage the environment and cultural heritage in what was then declared an archaeological area. The Reuters report called this a 'setback', but I am relieved that money can't buy everything it wants. I am grateful, at remote and half-abandoned Ayios Antonis, for a wasteland that shelters mysterious ancient remains, the landscape more than half reclaimed by nature.

The word abandon comes from Old French: to put your forest '*à bandon*' meant to open it freely for anyone to use as pasture or for cutting wood. It came to mean letting go, leaving, deserting, forsaking, giving up, with an association of recklessness, lack of control. The word was naturalised into the English language, and by the nineteenth century it also came to suggest freedom from inhibition and convention, a surrender to natural impulses, to nature.

Progress in much of the world is about acquiring more, but for some of us there's a liberation in having less, living without television and crowds and traffic jams, pointless noise and tiring time in transit just waiting. When I go back to England – a little horrified to glimpse my semi-feral state in a mirror – I gorge on tastes I can't get on my tiny island: Asian spice, pub grub and real beer. It's fun. But sooner than I expect, I've had enough. I am lost when I go to a big supermarket with my mother and she asks me to choose something for dinner – how do you decide when you can have anything? I'm happier having things when they are available, making do the rest of the time, living in a place where people aren't trying to sell me things I don't need. Most places continue to build and grow, offering more choice, more information, more things you worry you haven't done. Even the most restless of us craves emptiness from time to time.

Where disused terraces cascade down the hillsides I follow a track uphill, roughly parallel to a dry riverbed, and see a cylindrical, tower-like structure built into a terrace wall. I first think it must be a cistern or an animal pen, but there's a small hole at ground level. A friend later tells me it's a lime kiln, an *asvestokamino*.

I do some research. People created lime for thousands of years across Europe to use as construction mortar, to neutralise acidic soil and to create whitewash in order to protect fruit trees against disease and keep buildings cool. The white powder is made by burning limestone – the main substance of the mountains here, formed from coral and the shells of sea creatures aeons ago. The earliest recorded use was between seven thousand and fourteen thousand years ago in what is now Turkey. A waterproof cement was made by the Romans to build structures that have lasted millennia, using quicklime mixed with volcanic ash. This lime kiln above Ayios Antonis belonged to a way of life pursued for centuries, abandoned just a couple of generations ago. Perhaps I will learn more about this and other artefacts on the landscape by travelling to other islands.

On the horizon is the distinctive flattened cone of volcanic Nisyros, where I've found a wealth of deserted places in the past. On this clear day, it seems I could reach out and touch it. The forecast shows several days of clear skies and suggests the fierce wind will die down. When I go to Livadia to catch the boat a couple of days later, however, the horizon is bumpy and there's no electricity so I can't buy a ticket. A local asks me with wide eyes if I'm travelling, as she heard on the news that the gale's getting worse. Last week the boat reached the edge of the bay then turned around.

I decide to postpone my trip. In Livadia square there are vegetables for sale from the back of a farmer's truck, chicory greens and new potatoes, broccoli and mandarins. I hear the boat arriving but it struggles to dock and something breaks. I happily accept a lift back home and since the power remains out, I make the most of the sunshine, walking up the old riverbed with Lisa. It's very overgrown with mastic and kermes oak and in places has been used as a rubbish dump, but it's protected from the wind by old stone walls. We walk as far as an abandoned farm with big old olive trees. I gather sticks for the fire, and Lisa startles a hare.

In the evening at the kafeneio, men talk about the old bakery, now unused and cluttered with junk. 'Do you know how good that bread was?! Big loaves like this' – Lefteris circles his arms – 'made of barley, baked in a wood oven.' They talk about getting the bakery working again and tidying up the old footpaths. Manolis arrives now that his card game is finished. He was gathering mushrooms today. A young guy sips coffee while stroking the cat on his lap and asks if he'll show him the best places to gather snails next time it rains.

THE MAKER AND
BREAKER OF FORTUNES

NISYROS

The catamaran pulls away swiftly and I am left alone on the harbour. A few people were waiting to embark as the ferry pulled in, but now there's just me and Lisa and a delivery of boxes. I stand and enjoy the moment, the silence on the quay and the thrill of being the only person arriving on Nisyros on this calm winter day.

I've been visiting this island on and off for well over a decade, and I have stayed many times here at Mandraki. I love the sea wall with painted wooden balconies facing out over crashing waves, the clifftop monastery of our Lady of the Cave, the narrow winding alleys strewn with plant pots and overhung with washing lines. Through the summer it is busy with day trippers from Kos. Today there's no-one, and in any case I'm heading elsewhere.

My phone rings and a car approaches along the empty dock. Yiannis, my host, has come to meet me. With short dark hair and a beard, he's local and I'd guess in his late thirties, calm and genuine in his welcome. His friend from Athens has longer, straight hair and a slighter build and is delighted with Lisa. We drive to the bakery where I stock up on bread and pastries while the others head off to do banking and buy cigarettes. An old man is selling olives from the back of a truck, so I buy half a kilo. Back in the car, we set off for the village of Emborio.

While Tilos on a map is a ragged tilde, indented with promontories and inlets, Nisyros, being a volcano shaped by its eruptions, is almost round with few protuberances and barely any natural harbour. The road hugs the rocky coast for a few kilometres, following the curve of the island. Then, turning off at a junction, we start to meander up the slope, zigzagging higher. The old farming terraces on either side of us are thickly green, scattered liberally with flowers, and Yiannis points high up towards the ridge where we are heading, the white almond blossom so bright it seems to glint in the sunshine that is shyly emerging from the clouds. The car strains up the final stretch and we park on a slope just below the village. Emborio is built on the rim of the volcano, hundreds of metres above the sea and overlooking the caldera, the hollow, cauldron-like centre of the island.

As its name – like the English 'emporium' – suggests, in Roman times Emborio was a centre of trade. It continued to prosper through the Middle Ages and into the Turkish era. A century ago, the biggest village on the island, it had 2,500, maybe 3,000 residents – until an earthquake hit in 1933, also devastating Kos. World War II took its toll, too, and by 1950, the population of the village had dropped to two or three hundred people. Now the permanent residents number just seventeen.

Some houses have been bought and restored by outsiders, says Yiannis, mostly people from France and other parts of Greece, who visit for a few weeks or months a year. For more than a decade he and his brother and sister have run Apiria, the taverna by the church, and now rent out houses. In winter, theirs is the only taverna; with so few residents, it's surprising there's anything at all. We climb up an alleyway of stone steps, passing empty ruins and the former village school, before reaching a restored house of dark grey stone. The door is stiff from the rain, but with a shove it opens on to a magical bedroom with the stone arches, stone walls and stone ceiling of traditional Nisyrian houses. Stone is not a scarce commodity, clearly. The building is at least a hundred years old, says

Yiannis, which means it survived the earthquake of 1933 – making me feel a little more comfortable about the huge slabs of stone above my bed.

He hands me the keys and leaves to do his work. The decor is spare and stylish, with smooth-finished grey concrete and neutral cottons, old wooden furniture, IKEA cutlery stored in an antique icebox. Despite its contemporary touches, I am delighted to find I have neither phone signal nor Wi-Fi. I stand on the terrace, ruined walls in small fields to either side, the land dropping away beyond the edge of the ridge. The only sound is the buzzing of insects, and a dog barking. This is the last inhabited house at our end of the village. Having completed the bare essentials of settling in, I follow overgrown stone steps until the view opens up to reveal the flat caldera floor far below: the green winter fields of the plain, and white craters in the distance.

The caldera of Nisyros sits one hundred metres above sea level with lava domes rising all around to almost seven hundred metres, forming the rim where I'm standing. It is the youngest active volcano in Greece, none of its rocks more than 150,000 years old; an eruption just fifteen thousand years ago covered the existing land in another layer of pumice and ash. The last known eruptions were in the 1870s and 1880s. Today the volcano is scientifically monitored for variations such as increasing temperatures and surface cracks. This volcanic activity makes the island, at just forty-one square kilometres one of the smallest in the Dodecanese, uniquely dramatic and ever-changing.

The crater known as Stephanos is a cauldron within the caldera. Steep-sided, circular, like a vast cooking pot 180 metres in radius and 30 metres deep, it was formed six thousand years ago by super-hot liquid surging from the earth and blasting the rock away. The white, viscous liquid has cooled and hardened in the bottom of the pot, forming a thick crust, but under the surface it still boils. I have stood several times down there on the white dust of the crater, where vapour rises wispily from hissing, gurgling canary-yellow openings; as I lean in close, momentarily blinded by the steam, the hint of sulphur from the fumaroles transports me to a more elemental world. I get a sense of walking closer to the earth here, to the raw stuff it is made of. The steam, the mud, the formation of fine, fragile sulphur crystals – this rare glimpse of the planet as a living being is humbling.

It was hundreds of metres above this caldera one windy evening in 2015 that I first started thinking about the deserted places of the Dodecanese. Surrounded by warm orange light as the sun went down, I heard a cow lowing. My friend and I had climbed up the steps from Nikia, the other village on the rim of the caldera, and I contemplated the blue and white chapel, surreal in its perfection, dedicated in 2010 by a Nisyrian of New York. We had also visited the monastery of Panayia Kyra, destroyed in the earthquake of 1933 and rebuilt two years later by a brotherhood of Nisyrians in America. In the caldera, we'd seen abandoned farms: threshing circles, water cisterns and stone houses littered with animal bones.

The full moon was bright and yellow against a dusky blue sky as we drove by scooter to Emborio, where cats leapt across the alleys from one roof to another. Of the two half-empty villages that faced one another on the rim of the caldera, one – Nikia – had been endowed with the wealth of those who left for America, while the other – Emborio – seemed mostly dark and crumbling.

It struck me powerfully then that so many islanders left their rural existence for such a different, urban life on the other side of the world. But while science may reassure us today that the volcano is stable, a century ago a disastrous earthquake could have been enough to persuade people to leave. Just twenty years after the 1933 earthquake, another in 1953 led to further decline in the population of Nisyros. The effect was similar on Santorini, another volcanic island in the Cyclades just to the west, where an earthquake in 1956 also resulted in a wave of emigration. In a documentary about it called *5:12*, the old people interviewed say that after they saw houses turn to dust and people killed, from then on there was a fear of the volcano. It finished off a farming way of life that was already in decline.

The population of Nisyros has remained around a thousand for the last few decades, while the Nisyrians in the USA number around twelve thousand. One of them, John Catsimatidis, left the island as a baby with his parents in 1948, grew up in Harlem and worked in a grocery store, and is now one of the richest men in America.

This winter day, the sun is now shining and according to the forecast today is the warmest day of the week, so I have my sights set not on the interior of the island but its shoreline – and a particular beach. I stride the empty, open, curving road around the high rim of the caldera, the sea an inviting deep blue far below, the fields all green grass dotted with flowers, oak trees and spiky euphorbia bushes blossoming bright yellow. Eventually I reach the track that will take me hundreds of metres down to the shore. A man is securing a fence and I assume the goats on the road are his; I ask if I should keep the dog away, but he says, 'Not at all,' and shoos them off.

The track zigzags down, changes for a while to a path of white pumice, then to red and black pumice that feels crisp underfoot. Finally there's a scramble through sand and scrub, amid lavender bushes and olive trees, to the wind-sculpted milk-chocolate beach falling away into clear sea. I swim and then dry off on the warm, coarse sand, grains of black, red and grey. The sun will disappear behind the ridge soon and I can't linger, sadly. I risk a nerve-wracking pull up a sheer cliff using Lisa's straining on the lead to help with upward momentum, a more direct route up to the path that leads to the road.

The light is already fading as I return along the high ridge to Emborio. I see one car, one motorbike, and one black cow with very sharp-looking horns, pencil points sticking out of its head, refusing to budge from the roadside. I veer off into a sloping field to look at an abandoned square stone building with narrow slits for windows. Inside there's a deep, bath-like structure, its walls smoothly plastered white. A year before, I saw something similar beside a track among the farms above Mandraki; the drain hole at the front leading into a stone bowl made me think it might be a wine press. I pause to see a few other deserted buildings. The temperature has dropped so when I get back to the house I find the hot water switch, make Lisa some dinner, crawl under the duvet and sleep until it's time for the taverna to open.

I hear the high bleeps of scops owls. Outside, it's pitch-black and I realise that although my mobile phone is useless for making calls here, it's essential as a torch to light my way down the uneven old steps until I reach streetlights. I'm early so I walk around the village, seeing few lights on; some houses are derelict, some restored but empty. There's a strange smell, and I realise it's the volcano. In spite of the pervading dark here, strangely I can see the lights of Kos strung out in the distance, as if someone left the Christmas fairy lights on, and the red flashes marking its airport runway, close and yet a world away. The night is cold and windy, so it is wonderful to see the taverna illuminated within and the key in the door.

What a taverna it is! Perhaps the narrowest, cosiest restaurant dining area in Europe – there isn't space for two tables side by side. There's one table by the door, and another in the back. In summer they set up outside, but for winter nights this is enough. Yiannis invites me to sit in the back by the door to the kitchen, while Lisa makes herself at home on the stairs. Within half an hour, there are four customers (including me) and the taverna in the semi-deserted village is packed.

Sitting by the door, Stella and Costas have driven from Nikia, which has no taverna in the winter. They have brought fresh fish to be cooked, and order mezes and tsipouro, or raki – the strong, clear, pure liquor made from grape must, kept in big bottles in the fridge. Stella is a handsome Athenian woman who has lived on the island for twenty years; she has a shop in Mandraki and is also an artist. Costas is a Greek American, and I can hear he's not entirely comfortable speaking the language of his forefathers. As we strike up a conversation, he confirms he only comes here for a few months at a time, though for longer and longer every year, as he has returned to restore his great-grandfather's property. He has a nice sense of humour, and I'm interested to meet an American descendant of people who left.

Costas tells me that when he was growing up in Astoria, New York, there were more Greeks living there than in Athens. And that his great-grandfather's property was something he had wanted from when he was a kid. 'I said to my parents: give my sister everything, I just want the house in Nisyros.' For an American, it takes an incomprehensible length of time to get anything done here – but he's taking pleasure from the old things he finds. He often hears cows passing by outside the house. I ask him about the bath-shaped structure I saw this evening, show him the photographs. He and Stella are certain it was a *kazani*, which translates literally as a cauldron, for making wine and distilling tsipouro.

'I still have my grandfather's in the house,' he says. When his grandfather was ninety-three, he was making tsipouro one day when he lost his balance and fell into the *kazani*. He couldn't get out of the deep bath and was drowning in booze. Thankfully someone helped him out. 'That's how I'm going to go, though,' Costas says. 'Well, if I make it to ninety-three.' We laugh and drink to our health.

'What would make someone from England come to live in a place like this?' he asks.

I joke and tell him it's snowing in England right now; then I tell him about loving the wild, nature on my doorstep, a life that allows me time to write.

'Sometimes it's hard to get what you need here though,' says Costas.

'It depends what you really need,' I say, and Stella agrees.

My ears prick up again when conversation turns to a deserted harbour. Costas has another good story. He was there with a friend, a local character, but when he was ready to leave, he couldn't find him anywhere. Then suddenly his friend emerged from the sea, naked, carrying three fish to cover his private parts. 'How did he catch them, that's what I was thinking…?'

In October 2017, on a sharply cold, blustery morning in Mandraki, an exuberant wind was rattling the wooden shutters of our rented apartment and the waves beat noisily on the walls below as my mother and I left with Lisa in the dark. We watched the sun rise out of the sea, then we took the bus to Nikia. The well-kept village was empty, just a couple of Albanian workers hauling bags of cement up the hill. We gave up on any hopes of breakfast and started down the narrow footpath into the caldera.

The sun had not yet made its way over the rim or penetrated its depths, so a soft grey light prevailed. The earth was bare and brown before the rains; the only colour came from a few pinkish-red autumn leaves on the *gramithia*, or turpentine trees. The steep hillsides were littered with colossal rocks, some of which seemed to have crashed through terrace walls as they fell, though more likely the walls had been built around them. There was no sign of anyone. As we descended further, the loose path revealed small yellow flowers poking up here and there out of the earth, purple heads of heather and the green and pink of spiky euphorbia.

I also saw pieces of flecked black obsidian. In Neolithic times, obsidian was mined from the offshore islet of Giali to make into cutting tools; once, it also had an agricultural community. The other half of Giali is composed of pumice, and today the quarrying and selling of pumice for building material is on such a scale that it has chipped away that side of the island, turning it to brilliant white.

As we neared the flat plain of the caldera, I noticed an old farmhouse built from the surrounding stones, braced by a massive boulder, blending into the land. Although it looked rudimentary, inside it had the classic hooped stone arches of the *spiladi* or cave-house; all the old houses of the island were built with arches to be strong against earth tremors. Recesses in the walls made a simple fireplace and cupboards; small gaps between stones were filled with earth. Outside was a well-crafted circular water cistern, a threshing circle and a hole in the ground opening into a storage tank, the rounded interior plastered smooth. Just below the house was a simpler building, presumably for animals. As we stepped away, we saw rows of field terraces. Someone had lived self-sufficiently here.

Because of the fertile volcanic soil, the caldera and the steep hills surrounding it have been terraced and farmed since ancient days, and at times have been extensively populated. A deserted hilltop settlement, Nyfios, shows evidence of Neolithic and Minoan life; down below, just above Mandraki is a fort, a *paleokastro*, with giant masonry dating to around 800BC; and nearby are ancient cemeteries where people were cremated with vessels of olive oil, wine, honey, figs and olives. According to the account of *Martoni's Pilgrimage* from 1394, there was then 'an abundance of fruit' on Nisyros, including great quantities of dried figs produced for export. But also, at various times in the island's history, its fields have been poisoned and destroyed by falling ash. The volcano has been the maker and breaker of fortunes, bringing waves of prosperity and ruin.

Further down, we found a handful of similar smallholdings in various states of decay. The olive trees looked as though they might have been coppiced – instead of one thick, twisted trunk there were bunches of slender ones – perhaps to produce fence poles or firewood. Suddenly the sunlight reached us, turning the leaves deep green, warming the land, creating sharp shadows. Horned cattle wandered the seemingly bare fields among the olive trees and holm oaks. We had a sense of being alone in the volcano – as if we were the only people not to have heeded the warnings.

Our solitude was first broken by a lone motorcyclist. Then a car appeared, and as we neared the main crater I was surprised to see people carrying supplies into the café. Soon there were eight or nine coaches parked nearby, day trippers from Kos streaming out of air-conditioned vehicles. Assuming each of the visitors paid the entrance fee, the volcano earned about a thousand euros that morning.

In summer, up to fifteen coaches of tourists of various nationalities arrive daily. Once, I overheard two women comparing this with a 'better' volcano experience on another tour in another country; funny, but sad. The man who set up a refreshments stall beside the craters a couple of decades ago could never have foreseen the scale of the business he has today. Now, instead of farming, people own coaches and cafés and sell pumice.

You can package the wild and sell it, but it may still turn around and bite. That day, sections of the surface, including all the fumaroles, had been roped off, and painted red rocks were arranged in order to measure any movement. Kos, thirteen kilometres away, had suffered severe earthquake damage that year. The rocks are caustic, they can burn, and there is still an active hydrothermal system underneath. Ancient mythology, explaining the phenomenon, said the god Poseidon crushed a giant under a rock here, and that his hot breath surges out from time to time.

A kilometre along the road from Mandraki are the municipal baths of Loutra, constructed between 1885 and 1912. These warehouse-sized buildings, beside a small marina, housed a luxurious resort with three hundred beds. People came here from Egypt and Asia Minor to bathe in the hot mineral waters.

A building that once held baths is now a shell, the vast interior mostly stripped bare to the dark grey stone and white mortar of its walls. Squares of sunlight from the empty windows illuminate its disintegration: the wooden first floor gone, a wooden staircase falling to nowhere, metal pipes rusted. A middle section between two of the deserted buildings is missing its roof and façade, revealing the torn-off remains of plastered and painted walls, electrical sockets and holes for wiring.

The final building still functions, in a rather down-at-heel, old-fashioned way, offering 'sodium chloride sulphurous natural curative baths'. Its curving and polished wooden staircase, worn tile floors and tall ceilings, wooden washstands and paintings of the founders all evoke a faded grandeur. A sign handwritten in felt-tip pen gives opening hours and price: 5 euros for a bath.

During my 2015 trip I met a seventy-three-year-old gentleman sitting outside. Originally from Kalymnos, he had lived in Australia for fifty years, and was visiting the baths for his health. As a young man, he had been sent by his father to Australia to bring his brother home, but instead he ended up staying there. When I asked if he'd returned to the Dodecanese often, he counted off the year of every trip over the decades.

At one end of the functioning building I found a brightly painted café, decorated with antiques and run by Dimitra who rented it from the council. She told me she had come from the city of Thessaloniki in northern Greece for a holiday and decided to stay, living in one of the abandoned rural cave-houses or *spiladi*.

The only other customer that day, an older man with a grey beard and a sailor's cap, eating octopus cooked in red wine, looked up. 'In the old days people made things. Now we only break them. We only know how to sell things.'

A little way along the coast, the White Beach Hotel, something of an anomaly on an island without big hotels, looks to have been unused for decades. From there, the road descends to Palli, where the Romans built baths and then Christians built Panagia Thermiani, a cave chapel devoted to Our Lady of the Hot Springs.

It's speculated that when the founder of Western medicine, Hippocrates, established his hospital or health spa on Kos in the fifth century BC, he established one at Palli too. What is certain is that in 1910, a doctor named Hippocrates Pantelidis made use of the hot springs and built another therapeutic spa resort on a grand scale, even bigger than Loutra. The elegant Pantelidis Baths, advertised widely, attracted shiploads of visitors from all over the Mediterranean. But Hippocrates died eighteen years after opening its doors, leaving it to fall into disrepair. Its buildings, featured on many old black-and-white photographs and clearly visible from passing boats, have stood lifeless for generations. In the 1980s, one of Pantelidis's descendants attempted to restore the baths, but someone tells me that other local people, jealous of his business plans, launched obstructive lawsuits.

I walked through the gates, which were rusted and fallen open, although faded signs warned: 'Entry Prohibited, Danger'. A complex of buildings of varying shapes and sizes revealed itself, all built of black stone and white mortar, with sandstone framing the windows and terracotta-tiled gabled roofs. The downstairs rows of windows were mostly bricked up, while several further storeys stared dark and empty out to sea. A central atrium had soaring arches; I saw the sparkling reflection of water but found only a shallow, brown pool where I thought I heard the plop of a frog taking refuge. There was a gentle twitter of birds nesting somewhere above. Walking outside across a green verge to the rocks on the seashore, I saw piles of sand waiting to be used one day.

There are rumours that another of Pantelidis's descendants intends to finish the restoration and reopen. For now, the building is another haunting reminder of a century of change. Is the skeleton of the vast spa the remainder of a failure – or is it a symbol of human striving in a harsh environment? Those volcanic eruptions at the end of the nineteenth century had damaged people's livelihood; earthquakes and tremors troubled them for years. The Turkish and Italian regimes were harsh at times. People saw their resources depleted and went in search of better opportunities.

On the hillside behind Pantelidis Baths, above Our Lady of the Hot Springs, I saw the ruins of black stone houses, and as I continued around the coast, the settlement dwindled to nothing. Layers of pumice in the cliffs at Cape Katsouni, walls of black and red scoria, then a road seemingly to nowhere curving around the island, alongside a long stretch of wild beach where turtles sometimes lay their eggs. Birds of prey soared over the tree-covered slopes. I swam and fell asleep on the empty beach until disturbed by a noise – goats dislodging the rocks while reaching for caper bushes.

Morning of day two in Emborio. Wind rattles the shutters. From the terrace, the views are hidden behind grey-tinged cloud, the ruined walls all around making me feel as though I'm living in an old, forgotten castle. The green fields are strewn with rocks, walls knocked down by the goats and cows and no longer repaired. The roof of the house next door is gone, revealing a large stone oven that hasn't been used for decades.

In winter, there's nowhere to go to drink coffee in the morning, nowhere for people to while away a couple of hours in company. I'm happy to go back to bed and drink coffee alone under the duvet, as the clouds blow over the edge of the earth.

When Lisa and I leave the house around ten, it's so windy I don't plan on going far. At the other end of the village I find an old church but its gates are locked, so I keep walking uphill as the sun comes out and the sky brightens to powder blue. We find ourselves high on a hillside of bright green grass and yellow euphorbia, where tiny shepherds' huts are built into the rock facing into the caldera. Peeking inside, I find that even these shelters have archways to brace them against seismic activity, and roofs of heavy slabs of stone.

I sit in a curve of rock that protects me from the wind. Looking down to the sea, I see white waves crash over a shallow point where the island curves towards Pantelidis Baths and the harbour at Palli, where some of the people from Emborio moved after the 1933 earthquake. A bird flies up and away. All I hear is the wind gusting around the rocks, and the faint noise of work being done on a house. Emborio sits astride the ridge just below; a field juts out into thin air where the caldera rim falls away. I'm mesmerised by the sturdy terraces built all the way down the sheer hillside to create a tight horseshoe or amphitheatre, every flat surface carpeted with thick green.

Clouds return and I feel the cold. I'm not much looking forward to scrambling back down in the strong winds. Lisa suggests an alternative route, keen on following a goat-scent away from the village. It's only mid-morning, though I've no water with me, no map… But I've wanted to walk this way for a long time, and it's hard to get lost. As we head down the terraces dotted by prickly bushes, I'm excited to find old cave shelters, and stone steps leading from one terrace down to the next. This land was clearly loved once, and I imagine how gorgeous it would be in soft, calm weather. There's also the occasional dead goat, a reminder of neglect, but uplifted by the surroundings I continue descending until the land levels out somewhat, and I find an old pathway marked by solid walls on either side. Lisa eagerly pulls on the lead, enjoying the cool, breezy day and her own discoveries. In the direction of the sea there's the inevitable rubbish dump and a quarry. But inland, an abandoned farmhouse sits in an idyllic hilltop meadow, with curved terraces flowing steeply all the way down the slopes to the narrow valley below.

Following the well-defined path paved with smooth old stones, I continue towards Evangelistria monastery, thinking I might find water. A few fields here are used for animals, fences reinforced with wooden pallets, doors, fishing nets. The monastery, built of brown and grey volcanic stone with a church and living areas grouped around a courtyard with two cisterns, is recently painted but uninhabited and the tap is dry. I decide to continue, and spot one of the heavy-duty plastic tanks farmers use for storing water. I hope they won't mind if I take a little for my dog – and a cautious slurp for myself. Then I wonder about walking down to Mandraki to buy water, since it's only a few more kilometres. I'm enjoying the adventure.

Further on, someone's fenced in their field using old wooden bannisters, still painted bright blue, wedged between trees. Someone else has stuck a beehive between tree branches. Why do I like these things – just because they are quirky? It's also the sense of people making the most of what little they have to get by. We veer from the road down the more direct, steeper old footpath. There are more farms, some chickens, lemon and orange trees, a sunken church in a field full of fig trees – and gradually there are people. At last, we're at the edge of Mandraki, and I say hello to an older woman struggling up the steps with her shopping. I'd offer to help if I had the energy. Finding a route through the narrow lanes, I stagger into a shop and buy water and chocolate. A customer gives me a strange glance. I must look somewhat bedraggled and feel uncomfortably warm after walking for hours, so continue to Hoklaki cove, with its smooth soot-black pebbles, to dive into the waves.

I carefully retrace my steps through the winding alleys of the village. I pass the same older woman; but this time, she is running down the steps in tears, calling, 'I'm coming, Maria!' The church bell is tolling for a death.

We return uphill to Evangelistria and have a choice of three paths. The first is the one we came on. Another goes up the mountain to the deserted settlement of Nyfios – not for today given that the damp clouds are closing in again. I take the middle way, signposted to 'Volcano'. A well-built trail leads me through a lush landscape of olives and big holm oaks. It's easy to follow, pretty with the occasional deep red poppy or pink cistus flower, with its crinkled tissue-paper petals, and brilliant yellow Bermuda buttercups. I stop to investigate a stone building with its water cistern. It starts to rain and I wonder about sheltering but don't want to get stuck if the rain worsens and night begins to fall.

It's just after this that the path disappears. One moment it's broad, firm and clear – the next minute there's nothing but a scree slope at a forty-five-degree angle. I try going back a little, thinking I must have missed a turning, but this yields nothing.

I think I'll find a way through the stream bed to the left, but it's overgrown and impassable. I try clambering up the rocky slope beyond it, but that seems worryingly dangerous and I have to scramble back again.

Baffled, I look back to the scree slope and wonder whether I might be able to discern the thin line of a path through the loose stones, though it could just as easily be just a goat track. Still, it's the only option. Maybe a rockslide covered the path.

I follow it very carefully in the wind and the rain, and eventually it does, in fact, turn back into a path. But I'd rather not do it again. As I continue down the hill, I think how strangely scary an experience that was.

Then I realise it's a metaphor. For years, you follow a steady, traditional path – it may be strenuous but you know the way. You spend your life building something. Then suddenly, it disappears – an earthquake or a volcanic eruption or a violent invasion changes everything. You think: *I love this place, but I don't want to die for it, or to build it all over again just to wait for the next earthquake. New York isn't so bad, I've heard...*

We reach the road at last, and spot three little pigs, speckled pink and black, wandering in the fields beside us; I pass men in a field, building something, but soon hear them down tools and leave. Although it's adding unnecessary kilometres to the day's unplanned hike, I walk to the craters just to see that white landscape tinged with pink and yellow, to smell the sulphur and see the steam rising from the vents in the earth. I finally have the caldera to myself, just me and my dog and the pigs.

Later, back in Emborio, showered and changed, I'm ravenous. I leave the house and the steps are slippery from the rain, my legs tired from eight hours of walking. I hold Lisa's lead with one hand and my phone-torch with the other. As we descend the narrow alley, it feels darker than last night – the streetlights are out. I call Yiannis to check he's got electricity. He is coming soon, he says – it's just the streetlights that have a problem. I wait in the cold in the middle of the dark village and realise, looking up, that I can see more stars than usual, and the Milky Way spread out in all its glory.

Yiannis's friend Nikos arrives to open up, and it's good to get inside. It doesn't take long for the heater to warm the cosy, narrow space, and I help myself to a beer. Yiannis arrives and gives me a cheery hello as he dashes into the kitchen. The door opens again shortly after and a man walks in carrying a plastic bag with some green vegetable or herb inside which he says will be good for soup. Another man wearing a fleece jacket comes in and joins him at his table. We have a full house again.

I order the heaped salad I've been thinking about all day, and the garlic dip with almonds that's a local speciality, and bite-sized pieces of pork in a spicy wine sauce with ribbons of onion – too much, but I gradually devour it all, with a couple of glasses of raki. Lisa breaks the ice with the strangers, wagging her tail and gazing at them with her big brown eyes. I tell them I'm here to research deserted places, ruins. 'You've come to the right place!' they say, grinning.

We talk a little and then the man in the fleece jacket takes me up the stairs, where there are more tables, to show me photographs of Emborio as it was in the 1950s. There are women in white headscarves, and men in flat caps; men standing outside the school wearing suits and garters and big moustaches twisted at the ends; men holding musical instruments. And in one of the photographs, the people are standing just outside here, in the 'square': a big crowd gathered for a celebration in 1950. The two-storey building behind them is one I photographed this morning, with just the remains of a wooden door and windows, and washed-out paint with a faded ice-cream sign. The man tells me that the *kamara* or archway over the alleyway had a house over the top of it then. As we turn to go back downstairs, I notice a hole in the wooden floorboards, looking down into the kitchen. 'Bullet,' he says.

His father is still in Emborio. Few old folks live in these villages now, though a man who's over a hundred lived at Avlaki until recently and used to row to other islands for fishing. I talk about the stone buildings and walls, how they have lasted. He says yes, stone walls packed with earth are more flexible; they don't break like concrete does. As we discuss why people left the island, the two men tell me about another factor that hadn't occurred to me: rain. The people built terraces and field enclosures and barns for their farms. Yet on an island with no natural springs, a few years without rain would have made a big difference to the sustainability of those farms. 'They built those walls so they could eat. But they didn't always eat.'

On my third winter morning in Emborio, I wake again to wind and mist, and take my time with coffee in the warm bed, ready to pack up. The sea seems calm enough for me to take the midday boat. Then I hear it's been cancelled because of bad weather in Rhodes. So I have another day here, and will take the big ferry late tonight.

As I stand outside the taverna to get a signal on my phone, I watch a little black cat sitting in a hole in the wall. Lisa sees it and growls, and it jumps away. Yiannis, appearing from the kitchen, points to the hole. 'Put your hand inside.' I feel warm steam. It's a geothermal *apiria*, or blowhole of the volcano. 'There's one in the taverna also. That's where the name comes from.' Steam escapes through vents all around the island. One of them emerges in a small, mossy cave at the edge of Emborio, a 'vein' of the volcano creating a natural sauna.

Yiannis is rushing to take food to his chickens and donkey so I don't want to bother him with questions. 'Perhaps you would like to speak with my mother?' he asks. And so, in a little while, we walk up the alley and enter through a low doorway to Anna's house.

Anna, dressed all in black – dress, tights, shoes and cardigan – sits watching an old black-and-white film on television in a small room with photographs covering the uneven, green-painted walls, under a low wooden ceiling. It's funny, I think, to live in such a tiny space in an empty village on a semi-deserted island, but then I suppose it's easier to keep warm. There's just space for a sofa and a table and a few chairs, with a doorway leading through to the kitchen, and a lace curtain covering the window. She insists I take some sweets from a glass bowl on the table, and Lisa finds a bone under a chair, left behind by the last canine guest.

At first Anna seems reticent, but we establish that I know some relatives of hers in Tilos, and I tell her I grew up in a village in the hills in England. She confirms there were once three thousand people living in Emborio, *palia*, 'in the old days' – a fairly broad term. It was a big trading centre, she said, for crops like wheat and figs. When the 1933 earthquake hit, destroying the castle and some of the houses, people were scared and many moved down to the coast.

'But you didn't?' I ask.

'There, what can you see? Nothing! Here you see everything – the volcano, the sea, the mountains, the fields… And several years ago, some doctors came and they said the best climate on the island was here in Emborio.'

Others moved to America – or to Australia, she says. But her family stayed.

'And you don't worry about being so close to the volcano?' I ask.

'We're not so close. Nikia's closer.'

I'm not sure the volcano would respect the distance of a couple of kilometres. 'And how is it, with so few people?'

'We've learned to like the quiet,' she says, quite contentedly. She seems to have no complaints.

That's until I ask whether she still has fields. She can't work the fields anymore because of her legs and her failing eyesight – but that's not what she grumbles about. It's the animals that run wild. *Adespota*. 'They destroy everything. You work hard to grow things and then the goats, the cows come and eat everything.' For about ten years it has been like that.

When I mention my walk to Evangelistria, Anna says the building on the hill was a cheesemaker's. They had plenty of goats but they looked after them, kept them herded so they could milk them. People also had lots of vines, she says, and I ask her about the wine vats in the abandoned houses. They'd make the wine in there, leave it for forty days and it was ready to drink.

It's hard to imagine what it must have been like here with hundreds, even thousands of people – the noise! I say so to Anna and she points out there was the noise of the animals too, carrying things through the village and ploughing the fields.

When I leave, she says she looks forward to my return. I open the front door to a bevy of cats. Across the alley is a courtyard looking out into the caldera.

Quite a few of the houses were painted in bright colours, I realise, as I look around at the faded stucco on the walls and fallen to the ground. It would have been a colourful village at one time. Now, many homes sport large signs detailing how much money was allocated by the European Union and other sources to restore them. These mandatory declarations of funding detract somewhat from the beauty but that money has enabled local families to restore their property, and gives young people a chance to make a living here. There's one of those signs on the house where I'm staying; I am contributing to the gentrification and touristification of Emborio by staying in it, but it means Yiannis and his siblings are able to live year-round in the village of their ancestors and run a fantastic taverna that's used by the locals.

Anna's told me how to find the castle, or where it used to be – it's been bought by someone from Athens and converted into a house. I think about how people need to be able to move; how people from here were able to go to the New World and rebuild their lives, and people from cities have come here for refuge. I ascend the white-painted steps and look down at the village snaking along the narrow ridge in front of me, a few red roofs, a palm tree, the land falling away in tiers of green. The sun comes out as I reach the bright white church with white stone steps spiralling up to the belfry. Suddenly all the colours sharpen to magnificence and I must go out walking again.

As I set off, I have just the place in mind.

Taking the road along the high caldera rim in the direction of Nikia, this time I notice something different. Spotting a little opening in the hillside, I investigate and find it opens up inside into a shelter, like a bunker, a hobbit-house. There are several – probably used by people when they stayed to work in the fields. Another has an outer wall of black porous rock, with a back room that's almost hidden, built against the bedrock and braced within by arches that are white, black and red, the colours of the island. The roots of trees reach down into it from the hillside above. I continue, walking into mist. It seems that the fields under the oak trees are white with frost, but it's an effect created by little pebbles of pumice.

The houses on the slopes below Nikia are different, the stone softer for carving; doorways have post-holes and arches. The descent towards the sea is peaceful, the land gently flattening out, clouds obscuring the views out to Tilos but the sun shining through a gap to gleam silver on the sea. I sometimes take the road, sometimes find my way along the stone footpath, passing abandoned farmhouses and wandering cows. It's misty and damp and there are clouds of white almond blossom. I hear a donkey braying, goat bells, the hum of bees. The rock gradually becomes grey then black and suddenly deep red.

And finally, I reach the small abandoned harbour. Steps lead to a cove of jagged and pocked black lava. A few once-genteel buildings of sombre dark grey and red stone now stand desolate around a small boat ramp. Somewhere in the waters below, hot springs bubble up. Sulphur was mined here during Turkish times, and at one point by an

Englishman named Mr Martin. Until 1950, this was the main harbour for Nikia. Rowing boats ferried goods from big ships to storehouses on the shore, then donkeys carried them up the paths, and in return brought down figs, almonds and acorns to ship elsewhere.

It is just as beautiful as I remember. When I first came, I was in a hurry and promised myself I'd return to find the hot spring. This place is strange, lonely, frozen in time like the black lava, the movement of bubbling hot rock trapped in its shapes, shiny and wet against white crashing waves. Lisa jumps in for a swim, and I can't resist either. I strip off and climb down the metal ladder into the water, though we must leave quickly as the pale winter light is fading. Once again, finding the hot spring will have to wait.

FAITH IN WATER
KOS

It's a mild night, but it's late and dark and most of us on deck have dogs. They aren't allowed inside the ferry, and most owners like me are reluctant or unable to lock protesting pets into a kennel, so I've become used to travelling with a sleeping bag. Thankfully there are comfortable couches. I read for a while, and eventually the lights of Kos town appear. The medieval harbour walls come into view, and we wait for the ramp to go down, and stroll off into the night.

I expected Friday night to be noisy and lively, even in winter; Kos is the third largest island in the Dodecanese with the second biggest population (around thirty thousand) and is a hub for the surrounding smaller islands. But nothing is open close to the waterfront, and there's nobody around. The quay where tour boats moor is empty and the concrete path is broken – perhaps still not repaired after the earthquake of 2017. I am grateful to have found a cheap, pet-friendly studio within easy walking distance – and the key is on top of the box by the door, as promised.

In the morning, I head out to find the fishermen's catch laid out on stands on the waterfront. A portly, moustachioed man picks up two small fish and feeds them to the cats. In the sunshine, it's wonderful to reacquaint myself with Kos town, stopping every now and then to read the helpful signs that relate its history. I pause at a 1930s Italian-built villa, all curves and arches, white with pale yellow trim and dark green shutters. Lisa sniffs around a couple of overgrown parks with ancient ruins.

In 1933, the same earthquake that rocked Nisyros caused so much damage here that it uncovered the ancient agora built two thousand years earlier, one of the biggest in the Mediterranean, hidden by successive layers. The seismic destruction prompted the replanning of the modern town by the Italians, who were by this point governing after centuries of rule by the Ottoman Turks. In many ways, the town benefitted from the Italian makeover. But there are traces of the Turkish occupation also. I find a minaret, all that remains of a sixteenth-century mosque that was at the heart of the old Muslim Quarter. According to the sign, its fountain for washing was inscribed with a quotation from the Qur'an: 'My fellow man, since everything lives thanks to water, why don't you have faith in it?'

Under a deep blue sky, waiting for the newsagent to open so I can buy a map, I sit at the Ariston kafeneio behind the main square, drawn by its old-fashioned, brown-painted wooden tables. When I go inside to order, I'm engulfed by the heavenly, sweet aroma of a custard-filled pastry called *bougatsa*. A man sits in a corner folding little cardboard cake boxes. A glass of cool tap water accompanies my Greek coffee.

On one side of the square is the public market built by the Italians in 1933, now filled with mostly tourist-oriented offerings, while on the other side, the archaeological museum is housed in one of the last major public buildings completed by the Fascist Italian regime in 1937. I spend hours walking and marvelling at the curves and arches of Italian architecture under an Aegean blue sky. Most of the elegant buildings are well kept and in use; one is an apartment building, where I stop at a stall selling earthy, organic local farm produce and homemade wine. The hospital has a beautiful decorative tower with arches open to the sky.

The objects of my visit, however, are beyond the town. Curious about the feasibility of walking there, in the afternoon I venture beyond the modern outskirts until I encounter wide, brilliant green fields, the occasional old stone farm building and one or two nonchalant cows. Hills rise all around, some of them in Turkey; Kos town hovers between two Turkish peninsulas just a few kilometres away. But the traffic on the main roads is fast, and when I try side roads, big, garish new houses are guarded by extremely large and angry dogs. Lisa is sensitive to harshness from fellow canines and keen to get away. Back in town, we go to the beach instead. In summer you can barely see it for sun loungers, but now, ignoring the closed bars and restaurants, it's quite an exhilarating stretch of pebbles shelving down to blue sea. Lisa races around, making a couple of new friends.

Kos is known for mass-market tourism, and the publishers of my map write in scathing terms of how it has sacrificed its natural areas, that 'as is the case almost everywhere in Greece, the absence of political will' has led to overdevelopment, jeopardising vulnerable ecosystems. I know Kos town from years ago and I'm not expecting too much when I walk the next day in hot sunshine east along the coast to Psalidi to see the wetland, a natural wildlife habitat.

Beyond all the restaurants and hotels closed for winter is another long beach with an inflatable dinghy lying damaged and deflated on the shore and, rather unnervingly, a single oar and a pair of shoes abandoned on the pebbles. And beyond that is a closed-up visitors' centre with a broken fence. I look at the map and try to get my bearings, continue along the shore away from the graffiti-covered concrete blocks, enjoying the warm, salty sea breeze, and happen upon a small gate.

Following a straight path bordered by tall grasses, I glimpse the shallow lagoon and from a vandalised hide see in the distance pale shapes on the water. I walk on to get a closer look. There they are, white flamingos. The birds trawl the water in a line, heads down under the surface, like policemen conducting a search for evidence.

'Get it out,' says a surprisingly gruff, overweight bus conductor when he sees my lovely dog sitting quietly at my feet. The few other passengers have been petting her. 'It's not allowed.' I'm downcast but we return to the port and flag down a taxi, and surprisingly the driver agrees to take us when I show I have a blanket to cover the seat. We're off to Pyli (pronounced 'pill-ee'), in the Dikeos municipality, on another warm, sunny winter morning.

Mount Dikeos rises to more than eight hundred metres and spreads out in a solid, broad hump along the southern coast. It starts not far from Psalidi where I walked yesterday, at the eastern end close to Turkey, and stretches for more than sixteen kilometres. On the sheer side that faces the coast, a road cut into the mountain goes as far as the hot springs of Therma, which bubble up into the sea facing Nisyros. On the other side, the mountain's slopes are gentler. As we follow the main road, dotted with furniture stores and hardware suppliers, forest-covered hills rise up to our left, with the white splashes of small villages and smoke rising from chimneys. Within twenty minutes we have reached our turn-off, close to the far end of Dikeos, and are heading up an incline that becomes the main street of Pyli, a village with 2,500 residents. The taxi drops us in the main square at the top, between the church of St Nicholas and an ancient spring.

Across the square I recognise the house that will be home for the coming days. The owner, a local man in his late forties or early fifties, shakes my hand warmly. He and his wife manage their own restaurant just outside Kos town. The house has been beautifully restored, keeping the original stone walls but modern and comfortable inside.

'The house is very old, from before the war,' he says. 'It was my mother's, but she never lived here. She received the house from her parents to live in when she was married, this is the custom as you know, but then she and my father moved to Australia. That's where I was born, in Melbourne. When we came back to Kos, we lived in the town and this house was falling down. I decided to rebuild it a few years ago, and now she comes for holidays with us sometimes.'

I like Pyli from the start. It's immediately clear that this is a busy, ordinary, working-class village with bakeries, supermarkets and café-bars (all privately owned, no chains), schools and even a couple of computer repair shops. Yet the evidence of the past is scattered all around, even in its dilapidation lending the place a beauty without which it would be much the poorer.

Most of the cottages along the road through the village have been adapted, walls covered with tiling or cladding, purple or orange paint, doors and windows replaced with aluminium and uPVC or hidden under heavy ceramic-tiled pergolas. Local people rarely seem keen to have what their parents and grandparents had. Perhaps it's just because there's more choice available these days, and it's relatively expensive to build with stone and wood compared with cheap imported materials. Perhaps there's hardly anyone around who still knows how to build that way.

But here and there is an intact original. One has '1945' inscribed over the central door, a window either side, stone walls plastered and painted white, a capped chimney. To these simple houses, sometimes two smaller buildings are added. The windows are covered with wooden shutters painted green or pale blue, and often have a raised surround with a decorative arch or peak. The front doors have glass windows protected by wrought-iron openwork in mid-twentieth-century designs, painted to match the shutters. Some seem merely locked up temporarily. Others are obviously long abandoned, broken glass in the windows and rubbish in the garden. I tread carefully through tall grass to peek through an open window. There are black-and-white photographs on the mildewed wall. An old black travelling trunk sits open with a New York address painted by hand on the side.

I pass a small chapel beside a stream with a cistern and irrigation channel; the water supply here is probably one reason the village survived. There's a working flour mill – not an old windmill done up for tourists, but modern – standing by a small vineyard and wine press. Amid the mini-markets, butchers and modern cafés stands the entrance to a long-closed shop, with a rusted padlock and paint peeling from its carved wooden door, the sign still stencilled on the wall. Across the road, I glance inside an open door to see a room with one barber's chair and an old man plying his trade, unchanged for decades. It's as if two different villages coexist: the contemporary one and the one that people started to leave in the middle of the twentieth century.

There is a still-older incarnation. Beyond the eastern edges of Pyli, the road enters a rural landscape with smooth green fields and cloudy grey olive trees. From the settlement of Amaniou, it then leads up the mountain into dark evergreens and pale grey limestone until the walls of an eleventh-century fortress appear high above on a rocky outcrop. Paleo Pyli dates back to the Byzantines, and the castle was reinforced around the fourteenth century by the Knights of St John.

The place was a refuge from invaders such as the pirates that raided these islands in the seventeenth and eighteenth centuries. After such threats receded, some say, people no longer needed to live so high on the mountain; others say it was cholera that caused it; but by 1820 the place was deserted, and now there are just empty shells of houses among the trees, irregular pale grey field stones overgrown with bright green moss.

Footpaths and signs indicate Paleo Pyli is well visited in warmer months, but today there are just goats. The only sound is trickling water and the misty, grey afternoon adds to the calm but slightly eerie atmosphere. A building towers over the stream, perhaps a watermill.

The archway in front of a church is supported by blocks of inscribed ancient marble masonry, placed upside down. Beside a dried-up fountain is a low construction with two smooth domes built into its roof, and a tree growing through the middle. I duck inside the arched doorway to find plastered walls with waterspouts, and a handful of circular holes in the domes to let in light. It is a Turkish bath from Ottoman times.

The bells of St Nicholas's church peal a few times in the early morning; then the square at the top of Pyli falls quiet. It rained overnight and is still raining. The kafeneio is open behind a plastic awning but the clientele appears sparse. From the house I watch trim older ladies in black coats leaving church clutching umbrellas and handbags, splashing through the square in classic black high-heeled shoes and black tights, occasionally accompanied by a husband in black coat and dark suit.

A few minutes' walk away is the old spring, built in 1592 during the Ottoman occupation. A well-dressed, middle-aged man is filling containers. The water that continually flows from the spring is channelled towards the fields.

After the rain stops, the sun comes out. Up the mountain on a road leading west, littered with plastic coffee cups and snack wrappers thrown from passing cars, the pines and wild plants are dripping with rain, the cliffs above glistening silver in the light while clouds hang above, waiting. A brown-and-white goat trips down a grassy slope, as if in a scene from *The Sound of Music*. The colours are all bright greens and greys, the pines deeply fragrant. Daisies, half-closed, show the outer pink of their long petals. Bathtubs sit in fields for goats and sheep to drink from. Sandy hills fall away towards grazing lands and olive groves, then plains, beyond which the sea gleams flat and silver-grey.

It's odd to see two other people out walking, not dressed for hiking, carrying nothing. They approach and I guess they're Indian or Pakistani; they politely ask if they are heading the right way for Pyli, before continuing cheerfully on their way. One thing I noticed quite quickly about Pyli was the number of people from Africa, India and the Middle East walking up and down the main street. In recent years, this area was designated a 'hotspot' for refugees and illegal immigrants, with an abandoned military camp nearby transformed into a holding centre. The island benefits from a reduced tax status for hosting them.

The road continues to skirt the mountain, passing an area where a quarry has cut an entire piece of it away; at the westernmost point before the road heads down towards the south coast is a farm with a scattering of animals and a pen made from old pallets. There are distant views south to Turkey's Datça peninsula, Tilos, Yiali and Nisyros, west to Astypalea, north to Kalymnos, then Pserimos and east to Bodrum. Rain is falling out to sea, and coming closer.

A flock of fat, contented sheep in an olive grove tug enthusiastically at juicy Bermuda buttercups. I've walked down from Pyli to the flat plain criss-crossed by straight, long roads with fields on either side. One of the roads is named for the refugees from Asia Minor, who came here a century ago.

Heading towards Alyki, the large, oval lake that borders the sea, I'm soon in the resort of Tigaki, its hotels shuttered and locked for the season; some look so forlorn that maybe they're closed for good. After so much rain, the tracks that lead to the lake are deep in water and mud, so I continue around on tarmac and see a handful of sheep grazing in a hotel garden. A man with long grey hair looks on, somewhat unhappily: does he own the sheep or the hotel?

A sandy track leads towards the sea, through a patch of land covered in wild plants and reeds, beyond which are dunes. It's hard to imagine that the beach will have escaped development but hope springs eternal. And is, on occasion, amply rewarded. A pristine, pale sand beach scattered with papery brown ribbons of seagrass stretches in either direction, bordered by rough blue sea, white waves surging into shore. I let Lisa free and there is sheer joy as she races around and wriggles in the sand. Across the water are the gentle hills of Pserimos, empty except for an army camp at one end. Dark clouds contrast vividly with the brightness of the sea and shore. As I turn to look behind, I can see nothing but soft dunes covered in grey-green foliage, and the mountain in the distance. It's gloriously natural and beautiful.

Eventually we walk inland a little, finding a route to the lake. A white flamingo steps tentatively in the marshy shallows. I follow a thin path between low samphire-like plants tinged with pink towards the still water's edge and see a flock of flamingos in the distance, where the lake is fringed with tall grasses. It would be dazzling at sunset.

Suddenly I hear something, look around, and through the bushes I see a person and some sheep. Then all hell breaks loose as a dog dashes over and starts snapping and snarling at Lisa. I expect the fighting is just a warning and let go of Lisa's lead so she can take care of herself. The man approaches, shouting at his dog to come, and eventually it backs off. It's the man we saw earlier with the sheep in the hotel. His long grey hair sticks out from under a woolly winter hat.

'It's the breed,' he says, apologetically. 'They never listen. She was just protecting the animals.'

I smile and tell him I completely understand. I'm happy to see a farmer and his dog driving a flock of sheep around the salt marsh. It's like a parallel universe amid the resort hotels. He's quickly gone, his sheep disappearing into the bushes. And I find what I came here to see: a few graffiti-covered buildings, part of the old salt works.

During the lifespan of Paleo Pyli (perhaps earlier) and into its new incarnation as Pyli, this lake, which lies just below sea level, was used for the harvesting of salt, a vital resource before refrigeration. The Ottoman-built hammam in Kos town, after it stopped operating in 1948, was used as a salt depot, and this salt works was used until the 1980s. Plaster has fallen from one building, revealing dark stone walls with round windows. There are a few holding tanks, and long, straight channels lead to the sea between dark marsh, filled with water that reflects the silvery sky. Hundreds of flamingos spend the winter at this wetland.

There's too much mud to continue around the lake so I am soon back to the closed-up businesses, including a Chinese restaurant and a gargantuan supermarket. I walk to the busy main road and into the modern village of Zipari for something to eat, then escape the speeding traffic and tarmac by veering uphill to find country tracks. The landscape is immediately lovely again, lush and green with stone ruins, cows and olive trees, and quiet – except for the occasional gunshot from a distant hunter.

Two women and two dogs are walking towards me, and they stop to say hello. They are German, living in the mountain villages. The chattier of the two, who works as a tour guide in summer, says the hunters are supposed to stay on the mountain, but often ignore the rules and, adding insult to injury, leave their plastic bullet casings and plastic water bottles behind. It's a long hunting season here, from late September, mostly for sport. As I continue, the sun breaks through clouds and casts magical light on the hillsides. Next to an old stone barn is a big villa where a stark expanse of lawn is enclosed by galvanised steel and chrome fencing. Life has changed so much in a generation or two that people now spend money to protect useless land. But the springs keep gushing, and soggy chickens and cows and sheep saunter happily in the fields.

Back in Pyli later, I go to the mini-market. There are two; in one, the people are very chatty, in the other they're more reserved. The reserved one displays, as well as good stuff like local cheese, a frighteningly vast array of cleaning and hygiene products and plastic toys, and has a garish sign – but in the corner it says, 'From 1953'. I wonder if the owner feels like talking.

The upright old man behind the counter, wearing his coat because the door is always open, says he's been running the shop for fifty years. 'I got it when I got married. It originally belonged to my father-in-law.'

'Were there more people in those days?' I ask.

'No, fewer. Now there are lots of foreigners – German, Albanian… But it's steady, people don't really leave.'

I say I like the fact that there's still agriculture here.

'Oh yes,' he says. 'Also cows, sheep, pigs… The only thing we don't have any more is donkeys. They sold them. Everyone has cars now, they don't need donkeys to get around.'

A younger man, maybe sixty, is shopping and the owner asks, 'You were involved in local politics – do you know how many people live in the village now?'

'Ah, let's see, there are about eight or nine hundred registered voters – though not everyone votes, because what's the point, they think?'

I say it's the same in England.

'I don't remember much about the old days here. I went to Australia when I was a kid in the fifties, to Melbourne. Who would remember?' he asks the older man.

He shrugs. 'No-one, they're all dead, the ones who knew.'

After more rain, the day dawns sunny and warm with deep blue skies. We make an early start. A dog charges out of his house with the pained love-howl he makes whenever Lisa passes. By the church of St George, I duck into the bakery for fresh spinach pies and baked cereal bars for the long walk. The plan is to follow a road that meanders through the string of mountain villages two or three hundred metres above the plains. Dikeos rises steeply up to five hundred metres higher and its pale rock, partly covered in dark pine and cypress, provides a stunning backdrop.

Beyond Amaniou, the road curves into an idyllic place where old fields marked out by stone walls are scattered with boulders. I notice a ruined stone farmhouse with an oak and a cypress tree beside it; then look up the hill and see others. I stop to sit for a moment, stare out to blue sea and sky, islands in the distance. The mountain and forest would have provided sanctuary from pirate raids. I imagine people living here, looking down to their fields where they grew vines and tomatoes, olives and tobacco – not only for smoking, but also for tanning leather. They'd have gone down there by donkey, perhaps stayed in a stone hut for a while before returning home. This small settlement on the hillside was abandoned by the 1950s.

The next village, Lagoudi, is dominated by a huge white church with a blue dome. Down a narrow alleyway are small, closed-up houses with arches over their doors, one inscribed with '1897'. A few locals sit in a tiny café. Across the street, a woman is feeding chickens and hanging laundry. The fields beyond here are full of olive trees, the roadside tangled with blackberry bushes and a clematis vine with cream, bell-shaped flowers. The road skirts a deep ravine with a stream running through it at the entrance to Asomatos.

The lovely name of this village – derived from *soma*, meaning 'body' – translates as 'disembodied' or 'incorporeal', referring to the holiness of the archangel to whom the church is dedicated. There has been a church here since the eleventh century, its cells functioning as a school during the Turkish occupation. Now it is surrounded by holiday apartments and a café closed for the season. The hundred-year-old whitewashed stone houses are simple and graceful, immaculately kept, but except for some barking dogs and the ubiquitous chickens crossing the road, there's scant sign of life. It feels a little... disembodied, incorporeal; a perfect ghost town on this sunny winter day.

Beyond the top of the village and the remains of the old public washing place, the road skirts the treeline; above are steep cliffs and dark forest. Men pack logs into a pick-up truck. In a clearing with a picnic area, buildings have fallen into disrepair and rubbish has been tipped down the slope nearby. I've been walking for a few hours and am only eight kilometres from Kos town when finally the road turns downhill into olive groves, branching off to the abandoned village of Haihoutes.

At the entrance to the village is a gushing spring. This would have been a useful stop for centuries on the route from the harbour town to the mountain, and the church, St Dimitrios, dates back to the Byzantines. The village's unusual name is probably derived from its founding family, who might have been Armenian. In any case, a community began here in the 1820s cultivating olives and vines, and a century later there were almost two hundred people. It grew further during World War II, providing safe refuge from the town, and in 1959 its school had fifty students. But by then the exodus to cities and the New World had begun, and the population dropped over the following decades. Perhaps for the last people it seemed crazy to live a hard, rural life within sight of the bright lights of town. The final resident left in 2007.

Wandering through the village, I stop to look at a ruined house, an interlocking pattern of brown and grey stones with hints of pink and blue, interspersed with moss and delicate green shoots. Each wall is different, a work of art particular to the person who made it and the stones they used. The rocks of these islands are so varied, shot through with streaks of varying colours and textures partly thanks to volcanic eruptions. Each abandoned house owes something to nature, which is working its magic reclaiming it.

And every village has local characteristics. In Haihoutes, chimneys with triangular tops sit above wide fireplaces. A walled-off storage area inside one house was probably once covered with a wooden platform for a bed. And there's an arched recess, like a cupboard with a wooden shelf across, in the outer wall of the building – a shrine? I notice lots of wood: wooden lintels over the windows and doors, and wooden roof beams that are simply rough-hewn logs. I look across a green field to the pine forest just metres away. What a resource that was, providing roofs, furniture, firewood and food. The grass is now covered in the multi-coloured plastic cartridges of hunters' bullets.

In fact, Haihoutes is no longer completely in ruins. A few people have seen an opportunity here, and there is now a summertime café with a stone outdoor oven, and a little museum of traditional life, and a few houses have been restored and made available for rent. It would be a tranquil walking stopover in the spring or autumn, with the forest above, and a view of the sea far below.

On the way back, for variety I walk through Zia, with its springs and old water mills and path to the highest point on the island. The village was already commercialised when I visited fifteen years ago, and is now a concentration of shops and restaurants (albeit closed), so I hurry through. Just below, an old man is sitting in a field behind a bushy hide, holding a gun. He fires just after we pass, sending Lisa into a panic, tail between her legs. We swiftly descend to Lagoudi, stopping briefly at a farm with about a hundred chickens, a few goats and sheep and even a couple of deer. I've just tasted some wild myrtle berries at the roadside when a big black cloud moves in to shed its load. I'm drenched to the skin. Guys pass in a flatbed truck but it's filled with freshly sawn logs for the fire. I press on, working up an appetite for dinner.

The owner of taverna Drosos on Pyli square welcomes me warmly and seats me next to a barrel-shaped wood-burning stove, made for big logs. He introduces himself as Vasilis. While I sip wine and eat salad and fried potatoes and lamb chops cooked to perfection, I eavesdrop on a group of men and women. One man talks about repairs to the town harbour. After they leave, as he clears their table, Vasilis says they were local politicians and a member of parliament.

'The problem with politicians,' he says, speaking generally, 'is that they can never agree. The mayor wants to say *I did it*, the MP wants to say *I did it*, in the end no-one does it because they can't work together.'

He pours himself a small drink and sits on a stool by the fire. In his fifties, he has lived here his whole life, running the taverna for thirty years. I tell him about the things I've been looking at, comparing the old houses with the big new homes. One I passed the other day had everything from terracotta tiling to porthole windows, a Chinese pagoda and English topiary.

'The old houses matched the environment,' he says. 'They were made with the only things people had – stones, earth and wood. Now people have big houses, even though the families are much smaller – in the old days there would be eight living in a little house, but in the summer we mostly live outside anyway. And now they have all the extras, different colours, fake stuff, everyone wants to do something different. But the old houses were better at keeping warm in winter and cool in summer.'

The walls of the old houses are so thick: often an outer wall and an inner wall, the middle packed with smaller stones and earth, providing insulation and longevity.

Vasilis was at school when the first hotel opened in Tigaki in the mid-1970s. The government had given the fields to the people, but it was too wet to grow wheat. Gradually he lost track of all the different hotels that went up. It's a shame they've left the salt works to fall into disrepair, he thinks. He also hasn't seen as many flamingos as usual this year.

He clearly loves his village but says being in a smaller place has its difficulties – even Pyli. If you have children who need to go to classes or activities and meet up with friends, you need a car as the bus is so infrequent. It's different for me, with my kind of work and the fact that I don't mind walking an hour and a half to the port… 'And most people these days want everything right beside them, done for them.'

Having the same routine every day and seeing the same people, with few choices, can be tough. There aren't many options for a break in routine when you have a job or children in school. It's a good point. I know how different winter on Tilos felt to me the year I agreed to give English classes to the schoolchildren, limiting my ability to take the ferry to Rhodes when I needed to. Vasilis takes the occasional break with the family but tries to keep the taverna open as much as possible for the local community. 'The old guys come in for their coffee, play cards all morning, go home for lunch and then come back at five… It's not right to be closed whenever I want.'

Another winter morning in Pyli, and five bright-eyed, dark-haired girls in pink coats huddle under one umbrella to pet Lisa, telling me English words they're learning at school. I set out past the gushing old spring and then downhill on country lanes, cross the main road with its fast traffic, continue past more fields and hotels until I reach Marmari and a vast stretch of soft, pale sand. At this time of year, it is empty and natural – dunes covered in reeds, blue-green sea sparkling in the sun, and the empty hills of Pserimos and Kalymnos across the water, dappled by cloud shadows. Lisa races about and rolls in the sand. A north wind is blowing, and it's too cold to linger. I return via old Turkish storerooms and a derelict stone windmill.

Another day, encouraged by my explorations so far, I decide to go further afield and set out west in the direction of Antimachia castle. Saddened by a pile of plastic gun cartridges dumped on the ground along with plastic water bottles and coffee cups, I continue up a muddy track, passing olive and orange trees and a stream trickling through a valley. The damage of quarrying is evident, and all too late I realise that we are heading straight for the municipal dump. A field where a stone house stands has a sad crop of plastic bags caught on shrubs; a truck unloads air-conditioning units; at the rubbish processing site I have to run to escape the stench, looking back to a vision from hell. Nobody should ever see this much rubbish up close. Or maybe everybody should.

I continue past a cement factory, all the way down to the main road where I trudge by speeding cars and litter thrown from car windows. I seem to have found the grimmest walk. Finally, there's a turn-off to a quiet track leading north away through wild heathland towards the sea. I relax and breathe normally again. There's the gentle sound of sheep bells in the distance. I will walk to the sea and find an easier route. Along the track is a parked pick-up truck and the ruddy-faced, bearded driver says hello and asks where we're going.

I smile and say, 'Just walking.'

He says, gently, 'Well, go a little way down here but then, my love, can you turn back? I've got lambs down there, mothers with the little ones, and as soon as they see your dog they'll run. My love, I've got four hundred sheep in these hills and you'll cause me a lot of damage if they start to run. D'you understand?'

I almost cry. I'll have to walk for kilometres along that terrifying main road among the rubbish. But the day is redeemed by meeting a good farmer looking after his sheep.

'You're still here?' asks the lady in the other mini-market on the square. 'What a shame it's been raining so much, such bad weather…'

I've been checking boat schedules online, and then the weather, and have decided to stay longer in this comfortable house getting to know this part of the island. While I've encountered abandoned villages and salt works, I've also found strong vestiges of rural life remaining, surprisingly, alongside the new.

'It would be raining at my home in Tilos, anyway,' I say. 'And we have more power cuts.'

I feel a gentle tug on my coat, turn around and it's the lady's husband, resting in a chair. I met him on the first day, unloading vegetables from his truck.

'I went to Tilos once,' he says. 'Lovely beaches, but very small fields. Here, it's paradise if you're a farmer. I've got hundreds of chickens, and so much land for them to walk around in. I've got a hundred laying hens, and a hundred little ones. They start laying at six months, and when they're a year old, I slaughter them for food.' He makes the throat-slitting gesture. 'And by then the little ones are old enough to lay. Today I got seventy eggs.' He shows me a huge one and insists I take it.

Up above the village, I hear animals' bells as I pass the field where five bathtubs serve as water troughs. The wind gets stronger. I keep a lookout north towards Mastihari for signs of boats crossing to Kalymnos, planning to continue my journey north from the small port there. Whenever I call, they say they're not sure the small boat will travel because of the weather. I near the edge of the mountain and can't go further in the fierce wind. Eagles wheel overhead. I turn back and follow the road to the cemetery where hundreds of birds are trying to settle in the trees as dusk falls.

Later, Vasilis at Drosos taverna tells me all his siblings still live in the village, and some have greenhouses and supply him with vegetables. He talks about the traditional chicken soup local mothers prepare on winter holidays, which must be made with a fresh free-range chicken. First, they slaughter the chicken and burn off the feathers. Then they take out the liver, chop it up fine and fry it, add a little onion and rice, stuff it in the chicken and sew it up. They then boil the chicken for three hours at least to make the meat tender, and mix egg-lemon sauce into the broth.

'You can make it with a supermarket chicken, and it's good, but it's not the same thing,' he says.

Lisa is happy because he's feeding her treats from the kitchen, as usual. As I eat a good souvlaki with tzatziki and salad and potatoes, at a table on the other side of the woodburner I overhear a man mention the word *kamini*. I realise he must be referring to a lime kiln or furnace as he describes how they built the fire inside the chimney and then put in stones, and how they'd wear two pairs of trousers and thick shoes and be very careful. I ask him if he's talking about an *asvestokamino* and he says yes, his grandfather had one in Albania. When there was an earthquake in 1979, 8.1 on the Richter scale, it took a few men three months to tear down the remaining walls of a stone house made with sand, lime and *porselana*.

The others leave and Vasilis sits by the fire with a drink. I mention the beautiful stretch of coast between Marmari and Mastihari. He says for maybe two kilometres it used to be all open and natural beach. He wistfully recalls a particular spot.

'I used to go there before I met my wife, and then we went there together, when she was pregnant, and then with the kids. We'd go there and just sit in the shade of a tree and swim, and it was a special place for me, for us. Now in the summer, it's so covered in sunbeds and umbrellas that even the tourists can't walk down it and enjoy it. And that makes me sad.'

He's not complaining about the hotels, even though many are foreign-owned and all-inclusive, where people have already paid for their meals, so the local tavernas don't see them. They're very nice places and he's proud that Kos has more five-star hotels than Rhodes now.

'But the local people have lost their beach.'

In the morning, I call Mastihari about the boat; they'll know by lunchtime about the evening crossing, so I set out with Lisa for a walk east, taking dirt tracks through countryside. When I approach a deserted barn to take a closer look, behind it I find a large dome-shaped stack of wood, the branches laid vertically, in a circle burnt black.

I hear an engine and a man appears: greyish beard and glasses, sixties, padded rainjacket, jeans, boots and a woolly hat. When I apologise for intruding, he laughs. 'I tried to offer you a lift in my truck a few days ago when it was pouring with rain.'

I'd misunderstood and declined, thinking he was going in the wrong direction. I ask if he's the maker of this elaborate, intricate woodpile. He says yes, confirming it's a *kamini* for making charcoal. Picking up on my interest, he explains how it's done. I don't catch all the details in Greek, but I get the gist.

'I'll be adding another two car-loads of olive wood to this before it's ready. And every piece has to be cut just right so it lies flat against the others and doesn't stick out. When it's ready, I put these' – he indicates sheets of rusted metal – 'around the sides, two layers with earth packed in the middle, and these' – he picks up curved pieces of metal, perhaps old oil drums – 'to leave about twenty holes around the bottom. When I light it, it'll smoke, not burn but smoke, for four or five days, maybe a week. I'll wait for good weather because I'll have to be here at night to check on it. Gradually the pile gets lower and lower.'

On retirement from his job as a hotel cook, he decided to consolidate his knowledge about charcoal making, learning from his father and friends. He's now taught it to his sons, who work with him when they're not busy with other things – one is currently cutting wood on the mountain. The charcoal is in high demand, sold even before he makes it, mostly to tourism businesses – tavernas or boat trip organisers. Tourism is helping this traditional knowledge survive, passed down from father to son. 'Whatever you learn, it's good.'

He excuses himself to go and feed a young pig in a pen. 'All the other little ones got slaughtered,' he says, guiltily, 'but I'll move this one soon to be with the older ones. What can you do…? If you eat something you've killed yourself, you know what you're eating.' The pig grunts with excitement when it sees the food bucket. Its water trough is, as usual, a bathtub. Who knew there were so many old bathtubs? Maybe they came from the hotels, replaced by showers. I wave goodbye.

At the shop in Amaniou, I buy cheese and organic wine made locally. Back in Pyli, as I climb the hill, the pink-coated girls squeal, 'It's Lisa!' They crowd around to stroke her, telling one another not to be afraid. Finally reaching the house that has begun to feel like home, I call Mastihari again to ask about boats, and it turns out they expect the evening boat to sail. Quickly, I set about packing and tidying the house, and call to book a taxi, explaining about the dog. The controller says no problem, and at the appointed time I go to sit in the square.

A taxi arrives, but the owner takes one look at Lisa and says she's too big and will have to go in the boot.

The boot?

The controller promises to try to find someone else. The boat is due to leave in half an hour. Vasilis beckons me over to the taverna and insists I wait inside, saying he'll take us to the port himself if necessary, though I'm not convinced I want to go. His brother says, 'Why travel at night? Better in the morning…' A man with an American accent strikes up a conversation; he was a cook in a Chicago diner for twenty-five years before coming home to Pyli. There's another story here and maybe another night wouldn't hurt…

Then the taxi shows up, the young driver having come all the way from town because he likes to help people with dogs. The boat is due to leave in fifteen minutes, so he drives through the dark at top speed. I hand him a big tip as I dash towards the tiny hydrofoil. Half of the passengers are standing out on the back deck either because they're smoking (the lads in tracksuits) or get seasick (the woman in shiny shoes) or have a dog (me). We wait. And wait. Then we hear someone say there's a flight just landed from Athens. We wait for the last passengers to arrive from the airport.

Finally, engines fire up. In the dark, with a crescent moon half-hidden by cloud, we go fast, a wake rising high behind us, bumping across the waves. I'm delighted I waited to travel this way. A big wave crashes over the side of the deck, soaking a few people. Wheelie suitcases roll all over the place. Half an hour later we're approaching the lights of Kalymnos.

GOLD IN THE SEA

KALYMNOS

Happy to wake to the sound of waves, I throw on some clothes and take Lisa to the beach. Curtains of misty rain obscure the island of Telendos that sweeps up to a great height just across the water. This lovely west coast of Kalymnos has hotels built into the hillside shoulder to shoulder, the road lined with restaurants and shops; but the resort of Masouri, where we arrived last night by taxi, is closed and empty on this damp January day, just the occasional car stopping at the ATM or to fill bottles from the free dispensers of filtered water. I take deep breaths of pine-scented air and spend the morning walking up the west coast to Kastelli. Lichen-covered stone walls criss-cross the steep promontory, faint remains of a fortress used during Syrian attacks in the seventh century, with rainwater cisterns dug into the rock. I look around at empty mountains, sunlight streaming through dark clouds to illuminate the steely water with silver.

A small cove calls me down, the sea a powdery aquamarine after the rain, the pebbles many shades of grey streaked with white, scattered with mauve. The water feels chill at first, but I acclimatise. From here all I see are limestone cliffs streaked with grey, the bare rock hills of the north.

Kalymnos is an extremely rugged, mountainous island; the fourth largest of the Dodecanese after Rhodes, Karpathos and Kos, though much smaller than those, and the third largest by population. Most residents live in the sizeable harbour town of Pothia in the southeast, or in the old capital of Hora above it. There are vast areas to the north with only a scattering of people.

I'm hungry after my swim and this area of the coast has no shops, so a sign declaring that taverna Tsopanakos is open for lunch is a pleasant surprise. I ascend the steps and enquire. A young man shrugs and shouts for his mother, who offers what she's cooked for the family. 'No problem to bring your dog inside – we have lots of animals. She can probably smell them on our clothes!'

Her husband worked as a cook in France as a young man, but came back. 'Life's too expensive there when you have a family,' he tells me. They now have two hundred sheep and goats. 'I wake up in the morning, wash my face and I'm off to feed them before I feed myself. People ask why I don't take holidays… but you can't when you have animals.'

Grateful to find a good meal, I eat free-range chicken raised on their farm and cooked in tomato sauce, with pasta and their own cheese; fresh winter salad of lettuce, cabbage, carrot and onion, with bread and red wine.

All is silent except for sheep and goat bells as I walk south down the west coast the next day. Euphorbia, wild fennel, Mediterranean pine, salt cedar and olive paint the land. With businesses closed, it's easier to spot a few old cottages and faded grand villas amid new development as I walk through Myrties ('Myrtles'). At Elies ('Olives') there are genteel abandoned houses with olive trees, palm trees and the occasional cistern and well. Stylish mid-twentieth-century villas stand neglected.

A path leads up from Kantouni Bay into a landscape of thyme, grey limestone and thorns. High above are cliffs rising sheer and striped dark grey, huge hollows and caves hung with stalactites. The footpath forks with a sign to the airport – conjuring comical visions of wheelie suitcases being trundled through the scrub to the strip on top of the escarpment. The whitewashed chapel of Ayios Fotis comes into view, built into a fold of the bare rock face. The waymarked path continues, with hair-raising drops in a couple of places. I go as far as the point where it turns south, sunlit sea rippling into the distance far below. Returning the same way, I notice a well-crafted stone wall capped with rocks aslant and protruding to stop clambering animals, and cave shelters closed in by stone walls, blending into the hillside.

At the fishing harbour of Melitsahas that evening, taverna Fountagio is busy with a baptism celebration, and young guys wearing bright shirts and gold jewellery emerge from the party to smoke outside, one talking in an Australian accent about heading back to Darwin. A priest in a fisherman's woolly hat is among a group of men playing cards. Space will be found for me but I prefer to sit outside and watch the lightning over Telendos while I eat grilled *palamitha*, bonito tuna, with garlic sauce.

Telendos, a small island separated from Kalymnos in 535AD by a massive earthquake – they say there's a sunken city under the strait – is home to a few families living year-round, fishing and keeping sheep. Its school has three pupils and one teacher who takes the boat across daily. It is one of several islands within the municipality of Kalymnos; the smallest have very few services and the most basic medical care. Pserimos had an official population of eighty according to the 2011 census, though locals a few years later told me that about twenty actually lived there. Farmakonisi had seventy-four residents in a 2001 survey but now has only ten. Between north Kalymnos and the Turkish peninsula beyond Bodrum is Imia (as it is known to the Greeks – Imia/ Kardak is its official international name), a territory of less than 0.04 square kilometres spread across two tiny islets. Bronze statues in Pothia commemorate those who lost their lives in the conflict with Turkey over Imia/Kardak on 31st January 1996; it remains on the list of 'disputed' islands and is protected by the Greek military, its only inhabitants.

Back at my room, I sleep a long, deep, winter's sleep, waking when it gets light around seven. From the balcony I look to the northern finger of the island, all the land seeming empty, where I walked the previous summer.

On a hot August day, I followed a path among old village houses and their gardens, then gradually ascended the hillside over a ravine to a cluster of huge olive trees. Their wide trunks were twisted into filigree threads, haunting shapes. A couple of stone wells were sunk in their midst. Though the ground was now disrespectfully scattered with plastic gun cartridges, I sensed this stand of olives above Arginonta was once an important place.

Arginonta is a little settlement in an inlet beyond Kastelli where the west coast meets the far north. Even in August, it felt excitingly wild and empty. The land was dramatic, fearsome even, with craggy grey cliffs, rust-streaked, dropping down steep inclines almost five hundred metres to the sea. Waves surged relentlessly from the northwest into the narrow inlet where aquamarine water almost glowed. I saw a diver in a wetsuit swimming close to the black rocks, then I watched it moving and realised it was a seal.

My friend found us this place as a refuge from the crowds of summer. There was no bank machine, an irregular bus service, no shop, but a woman sat at a roadside stall with thyme honey and homemade cheese, proud to have lived her whole life in this village. 'Here you wake up in the morning, open your doors, and leave them open.'

The owner of the roadside taverna where we went for dinner was also sanguine about life in the quiet north of Kalymnos. 'Things have been hard in recent years, but it's OK to live on a little here.' While his teenage son prepared the food, he showed us photographs of his climbing friends. I think a lot of Greek men run tavernas just for the company.

The peaks of Kalymnos may look severe, but they make rock climbers salivate. Since the late 1990s, the island has been extensively remapped by climbers, especially in the north. White posts indicate the way to climbing areas, and signs give affectionate names for crags. The busy season is in the cooler autumn, and an international climbing festival takes place every October; but even in summer, I looked up to the high cliffs and saw tiny, brightly dressed humans clinging to the orange-tinged limestone.

The road north, cut into the rock, was lined with flowering oleander. On a discarded fridge, someone had affectionately written in English, 'Fridges of Kalymnos'. The occasional truck passed, selling vegetables. For several kilometres there was nothing but wide vistas of rock and sea, until a few houses started to appear. Those by the road were mostly modern; a private road led to something that looked like a Disney version of a Scottish castle with a swimming pool and tennis courts. But higher up the hill I spotted ruined stone barns, while a stone path downhill passed cottages hidden in gardens and olive terraces to reach the early Christian church of St Nicholas and a sliver of beach where a fishing boat idled with engine problems. A cry like a dog's turned out to be a lady calling her goats.

It was hot for walking – we'd left Lisa behind, knowing she'd struggle – so we were grateful to see a stand selling cold drinks. The proprietor, a woman with bushy dark hair, took my money for a can of lemonade then poured us cup after cup of delicious, ice-cold spring water from an old Coke bottle, pointing out the path to the village spring that flowed all year. She and her husband had just reopened the stand after twenty years of living in town for their children, and they took turns looking after it while she cleaned hotel rooms and he tended to the sheep. At that moment it was a venue for the local committee, including the priest, to plan an upcoming festival. Intrigued about the vestiges of an older way of life here, I asked when the road was built. She stopped to think.

'Well, I'm now fifty-six and I was seven when they built it, so it's forty-nine years old! I remember because all the children used to walk along donkey tracks from the other villages to the school here.' That would have been the 1970s. She added that even then, people here still produced most of what they needed. They would take their mizithra cheese to sell in town, travelling occasionally by boat but mostly along the paths on foot with a donkey. That way of life disappeared along with the school and many of the people. But some were moving back.

We walked over the mountain ridge and down past more abandoned stone huts to an empty green valley and a bay with a chapel. The north wind and currents carried rubbish here, but a little further was a cleaner pebble beach from where climbers made their precarious way up a cliff while rough, wild-looking goats mooched about stone pens. There was something built of red rocks and handmade bricks at the water's edge, strewn with shards of earthenware pottery; an oven, a kiln? They made ceramics in this area. I looked at the hillside covered in green shrub and thought someone could live here for a while on sea urchins and fish and goat, capers and thyme and oregano.

On the way back, hearing bells, we looked up high and saw sheep passing single file along the mountainside. While the glowing orange sun dropped into the sea and the bay below rippled with the wind and the hillsides turned golden, goats and sheep headed home for the night, surrounding us. Listening to the music of the bells, I wondered who would keep animals in years to come and if we would be the last generation to hear this sound as we walk.

The next day of that same trip, we made our way further north to Emborio, a harbour sheltered by a spit of land. Its name suggests it was once a trading centre, and we saw etched lines of old terraces on the slopes. I knew there were remains of an ancient castle high above, and early Christian baths nearby. Now it was a tiny settlement with seafront tavernas and a handful of pensions, sailboats moored in the bay. Beyond, there was little but windswept bays and fishermen, a fish farm, beehives and goats.

A handwritten sign on a gate offered fresh eggs and vegetables for sale. Ringing the bell, we met a man in his forties from Melbourne. My friend got chatting with him and he told us his parents had come from Kalymnos and moved to Australia, but he had loved spending holidays here as a child, so when he had saved a bit of money from his business he moved to Emborio, met his wife and set up a farm supplying the local community. He'd been here about ten years now, his gardens well kept and flourishing.

The maritime people of Kalymnos have a history of coming and going. That night, we took a taxi across the island to the big, busy harbour town of Pothia. Inhabitants of rocky, mountainous islands often turned to the sea for a living and Pothia, established in 1850, has many old mansions dating from when it was the centre of Greece's sponge industry. In the late nineteenth century things had begun to change and many people left for the New World, but it's still a lively town.

At the end of the harbour where fishing boats sat in the inky water, lights glared over a café table. Three men – one slender with long grey hair woven into plaits, one with a prodigious belly, one smartly dressed with a hooked nose – hung on every word of the fourth. His bare back was tanned deep chestnut, tight with muscle and lean down to the narrow waist, his broad shoulders hunched over the glass in his hand, and his head was covered by a stars-and-stripes scarf. He held them spellbound with traveller's tales.

That summer night we found a taverna among derelict buildings behind the waterfront, with tables spread out along the meeting of two alleys where musicians played. The owner found us a seat. Across the alley was a big table with what I guessed was a family of Kalymnian Australians back here for a holiday, the older generation born on the island and the younger in Australia.

The eldest man, with white hair and bushy moustache and his paunch held in by a pale blue shirt, got up to lead a dance with a woman of the same age wearing a knee-length dress and the kind of comfy sandals you see for sale in chemists. The young women joined in, including a beautiful, shy woman with sleek black hair and pretty sandals. She had perfect footwork, tiny steps, understated; she had clearly taken lessons since she was a child. But the elders danced smoothly with a natural joy as if this was how they met.

The song was one I knew: a man who lives far from home reminisces about the taste of the water and the wine from his village, and the kiss of his girl.

Over ninety per cent of the world's natural sea sponges come from the Dodecanese, and they were harvested from ancient times, mentioned by Homer and Aristotle. Naked divers used stone weights to help them descend and would hold their breath like the *haenyo* of Korea as they cut sponges from the seabed, leaving the base of the sponge intact so it would reproduce. It was hard and dangerous work, but local men learned the skills and were proud of their fearlessness.

In the nineteenth century, along with trading and boat building, sponge diving was the major source of the island's economic and social development. Black-and-white photographs show boys holding sponges half the size of themselves. The team on the boat would scout for the sponges using a glass-bottomed cylindrical tool; the diver went down as far as thirty metres and would stay three to five minutes, depending on lung capacity, cutting them loose and gathering them in a net. Merchants made great profits from trade and export. Like the pumice of Nisyros, it seems a surprising source of prosperity, but before synthetic substitutes, sponges were used for padding and filters, for cleaning tools, applying paints and glazes, and even as contraceptives.

Wealth from harvesting a free natural resource, however, brought greed and competition. In 1865 the diving suit or *skafandro* was introduced, enabling divers to stay down for longer, and deeper – as deep as seventy metres. Large fleets took over from the small boats; there were maybe three hundred ships, most with six or more divers, some more than a dozen. Trawlers were also used. They crossed to the southeast Mediterranean, which had the best sponge conditions, and stayed up to six months, stopping in Syria, Lebanon, Egypt, Libya and Tunisia. The week after Easter is still celebrated as the time when the sponge-divers' boats set out.

The diving suit came with great risks, and mistakes led to accidents. The men had to make several dives a day at greater depths without decompression pauses; decompression sickness led to paralysis and death. In 1884, a law was passed to regulate the use of diving apparatus, but between 1886 and 1910, around ten thousand divers died, while twice that number were left with permanent disabilities. Every household on Kalymnos was affected. Thanks to pressure from the women, in 1882 the Turkish sultan banned the suits; but that led to widespread concern about the economy and they were used again. On Symi, another important sponge-diving island, the sponge fishermen rebelled and destroyed the suits, but there the Ottomans sent in a warship and the rebel divers were arrested. Divers continued to be paralysed, but businesses flourished, using their fortunes to fund education and health care.

In the first decade of the twentieth century, as desire for union with Greece grew across the Turkish-controlled Dodecanese, Kalymnos and Symi started literary and cultural societies to reinforce the spirit of independence. But it was to no avail and many of the islanders gave up and left. One John M. Cocoris emigrated from Arcadia in the Peloponnese and founded the sponge-diving industry in Tarpon Springs, Florida in 1905, recruiting divers and crews from the islands of Kalymnos, Halki and Symi. It was extremely successful, and Tarpon Springs remains today a slice of Greece in the USA. If you Google 'Tarpon Springs sponge diving' you find businesses listed on Dodecanese Boulevard.

Meanwhile in the Mediterranean, the renewable resource of the sponges had been endangered by overfishing and trawling, and in the 1980s, a marine disease brought them close to extinction. Harvesting continues today on a smaller, safer and more sustainable scale. Natural sponges are highly absorbent and an environmentally friendly alternative to artificial versions. The unbleached ones can last eight years if left to dry out after use. They have enzymes that inhibit the growth of mould and bacteria and, once discarded, they decompose organically, leaving no trace.

When I was leaving Arginonta on that trip, Antonis drove me and Lisa in his taxi up the mountain road, blocked at one point by goats that seemed settled in for the night, and on to an empty plateau. All around was dark but I knew the route, having walked it with my friend a couple of days earlier.

Antonis told me that when his grandmother was born in the 1930s, the population of the island was about 35,000. 'People had big families, between six and twelve children. They had farms and produced everything they needed themselves,' he said as the road turned down into the valley where most of the farms used to be, kilometres of flat and fertile land stretching all the way to the inlet of Vathy.

'Prosperity still came from sponge diving. Sponges were like gold. But life was hard, and Australia and America needed people.' Men from Kalymnos joined sponge-diving communities in Florida and pearl-diving communities in Australia, grasping the opportunity to make their fortunes. Many married and had children in the countries where they had found work. 'First one brother went away, then another. My grandmother was one of seven children, but in the end she was the only one left on Kalymnos.'

In the 1970s, Kos began to invest in the burgeoning tourism industry. The lights of its northern coast were now visible across the water. Young people didn't want to earn their living from the sea as their fathers and grandfathers had. Some of those who had remained on Kalymnos went to Kos and earned their living from the sun.

Around 1980, people from Kalymnos began returning from the New World to build houses on family land. Probably after what they had been accustomed to, they didn't want to go back to the compact, traditional stone houses they'd had before. Maybe their children were taller, although the families were smaller. They built their dream houses in various styles; there was a building boom. But over the following decades, the boom started levelling out, and soon the country's economic difficulties began to take hold. People began leaving again for Australia and America, wherever they knew people and could find work.

The population had fluctuated up and down, but was currently around twelve thousand, or one-third of what it was in the 1930s. And although Kalymnos was a rich island compared to many, the cost of living in Greece had become higher, especially since the euro. 'There's always work on islands like Kos and Rhodes,' said Antonis, 'but these days when people leave for work, they don't get rich. They just make a wage.'

Antonis had taken out a loan to cover more than half of the 80,000-euro taxi driver's licence, and in winter supplemented his income by driving the school bus. Like all the taxi drivers I met on Kalymnos, he was eager for business, would drive twenty kilometres across the island for a fare and be there early.

I talked a little with him about the old skills lost when people left, and today's throwaway, imported plastic things.

'Fake stuff,' muttered Antonis quietly in agreement. He cared about the environment, though 'up to a point', because why do something if no-one else does? 'Look at this,' he said as we drove into a cloud of smoke. 'This is where they burn the rubbish,' he said. There were plans to make a recycling plant, but who knew when that would happen. A few minutes later we were relieved to be back in clean air, and soon descending into the bright lights of Pothia. He petted Lisa, cheerily waved goodbye and drove away to his next booking.

Lisa and I found our way through dark streets, chased by barking dogs, to the Villa Melina, a hotel where I'd booked a room for that night: a gate, a path through overarching trees, a tall darkened mansion, the setting for a ghost story.

The next morning, I saw the villa was painted salmon-pink; with a swimming pool surrounded by bougainvillaea and palms, it had an old-fashioned, slightly off-kilter charm. While waiting for breakfast, I met the owner, a man called Antonios with long grey hair. Relaxing at a large table on the veranda, he told me he lived in Germany for over forty years. I asked why he decided to come back.

'I always wanted to,' he said without a moment's hesitation. 'I went there to study, stayed to work, started a restaurant. Then I met my wife back here on a visit, and took her to Germany. We had a couple of children but I didn't want them to become *Germanakia*,' little Germans, he said, grinning, 'so my wife came back with them and they went to school here, and I stayed on for a while to continue with the business.' In the meantime, he bought this house, gradually turning it into a hotel.

We were joined by a plump woman from the north of Greece who was here for the saint, the miracle-working healer Ayios Savvas whose church was on the hill across town. She booked to stay for a month but was finding it expensive and wondered if she could find a cheap flight home – to Belgium, where she'd lived for fifty years.

Another man sat down at the table: slight, fair-haired, with gold glinting on his wrist and around his neck, he was from Kalymnos but had lived in Sydney for fifty years and made money in mining. He came back every other summer and would spend three months here this year. 'I spent 450 euros last night. I like throwing money for the musicians, and then of course there was the food.' I thought he was deliberately being nonchalant, as if this was perfectly normal – although Kalymnos is known to be a wealthy island.

I noticed a little tension in the face of the woman who couldn't afford to stay. 'Well, if you have that sort of money…'

'I'm sick,' he said. 'Cancer.' He was having chemotherapy and the tumour was getting smaller but he decided to spend his superannuation, his private pension, on having a good summer.

Soon they were both talking about miracle-working saints, and I was thinking of all the people who left and came back.

As I wander the backstreets in January, Pothia's legacy from the golden days of sponge diving is clear to see: sturdy stone mansions with a reserved elegance, wrought-iron balconies with flower motifs on the underside, half-circle windows with metal grilles over the doorways. Many have been renovated, others are derelict.

There are signs of twentieth-century abandonment too, though. A two-storey white house with balustrade and ornate details has 'For Sale' and a couple of phone numbers scrawled by hand on the front. Along the street, every other house is either boarded up or locked. These empty houses have a sense of calm prosperity: classical columns in bas-relief, tall louvred shutters, wrought-iron openwork, symmetry and proportion; but plaster has fallen away, paintwork is faded, a staircase hangs askew. Electricity boxes fixed near the doors are evidence of recent habitation.

There's a lowly stone cottage with a wooden platform for a bed inside surrounded by rubble. 'No Parking, Private, No Rubbish' is scrawled in spray paint on the outside and ignored; an abandoned car is sunk into the ground. On a forlorn façade nearby, with a fig tree growing through an open window, someone has stuck a sign advertising a language school for English and German lessons, as if to make a point. In a deserted playground, the swings have fallen from broken chains and lie amid grass and gravel. A sign on the locked gates announces a temporary closure for improvement works, but it's dated five years ago.

I happen upon the 'Neoclassical Museum'. A man around sixty years old with keys and a motorbike helmet in his hand seems about to lock up.

'Don't worry,' I say, 'it's OK if you're closing.'

'No problem, come in…'

The man introduces himself in English as Michael, a retired schoolteacher, and says the house was built by his grandfather. I'd assumed the museum would tell me something about Pothia's old houses; in fact, it tells the extraordinary story of his family. The rooms are filled with furniture, household objects and lots of photographs – of his parents, grandparents, aunts and uncles. And a gramophone from St Petersburg.

In Kalymnos around 1880, says Michael, some people were making money, mostly the big merchants, but many weren't, including his family. And so they took their sponge-diving money and were among many who moved to St Petersburg. They set up restaurants and pastry shops, and gradually learned the cigarette-making business there. Greeks felt somewhat at home in another Orthodox country and it wasn't easy to return, so they stayed. They spoke Russian, he says, and there are still many Greek descendants in St Petersburg. On the wall I spot a photograph of Greek shoemakers in Sebastopol, taken in the early twentieth century.

Michael's grandfather's name was Kyrannis; the pictures show him as a portly gentleman with a handlebar moustache. He was among those who saved Queen Olga, who had been married to King George I of Greece, when she sought refuge in the Greek Orthodox church in St Petersburg during the Russian Revolution in 1917. It was then, when those involved in trade were seen as enemies of the Bolshevik government, that Greeks had to leave behind their businesses and property and return home. His family were among them, though they took the gramophone, religious icons and cigarette machines. Kyrannis built a new house in Pothia and the family set up their own cigarette business, using tobacco grown on Kalymnos and around the Mediterranean, selling locally and to the other islands. It continued until the late 1950s when competition from the big companies made it no longer commercially viable.

Another of Michael's relatives, Drossos Skyllas, born in 1912, had been forced by his father to train as an accountant and work in the family tobacco business from a young age. But after World War II, he was finally able to emigrate to the USA and follow his dream of becoming an artist. Although with no formal training, he was meticulous about his painting, even making his own brushes to create the finest brushstrokes in his pursuit of photographic realism. His vivid self-portrait now hangs in the American National Gallery of Art. A print of it stands in this wonderfully quirky museum.

Michael is keen for the young generation to keep in touch with its heritage and the museum shows a domestic life now lost. In the kitchen, there's a tank with a tap over the sink for 'running' water; everyone had a tank for collecting rainwater. There's a small, low table for eating around – they didn't have dining tables or chairs – and implements for baking bread for the week, and a big pot for cooking *muuri*, goat stuffed with rice and roasted overnight. The collection includes pottery from the last potter on Kalymnos, whose kiln was near Panormos, and bricks made at Taphos in Pserimos, and tubular earthenware beehives that were laid flat but not as efficient as modern ones, he says, and easily broken. There's an earthenware bottle for keeping water cool, with a stopper made from natural sponge.

Back outside, I look across the water and think about my continuing journey. I have an option to stay another night here at the dog-friendly Archontiko Hotel, an old sponge-merchant's mansion owned by an Italian family since 1912, and to then head north to one of the less populated islands. On the tiny island of Arki, a lady called Evdokia is standing by to open her rooms especially and will cook for me. Her brother should come back soon and open his taverna, but then she is leaving until the spring. We speak again on the phone. The wind was bad last night and today, and more rain is forecast. It might not be the best time to go. I'm also feeling drawn in another direction, to the west this time and an island I've always wanted to visit.

BEE WINDOWS AND
BURNING ROCKS

ASTYPALEA

Close to midnight on a perfectly calm night, I'm on a familiar couch of the empty covered deck of the Blue Star ferry. Decadently comfortable with blankets and wine, and Lisa curled up nose to tail beside me, I write notes in the fresh air while my friend sleeps downstairs. For the first time in a while, I am heading away from the Turkish coast towards the middle of the Aegean.

Astypalea is the westernmost point of the Dodecanese, a stepping stone into the next group of islands, the Cyclades. Big ferries pass through in the middle of the night, stopping only at a little purpose-built concrete dock, so I've never seen the main village, six kilometres away. Shortly before 2am, we're met at the port by a young woman who has kindly waited up to drive us to our studio apartment. She says rain is expected; I groan a little but she assures me the island needs it to top up the water supply.

And she must be pleased in the morning because when I wake, it is pouring. A break fools me into chancing a walk to the shop but I return soaked to the skin and stay inside with the air conditioning on warm, trying to dry my clothes as I watch gauzy cataracts blown by the wind across the valley between me and the village.

The Hora – main village – of Astypalea is one of the most striking of all the Dodecanese. Sitting atop a small, steep hill with harbours on either side, its densely packed white houses are clustered below the brown stone walls of a Venetian castle. The architecture has a Cycladic flavour: all the buildings except the castle are painted white, many with triangles and rectangles cut out of the balcony walls. The white looks flat with the grey clouds above, and I wonder idly if it's all too perfect and obviously pretty for my taste. But first impressions on a cloudy day are often wrong, and anyway I have to laugh at where this journey is taking me if I can prefer tumbledown walls in a field to this. Will I ever recover from my obsession with dilapidated barns and threshing circles?

Astypalea is rich in remains of basilicas, mosaic floors and partial columns from the late Roman to early Christian era, a prosperous time for the island. Its history varies slightly from that of the rest of the Dodecanese. It was never ruled by the Knights of St John but was occupied by Venetians from 1207 until the Ottoman invasion of 1537, and again from 1648 to 1668. In the following centuries, people built their homes in the castle to be protected from pirates; otherwise, the only refuge was in caves in the high escarpments at the extremes of the island. The whole island may have been abandoned for periods due to invasions, but as the threat of pirate raids waned, people began settling all over the island again.

Records vary, but the population was probably around three thousand when the island joined the revolution that became the Greek War of Independence; after the 1830 negotiations, it was returned to the control of the Ottoman Empire along with the rest of the Dodecanese. The shocked islanders began to leave for other parts of Greece, North America and Australia, where Astypaleans helped to build the railways, settling in Fremantle and Melbourne. Those who stayed continued to work the land and the sea, but by 1910 the population had dropped to two thousand. Emigration continued through the twentieth century and in 1956, an earthquake toppled many of the houses around the castle, leaving it mostly deserted; a tsunami followed, destroying fishing boats and crops.

Around the 1980s, however, the population began to increase again and has remained steady at about 1,200–1,300 for the last two decades. Most live in and around Hora, where tourism provides another stream of income. There's a hospital, schools and an airport. For us, it will be a good base, with shops, cafés and tavernas – even in winter – including a pet food shop which Lisa sniffs with interest. The deserted places are further afield.

When the clouds clear I make my way to the castle, following the line of restored windmills to walk through the narrow alleys, well protected from the strong winds, heading gradually higher. Passing under the archways of a large church with a sky blue domed roof, I find an open area surrounded by the walls and arches of ruined buildings, their windows looking out to sea.

In the evening, my friend and I find taverna Maistrali (the name for a strong northwesterly wind) in a backstreet behind Pera Gialos, the old harbour. After such a cold, damp day it's wonderful to see a log fire burning and be invited to sit by the hearth by Dimitris, the owner, who has a square, tanned, unlined face and cropped, tufty, light grey hair.

'We need the rain to fill the dam,' he says. 'Otherwise when the water level gets low as it has in the last few years, the water's as brown as this table. We need it for the bees, and for the animals, and for tourism.' The reservoir is being topped up by the heaviest rainfall in years, but the tap water, although filtered and fine for cooking, is still discoloured and people have got used to drinking bottled water.

Dimitris fries tender calamari in a melt-in-the-mouth batter, while Tani, a woman with henna-red hair who works with him, heats up bean soup. Then they both sit down again by the fire. Dimitris pours himself a small glass of dark amber wine. Tani, who has topped up her large glass of red and is smoking a cigarette, asks him how it is.

'Vinegar,' he says drily, looking at the glass. 'But good vinegar.'

I laugh, and he explains it was made by a friend of his in Santorini and this is the last of it. He asks me about how I speak Greek and we get talking a little about Tilos.

'I went there maybe forty-five years ago,' he says. 'My father had a big wooden caique and used to deliver dry goods to the other islands. Tilos has the same sea bed as Astypalea more or less, rocks, *asvestolitho*.' Limestone. 'It must be nice there. Nothing to do except fishing. One day when my children have time, I'm going to fit out the boat with a bathroom and kitchen, and just take off. A few days here, a few days there... Nisyros, Tilos, Kos maybe – though I don't know if I'd like it...'

I tell him about the empty winter beaches and he sighs and smiles. Tani brings cake with whole walnuts inside, and Dimitris tells her to bring extra wine on the house.

'Now is the best time,' he says, 'in winter when there aren't many people around and there's not too much we need to do, just a few chores in the morning. Now I can go out fishing every day in my wooden boat and get a few calamari, octopus, maybe cuttlefish.' He warms to the topic of fishing with enthusiasm. 'One day I was fishing deep, eighty metres, so I didn't know what was on the end of the line. It could have been anything, slippers, a sack... But I started bringing it up, slowly. And the sea was perfect that day, glass, a mirror. I gently reeled it in, and as it got to about ten metres away I could see what it was, a monster of an octopus, and I'd caught it by just one of the suckers on one of its tentacles. Remember?' he asks Tani. She's heard the story before but smiles and searches for the photograph on her phone.

'There used to be a lot more fish,' says Dimitris. 'Before, people only took a few, maybe a few kilos each time, because there were no refrigerators, no ice to keep them – you just caught enough to eat that day. Now, the big boats take ten times the amount, pack it all up in ice and fridges and send it off to sell elsewhere.'

We hear the rain beating down on the roof of the terrace as he tells us about the cove where his kids learned to eat sea urchins and limpets. 'But it's not the same in summer now – it's full of people and sunbeds.'

Tani says, 'We're busy here now from June until the end of October, the season's getting longer. It's good for business, but it's changing the island. In August, I look up and suddenly the restaurant will be full and everyone wants to eat at the same time. People need to eat when they're hungry, but it's stressful. We enjoy the winter, the peace and quiet.'

That's why I wanted to come now.

A young woman comes in and flops down by the fire, stretching out and getting comfortable. Dimitris is soon engrossed in conversation at a speed I can't follow. I assume she must be a relative, but it turns out she's only been here a few days; a contemporary dance teacher from Athens, here to hold special classes for the kids. It's a programme designed to bring different activities to the remote islands.

The next morning, the sky has cleared to blue with a few little puffy clouds. The sun comes out and shadows break up all the blocks of white. The beautiful shadows make all the difference.

A row of scooters is parked on the edge of the cliff, looking down over denim-blue sea sparkling with sunlight. The scooters belong to the old men of the village, who zip around identically bundled up in thick winter clothes, though one wears a blue-striped woolly hat. I tie Lisa to a tree while my friend and I go into the supermarket for supplies, then

I roll up my sleeves and leggings, pack water and food among warm clothes in my backpack, and we set off walking east towards Steno.

Steno ('Narrow') is an isthmus of land in the middle of Astypalea, from which the island spreads out at either end to create its distinctive butterfly shape, rising into limestone peaks. Gently undulating and indented with bays, the isthmus at its narrowest is only a hundred metres wide, and it's a pleasure to follow the quiet road. At one point I look up at the ruins of a farm building with 'For Sale' and a phone number painted illegibly on its stone wall, and spot curious, square, window-like openings in the hillside framed by rough blocks of stone, loose rocks stacked around them. It's something to ask about later.

After walking for a couple of hours, we enter Maltezana, also called Analipsi, a fishing and farming village with only eighty permanent residents, although plenty of tourists in summer. A grassy patch of land is covered with the clover-like leaves and yellow flowers of Bermuda buttercups. Pretty as it is, the village seems slightly overwhelmed by tasteful tourist accommodation. Set back between studios stands an old house, plaster worn away to a wall of expertly laid grey field stones. The wooden frames of the windows and door are faded, half of the shutters open to deep blue sky behind. On a wall, political graffiti is sprayed. We continue down to the bay, its shallow waters revealing the rusted workings of a sunken ship.

Near the jetty, fishing cottages overlook the water; on closer inspection, I notice they each have a number on the door, which is unusual on small islands, and that their pergolas, though different colours, are all the same design. I realise the cottages have been converted into more tourist accommodation. Over the headland, the marshy shore is dominated by attractive but intrusive villas, though sheep graze unfazed.

This feels like the sleepiest place in the world on this out-of-season day, but the taverna overlooking the jetty is open and an Italian man with a red rental car, seemingly the only other visitor on the island, relaxes at a table in the sunshine. We sit down and the old owner asks where we're from, lighting up at the mention of England. He worked on ships.

'I was in Manchester, Liverpool, and…' He tries to remember, goes inside to fetch something and returns. 'Hull, that's it! And the river in London.'

'The Thames?' I prompt.

'Kent. We carried sugar from Dominica, the West…'

'West Indies?' I prompt again. 'How long did you work on the ships?'

'Seventeen years,' he says. 'I travelled everywhere. That was enough. I retired, built the studios next door and the taverna, and now I don't want to go anywhere.'

I watch a man row a wooden boat to another little boat. He sets up a pump and starts bailing out rainwater. Another man is mending fishing nets. A scooter approaches, driven by an old man in a thick checked shirt holding a handmade walking stick. Sitting behind him is a woman wearing a headscarf, a dress, tights and boots. He stops to let her off and she takes her time getting up the steps, then sits down and smiles. Having parked the scooter, her husband arrives and suggests she move into the sun. The owner greets him as Michalis. Michalis pulls his phone out of his pocket and talks loudly to someone. 'We have to take care of our women! We can't just be going out all the time on our own without them!'

The taverna owner talks with the Italian, who is interested in renting a place here long-term. The owner tells him in English about a big house, fully equipped with bathroom, kitchen. The man says he wants just a place to store his things.

'Michali,' says the owner to his old friend with the stick, 'what about your place, is that available?'

'He won't like it. It's fifty years old and hasn't been renovated… Upstairs where we live is nice but… These people have money, they have certain expectations! He might want to bring his family…'

They make a plan to see the two places tomorrow; I intervene to translate when Michalis's wife worries they might have to miss their check-up at the hospital. The Italian leaves soon after, and the owner offers Michalis a coffee.

'No, no, I had one at lunchtime. If I have another I might not sleep.'

'Look, I'm going to go inside and make us two coffees…'

The two men sit with their coffees. The woman sits on her own in the sunshine, still smiling.

In a field near the taverna beside a stand of bamboo are some late Roman baths from the fifth century AD. The site is fenced off and locked, but I see a pool filled with rainwater. A little way on, there's a twentieth-century well with a heavy iron mechanism made of intersecting wheels. The hinterland of the village is gently undulating, pale green hills with old stone field walls and the occasional farmhouse. A field of fig trees is bounded by bamboo and prickly pears.

We make our way around to the northern shore and a beach swept clean by gusting wind and the waves surging in. The pure white of salt, pumice, shell, bleached wood, fragments of white plastic – all is washed smooth and clean by the unstoppable force of the clear and ever-shifting sea. I lie on the coarse sand to see the grains of stone and shell, yellow and grey and white.

The rock is eroded, fragile, with a thin white crust as if the surface dissolved then hardened. Up on the headland, volcanic stones of red and grey-black once hefted into walls have been left to fall, interspersed with fragments of brilliant chalky white. Beyond, the rock forms thousands of sharp knife points against the sea. A cormorant flies up from the water. The sun and wind make this place feel brightly alive, imbued with energy. On this January day the only sounds are the sea and an orchestra of bells as sheep and goats roam scrub-covered hills.

The days are short and it's time to head back. As dusk approaches, the colours fade, the sea grey with tinges of blue and green. The land gradually falls dark, beautifully empty, rocky points reaching out into a serene, dull-silver sea. The sunset turns the water to gold, then rose pink; eventually I see the half-lit houses of Hora.

When we stop at the pet food shop to buy Lisa's dinner, we find out that the young man who runs it is a beekeeper, and he confirms that the stone windows or openings we saw built into the hillside at Steno are old beehives.

Stone hives were durable, hard to move but also hard to steal, he says, though they weren't very efficient because it wasn't possible to check on the bees. Cylindrical terracotta hives, which came later, were portable but broke too easily. They were replaced by today's painted boxes with removable hanging frames.

I learn that stone hives were used from antiquity and through the last few centuries up until the 1940s in the islands of the Eastern Mediterranean. Varying from small houses to cupboard-like recesses in stone walls, they were built from basic raw materials on islands with few trees where wood wasn't easily available and clay was expensive. People used what they had.

At Ageri, another taverna named after the wind, positioned near the windmills, most of the tables are full. Lisa is allowed to sit at our feet under the table. We order salad and white wine, pork baked with tomatoes; stuffed cabbage leaves arrive on the house. Our hostess is petite and thin with stylishly short, tousled grey hair, and when she finally has time to sit for a little while, she's clutching an electronic cigarette. A couple have just left and she says they own a house here; most of the old houses of Hora are owned by foreigners, Europeans. 'There are a few old people still living there but locals can't afford to restore the houses. We have to work hard, pay too much tax, you can't imagine.'

She grew up in Athens, like many people from Astypalea, including her husband. He became a captain on a Greek merchant ship and they travelled around the world. 'Then we started a family and decided to follow our dream and come to live on our island.' It had barely begun when she got a call: he had suffered multiple strokes and was found to have a cyst on the brain. He came home in a coma and she looked after him until he died a couple of years ago. She gets up and sends over more wine. 'I want to write my story,' she says, smiling. Her name is Terpsi – short for Terpsichore, the ancient muse of lyric poetry, song and dance.

The shadows make all the difference.

Beyond Maltezana, a new asphalt road winds up and around, past a solar farm sitting in fields surrounded by stone walls, into a virtually deserted part of Astypalea.

This northeastern of the island's 'wings', designated a conservation area, is largely wild and untouched by recent development, although there's a small fish farm just off its western coast. And at the north is a natural harbour with a village that is almost abandoned. It's too far to walk there and back from Hora in a single day, the road twisting and turning for over twenty kilometres, so I've rented us a jeep.

All around are slopes of pale grey limestone covered with low, dark juniper bushes. Under a cloudy grey sky with not a soul around, it feels beautifully desolate. I drive slowly, looking around. An abandoned quarry, an abandoned army camp, and across the road, some intriguing piles of rocks. I stop to investigate. Through a gap in a fence is a long building made from the surrounding grey rock, unusual in that it has several archways along the front made of sandstone blocks; inside are lower archways at right angles to these, leading from one room to another. The vaulted ceilings are plastered. I later learn this was a basilica dating back to the sixth or seventh century, built with lime mortar. Most of the building is ruined but among the fallen stones I make out a flat stone floor sloping towards the opening of a cistern for catching rainwater. Not far off, among the golden-orange tinge of lichen, there's a threshing circle and an animal pen with rounded ends and very thick walls.

I park the jeep and we get out so we can walk the rest of the way. The rock was blasted quite recently to build this road. Occasional spray-painted messages range from the mundane to the poetic: 'Your eyes are the window to my chaos'. An old man drives by on a scooter, the first traffic since Maltezana.

Near a bend in the road is a *mandra*, a farmyard. The drystone walls that curve around deserted animal pens are whitewashed and, under pale grey cloud, give the illusion of being covered in snowdrift.

They are topped with dry, dove-grey branches, the gates weather-bleached wooden pallets. In a few adjoining huts painted white over rough plaster, the ceilings are made of faded grey bamboo, and thick knotted ropes hang from timber beams.

The sun begins to part the clouds as we descend the final twist in the road to see a valley divided into fields, some brilliant green, others sand-coloured, scattered with pale rocks. This is the start of Vathy ('Deep'), and the road becomes a rough track leading down to the shore of a long inlet. It was always a natural refuge in stormy weather, and excavations around it have revealed prehistoric, Minoan and Hellenistic settlements. Parts of a Byzantine chapel lie scattered. There are deserted farmhouses in a distinctive design: a main house with rounded corners, almost oval; a second almost the same but a little smaller; and circling them, a walled enclosure for animals. The roofs have timber beams with thin branches laid crosswise, then a layer of packed earth, sometimes grass. Many have fallen in.

We follow the wet track along the pale blue water's edge with wild hills either side until a massive, incongruous brick chimney appears. Rising from a large building beside the water, this was an industrial lime kiln, the last incarnation of the timeless circular stone structure, the *asvestokamino*. The natural resource is all around us: limestone. This kiln, where rock was burned to create *asvesti*, lime, for construction mortar and agriculture, employed two dozen men a few decades ago. Through an empty window frame, I see the brick chimney encased in rusted iron, rusted pipes hanging down to three arched openings. After the kiln closed in around 1980, Vathy was mostly abandoned. From the smell and the mud inside the building, it seems to be used for pigs.

As we draw closer to the mouth of the inlet, where a narrow strait gives on to open sea, the sky has cleared to deep blue and the rippling water sparkles. There's a handful of houses and a taverna by the dock, and a brightly painted fishing boat moored up. It seems impossible that anyone would be here, but voices can be heard through the open door. Inside, three men in thick fleece shirts and hats sit around a table with heaped plates of fried fish, the steamed spinach-like greens called *horta*, and potatoes. Sunlight glints on glasses of pale-yellow wine. Another table is covered with mandarins and jars of aromatic wild narcissus. I leave Lisa by the door.

A woman with dark hair emerges from the back room and invites my friend and me into the bright, sunny kitchen to see red mullet caught that morning. There's no more *horta* but we can have some of theirs. While she stands at the sink washing potatoes, I spot a pile of fresh cabbages and she cuts one into a salad with oil and lemon. When she's filled our table with a perfect meal, Maria sits down with the men to eat her own lunch, though she insists on giving us another fish from their table to taste. Gradually two men get up to leave. The third, the eldest, is her husband and she suggests he rest for ten minutes. He disappears inside, and precisely ten minutes later he's heading out to his fishing boat.

Maria says, 'My husband isn't a professional fisherman, just does it for hobby. But he's mad about fishing, he'll go out even in six Beaufort. In the season we buy from different fishermen, we need ten kilos a day. The fish farm is good, it's clean because of the way the sea washes it. But I don't buy fish from there.' She gestures with a hand pulled over her chin and says, 'I'd be ashamed. We offer whatever food we have locally, octopus, potatoes, goat from the farmers you saw here earlier – they have a couple of hundred animals – roasted vegetables, whatever I've cooked that day.'

Maria eats the fish with her hands, as do I, and she laughs at my friend who doesn't. She says it's the only way. 'Once, I was at a big hotel in Athens where my sister was working, and there were hundreds of Chinese people there for a conference. We sat down in the restaurant, and I ordered a leg of chicken. I tried eating it with a knife and fork, but it was impossible, so I picked it up with my fingers. Everyone in the room stopped eating and looked at me...' She mimes how everyone stared. 'Then they put down their knives and forks and started eating with their fingers too.'

Here in Astypalea, everyone who runs a taverna seems a born storyteller. I ask her about life in Vathy. There were about two hundred people living here a century ago, she says, and a long time ago they grew cotton in the fields.

'People started to leave after the Italian occupation and then the German invasion, moving to Hora or to Athens. The school closed in the 1970s. Now – all together, in the whole area – there are eighteen, maybe only fourteen people for certain.'

But I get no sense that this is a problem. She goes into Hora a couple of times a week maybe for the bank or the post office, a bit of shopping.

There's just the sound of water lapping outside, the sunlight pouring in through the windows and the open door. Lisa is snoozing outside in the sun.

'My husband gets up in the night and comes and sits here, drinks a coffee and smokes one cigarette, and looks out of the window over the bay. Then he goes back to sleep for a couple of hours, gets up and does the same.'

'Like a king,' I say.

She tells me they only got electricity around 1987. 'How long ago did they build the new road?' I ask.

'They finished the asphalt three years ago. To tell the truth, it was better for us before. Before, the boat used to come across, and visitors would spend the day here, have a swim, get a feel for the place before taking the bus back. Now they drive down the road, take a few pictures and leave. But still, in general the people who come here are people who really want to come. And life here won't change while I'm around.'

She clears our plates, putting the fish bones and heads to one side for the chickens and the mandarin peel on another plate for the pigs. When we have to leave she kisses us goodbye, showing us photos of her family and the empty stone building next door that was her grandfather's kafeneio, where a cat now sits in the bare window. Beyond are ruined stone buildings, a church, a couple of little farms, rocks. The sun casts a glorious warm light. There's a grey donkey wearing a wooden saddle. Partridges waddle across the road and take off noisily. The light is fading as we return to the jeep and drive back. An owl flies up from the road.

In the evening, behind the closed-up terrace with stacked tables and chairs at Maistrali, the light is on and we see Dimitris's tanned face and cropped grey hair through the glass. He's sitting by the fire.

'How are you finding our beautiful island?'

I tell him about our day in Vathy.

'That's where I went to school,' he says.

We order retsina, and sip it from small tumblers.

He estimates there were around a hundred people there when he was growing up. 'No road, no electricity, no running water…'

'Was it difficult?' I ask.

He pauses. 'To be honest, no. We had everything we needed. Fresh fish, tomatoes, cucumbers, animals, wheat for making flour for bread, vines. Sure, there were little things that would have been hard, like…' He stops to think. 'I don't know. No, there wasn't anything we lacked, really.'

I smile. 'So, why did people leave?'

'The lime kiln closed, and that was the only work.'

'But what work do you need if you have everything?'

'Well, you need to have a bit of money. After it closed there was nothing. My father used his wooden boat to transport the lime. We'd take it from here to sell on Rhodes. It was very good quality, but because of the rising price of oil to fuel the kiln, it became expensive. So then instead of selling to Rhodes, we bought the cheaper, less good quality lime from Rhodes and sold to other islands.'

It's sad that people left; but they'd have needed some income to pay taxes and soon electricity bills, to get to see a doctor or dentist, and for water unless they had their own supply. To me, places like Vathy are romantic. But for local people, after the kiln closed, the only options left were keeping animals and fishing. The Greek tax system doesn't support entrepreneurialism. Tourism has brought money, but also problems, with people working non-stop all summer and with virtually no income in winter – and losing their beaches where they taught their children to fish.

'We were poor,' says Dimitris. 'We didn't have a real house.' He says they lived in a shelter under a very large fig tree, built of bamboo and lined with cloth, with mattresses inside. 'But it was fine,' he says, *mia hara*, implying *what more do you need?* I remember his dream to rig up the boat and just take off for a while.

It's a misty day when I park the jeep again on the road to Vathy and look down to Agrelidi. The inlet is so encircled by land it is almost a lake, silver-blue in the muted, hazy light, surrounded by low, smooth hills half-covered in dark mastic and juniper. It was an early Christian settlement, the area continuously inhabited until recently.

My friend and I walk down to the shore and follow the waterline to the red brick chimney of the Agrelidi lime kiln, standing proudly with the rust-red cliffs of a quarry behind it. As at Vathy, but larger, here are the workings of a modern, industrial lime kiln, deserted since the 1970s. Beside a chapel, the remains of a slipway for boats poke out of the water.

In the fields here, people cultivated olives, almonds, figs, pomegranates and quinces, and earlier also wheat and tobacco. Quarrying provided stone for building, broken up by dynamite and carried by donkey. Brilliant green grass grows between the pale grey rocks scattered everywhere. I find a small barn with walls more than half a metre thick held together by brown mud. A roof of bamboo covered in branches and earth and pebbles has fallen in. Barns and poor houses were held together by mud and wood; the plaster, made of mud and straw, had to be replaced often. When people could afford it, they mixed lime with the plaster. The next building is more substantial, walls of irregular limestone fixed with pale grey mortar.

Low stone walls demarcate a route down to the sea; but the path's now filled with rocks. On the other side are a couple of houses inhabited not long ago. I approach the first, painted white with faded blue wooden shutters. Above a wood lintel, a rudimentary star-shaped hole let air in and smoke out; the year '1949' and some initials are handwritten into the plaster half-moon above. Inside, a rug and wooden steps and wooden door are messily piled behind the wooden balustrades of the platform bed. A short embroidered curtain still hangs from a picture rail, but wooden cupboards are bare, paint and plaster worn to expose the stone wall. The ceiling is bamboo held in place by timber beams. Iron hoops are built into a plaster ceiling in another room for hanging food; iron or wood protrusions on the outside walls were used for hanging tools or tying animals. There's a wood-and-rope contraption hanging down, a wooden worktop, a stone hearth. In the corner of the yard is a covered cistern, with water in it.

It begins to drizzle as we make our way back to the jeep and, passing an army building that seems to have been abandoned, drive up a track to the top of Kastellanos (at 366 metres the highest hill on this part of the island). Visibility is reduced by the eerie white fog, a dust-cloud from the Sahara, and there is no sound, no sign of anyone.

The imposing building on the peak is another abandoned military station. It was used during the period of the Greek Junta, the right-wing military dictatorship that lasted from 1967 to 1974. The base was already derelict by the early 1980s, becoming more dilapidated as the decades passed. The concrete is mottled and cracked and discoloured with mould. Wooden shutters are broken, empty windows filled in with stones, wires hang askew, plaster is broken away. Behind are tunnels that burrow deep into the mountain.

Leaving the jeep again, we follow the track downhill, coming to the chapel of Poulariani just as a rainshower begins. It's also a farmyard, with circular drystone walls painted snow-white, and gnarled branches, dark with the rain, laid crosswise on top and held in place by more stones. Beyond grazed green fields, a large yard uses the natural slope of the hill to collect rainwater into a cistern. A ewe and lamb watch us curiously. I'm mesmerised by the curving thick walls of an old tower or kiln, echoing that of the bay below.

There's still just enough time to drive up to Vathy again. The inlet is aquamarine, and a rainbow emerges as we arrive at the taverna, where Maria is outside sitting on the ground, applying duct tape to the back of a car. She says it got damaged and the duct tape is about the same colour as the paintwork.

She gives me a hug and I pick a stray bit of tape off her trousers as she invites me inside. Manolis has gone into town and she was supposed to go too and visit the hairdresser, but ended up mending the back door, which wasn't closing properly, and some leaks in the roof instead. She promised her late father she'd keep her hair long, anyway, and she likes it that way. 'When my mother got married, she had hair down to her knees, and she had it all plaited around her head for the wedding.'

There are narcissus on the table again, and she tells us the name for them, and then, 'Here they call them something else.'

'But you don't?'

'My parents were from here, but I was born in Athens, and I grew up there, went to primary school there. After that we were back and forth all the time.'

She wasn't allowed to finish high school because it would have meant going away to Kalymnos; instead, her grandparents married her to her first husband at the age of fifteen. Her daughters, a literature teacher and a doctor, both live on Rhodes.

'Sorry, I've been talking away and haven't offered you anything! Would you like anything to eat, to drink? It's OK if you don't.'

She brings homemade bread and spinach pie. The sun is turning golden amid the clouds. Before we leave, I ask Maria if she's going to the upcoming festival, the celebration of Panayia Flevariotissa, at the monastery in the hills on the other side of the island.

'Oh yes. I'll be going barefoot. I made a vow to God when my daughter was sick that every year I'd go on foot, without shoes. It takes two and a half hours from Hora. I've been doing it every year for eleven years now.'

And I'd had doubts about going to this festival, in the dark, in the middle of nowhere.

Leaving behind the lights of Hora, and leaving Lisa in the rented apartment for the evening, my friend and I walk (wearing walking boots) under millions of stars and the Milky Way towards the monastery of Panayia Flevariotissa. The rocky track, uneven and muddy from rain, heads into the high, pitch-black hinterland.

For Astypaleans, this annual celebration of the Holy Virgin of February is one of the most important occasions of the year and people travel back to the island for it. Most festivals tend to take place in summer, so I'm intrigued. Some attend early for the church service; others go late for the party. After an hour of being blinded by headlights, we're happy to accept a lift in a jeep the rest of the way. The road is slippery with mud on the final approach, and there are seemingly hundreds of cars, all the cars of the island and more.

We smell fresh grass from the surrounding fields. Children mill about on the steps, and down in the courtyard tables are filled with people eating. Light spills out of the open church door. Greeting familiar faces, we enter the main hall where the musicians are playing; more tables are crammed with people eating, while others carry trays of food. Maria and Manolis from Vathy wave us over, finding spare seats and glasses of wine and plates of roasted goat with rice and liver stuffing, here called *lambriano*. Maria is all dressed up, though she's lost an earring. It's too noisy to talk much, so I eat and drink, listen to the music and look around. At the top end of the table is a striking couple in their forties, he a smooth-faced bodybuilder, she pale and reserved with straight hair to her shoulders, most likely here from Athens for the weekend.

Manolis, with his hooked nose and sparse teeth, still wearing his woolly fisherman's hat, enthusiastically applauds a song or dance he likes, tops up glasses of wine and beams, saying, 'To the next year!' He says to his friend opposite, 'It's only women dancing. Shall we get up?' His friend is less keen on the idea but Manolis wants to dance. 'We'll be too late…' Eventually he gets up to join the line of people on the tiny dance floor, leaving his cigarette burning. Maria stubs it out. The large ladies at the table behind keep pushing past me to get up. One asks if I've finished with my second helping of goat, then empties it into a plastic bag to take home for her dogs. More trays of food arrive, including big sweet potatoes charred in the fire.

Someone comes around selling tickets for the night's fund-raising lottery, and we buy a couple. Manolis buys a lot, and Maria guards them carefully. When the prizes are announced, she flips through them over and over, checking. Manolis wins something, a religious icon, and he's very pleased. No-one claims the top prize, and the ladies opposite check we don't have the winning number. For the next hour, every now and then Manolis asks, 'Who got the Virgin?'

I'm so relieved I didn't win an icon of the Virgin Mary.

The next day, we don't feel like going very far. We take Lisa down to the expanse of concrete harbour at Pera Gialos to let her run free. In a backstreet is an empty, overgrown stone house for sale with a wooden floor and ceiling, a view of the sea, and a Venetian crest on the outer wall. On the track to the castle we notice broken pottery and deep, plastered cisterns, then we continue around to the other side of Hora.

In 1996, someone was digging a foundation for a new building below the old village when a cemetery was uncovered. Known as Kylindra, it now looks like abandoned foundations with bags of materials left inside, a smattering of litter. But archaeologists found the skeletons of eight hundred or more babies and infants here, buried in clay pots over a period of six hundred years until a few hundred years before Christ. Research in the UK and Canada has shown that most of them died around birth, while some lived months, up to two years. Similar cemeteries have been found in Sicily, Sardinia and Tunisia, but nowhere have so many infants been found buried in one place. As on all these islands, Astypalea has more remains below the surface than we will ever know. In the centre of the Aegean with its ancient trading routes, the natural harbours and islets offered useful stopping places for sailors. Obsidian, pottery, tombs, bronze tools and lead fishing weights have been found around Steno in the middle of the island, and at Armenochori.

My friend introduces me to Astypalea's library, and I borrow a few books of local history.

'If I'm not here when you leave,' says the curator, who wears a cardigan, woolly tights and slippers, and has a blue ink-smudge on her nose, 'just leave them in the supermarket across the street.'

Back down by Pera Gialos harbour at 'The Parliament' café, Laura, a blonde English woman who has lived here for decades and runs the establishment, makes me a coffee and serves my friend a soft drink. The old men are discussing last night's festival. A couple of them flick their *komboloi*, or worry beads.

Laura explains that musicians had been booked to come from Kalymnos, but the boat couldn't travel so alternatives had to be brought in at the last minute from another neighbouring island,

Amorgos. There's only one musician on Astypalea and he was away. She disappears into the back to clean up, and the men continue talking, voicing disgruntlement over this or that. Some are unhappy about the food that was served, others about the low number of visitors. 'People don't have money to fly these days.'

Someone mutters, though, as if to himself, 'It was a good party.'

One man leaves, taking his shopping. Chat goes quiet for a while. A fat man in a beret, holding his stick, says to the younger man across from him, 'We should go to Vathy sometime.'

The other agrees. 'When the weather's good, we'll go and spend all day there, drink, eat, make a day of it.'

'Will you take Laura with you?' says someone else, grinning.

Laura shouts in Greek, 'I can hear my name and I'm worried! I'm off to do the shopping.' Carrying a list, she crosses the street to the mini-market.

There's a lull for a while, and the fat man says to the other that the flowers are blooming in Livadi. Then he talks about something that's good medicine for goats, for cleaning out their insides. His companion gets up to go.

'Why are you leaving?'

'I've got jobs to do, and you're talking about manure!'

'Stay a bit.'

'I've been here an hour. I'm off. Manure!'

'Well, I'm going to stay a bit,' says the fat man defiantly.

It's quiet now, just the television and the click of a *komboloi*.

I pass a farmyard with a couple of wooden saddles hung in a tree and a fence decorated with goat skulls. Beyond trees bright with almond blossom and a chapel used to store the dark and waxy hanging panels for beehives, I see the monastery of Panayia Flevariotissa by daylight, across the valley, high in the gully of a stream surrounded by ladders of terraced fields. Perhaps the festival originally celebrated the winter flow of rainwater, fertility. To the north are the rounded backs of limestone hills falling away in steep cliffs and caves, the only modern, man-made intrusion a line of solar panels.

The furthest reaches of the western wing of the island are mostly empty except for scattered churches or farms built of field stones, blending into their surroundings. Little is grown now, leaving the hillsides bare, patchworks of old cleared land. The winter winds can be too fierce for walking in these exposed, mostly treeless hills, but I do it gradually over a couple of weeks, often wrapped up in many layers, sometimes renting the jeep for the first section and then walking two or three hours as a road turns into a track that turns into a path. The benefit of being here when there are few people around outweighs the weather.

On the road beyond Livadi, the farming settlement just to the west of Hora, tourist accommodation has been built along the shore, looking across to the castle. But when the road turns inland there are no more hotels, just a hillside with rocks as rough and brown as *paximadia*, the traditional bread rusks. The tarmac runs out at a chapel. There are ruined stone houses, 'bee windows' in the hillside, a fence of prickly pears. Broken walls, broken homes, humble places.

Smooth brown hills glow in the clear sunlight like nothing I've seen before in the Dodecanese. Ploughed fields in whimsical shapes curl around on the lower slopes without a single straight line, as if the tractor's steering was skewed or the driver tipsy. Borderless, they are probably planted with grass for animals. Deep fissures of streams zigzag down, marked by oleander. Only my footsteps are loud on the rough track; when I stop to watch a barn owl, I hear chickens and goat or sheep bells in the valley below, and the trickling of water. From the crest of a hill, the land falls away in rugged limestone cliffs all the way to the sea, the site of a World War II battle.

North of the cruciform white church of Ayios Yiannis, with its waterfall cascading over the cliff, a stone shelter built into a cave and gnarled olive trees, I find an abandoned farmhouse standing on a spectacular cliff. There's a timber-and-bamboo ceiling, a still-strong timber platform for a bed, views of empty hills and sea in every direction. The wind is howling and the shutters and doors are missing, but within those thick walls it feels warm and calm.

Heading south another day, the track winds over the hills with stone hives in fields where bathtubs are given a second life as water troughs and fridges are also being recycled, perhaps for storage. At Agios Konstantinos is a well with its mechanism still mostly intact – a lever, sprocketed wheels, swinging buckets – though completely rusted. Heading further along the coast my friend and I find a clearing covered in pale stone, an amalgam of quartz and something reddish, molten. Standing over a tiny bay is another shell of a house that once had a pitched roof and large windows looking out to sea. With steps leading up to the door, it's built from its surroundings – the yellowish pale stone, the dark greenish grey of the cliffs opposite, and concrete made of sand and pebbles. It wouldn't be remote if you had a boat; an easy journey to Agios Konstantinos or across to Hora. As we retrace our steps, I notice terrace walls blending into the high hilltop and cave-shelters, a stream bed filled with oleander and cut bamboo rattling in the wind.

Hens scurry around an old shipping container, oil drum and wooden pallets. Someone is calling to his goats and we see a figure with a stick – grunting, shouting, trilling – and throwing stones occasionally to direct them. Their bells come in all shapes and sizes and pitches. I wonder how the farmers choose them.

At the mini-market in Livadi, the owners proffer a gift of freshly made pastries – called *bougia* here, filled with local cheese and *horta*. I ask if it's possible to buy the local cheese, and they offer to call a man who makes it. I thank them but say we may be leaving tomorrow.

'With which boat? The little one? You'd better check, but I've heard it's gone for service. You could have left last night…'

But last night seemed too soon.

Later Verginia at taverna Argo, bringing a carafe of filtered water, confirms that the small boat, the twice-weekly *Nissos Kalymnos*, goes for service around this time of year, often without warning. Without that, there's only the big ferry. Astypalea is cut off from the rest of the Dodecanese for a week.

The kafeneio in Maltezana was in ruins until Panayiotis decided to fix it up. His father was from Astypalea but like many from the island they lived in Athens. Panayiotis, wearing leather boots, his black beard knotted under his chin, grew up in the city and did building work, but there wasn't much going on after the economic crisis so ten years ago he came here and restored this café-bar. He kept the original stone building from 1956 but added his own touch of colour.

A guy comes in for coffee, a woman plays with her phone. Lisa and another dog sniff around, looking for food and attention. I eat a delicious *saganaki*, made with local cheese lightly pan-fried. Panayiotis says if I want to buy some, he can get in touch with the cheesemaker.

'What I'd really like,' I say, 'is to go to where he makes it and see how it's done. But I don't know if that would be possible.' As I'm finishing a salad of tomatoes and *paximadia* with lots of oregano and olive oil, a large man in a rain jacket walks in and sits by the wood-burning stove with a beer.

Panayiotis says, 'This is the man who makes the cheese.' It's a small island, after all.

The cheese man is talkative and full of stories, like a lot of the people I've met here. He went to school at Vathy and used to work on boats; like Dimitris's father – Dimitris is his cousin – he had a boat that travelled from island to island with goods including lime. Since retiring, he raises sheep and goats, and makes cheese regularly from Easter onwards, though just in small quantities at this time of year when the animals need their milk to feed their young. The fresh, unaged cheese is called *chlori*. He keeps about five hundred animals, and it was a big problem when it didn't rain for the last three years. Without rain, there's no grass. 'There are twelve and a half thousand animals on the island. They mostly belong to the church, but there are farms with animals all over.' He reels off a list of places.

Life here has not changed that much, he says, except for tourism. The young people are seamen, and those in their fifties and older raise animals, are farmers. 'When we're gone…' He trails off, suggesting that then things might change, the skills lost. He's taught them to his son, however.

If I want to see his cheese factory, I can come here any day at ten. But when I arrive at ten on my last day, the cheese man isn't there. In fact, the door of the kafeneio is padlocked, and on a table by the door are some remains from the night before: a glass, a bottle and a cigarette lighter.

It's a beautiful day and perhaps it would be a shame to be indoors watching milk boil. Maybe he's out fishing instead.

WHEN THE BIRD FLIES
RHODES

I'm at Tilos harbour at dawn, waiting sleepily in the dark, listening to the sea slap against the concrete dock. Men lean against trucks, talking.

The big ferry leaves Piraeus, the port of Athens, in the afternoon and travels south overnight to the Dodecanese. Rhodes is the end of a route that takes twenty hours or so (stopping at Tilos along the way, and sometimes continuing to Kastellorizo). There's a flurry of activity as it comes into view around the edge of the bay; the great vessel speeds towards us and nimbly turns. Men secure the ropes, the ramp comes down and there are shouts and whistles. As we pull away into the wind, daylight is appearing over the jagged points of hills, the pale grey rock. The edge of the island a dark shape, a curve submerged, the twinkling of electric lights soon distant behind, blue-grey horizon ahead. Faint land-shapes around us, otherwise sea-emptiness. I find a bench on deck and sleep for a while.

It's a few hours to Rhodes, stopping at the spectacular harbour of Symi along the way. We pass close to Turkey, close enough to see houses and cliffs and green valleys this morning. It's strange living so close to a border, but of course at times it wasn't a border at all. It's changed back and forth over the millennia. From the fifteenth century, much of Greece was within the Ottoman Empire; before that, Anatolia had been part of Ancient Greece and the Byzantine Empire.

The largest island in the group, up to forty kilometres wide and eighty long, for many centuries Rhodes was where people from much smaller islands came for protection from invaders. Now it is still the administrative centre, the place we come to run errands; many people from smaller islands live here in winter for schools or work or healthcare, access to supermarkets or because they like having a few more people around. Young people unable to find work in mainland cities often come to Rhodes. There's a permanent population of around 120,000, and when the numbers of British holidaymakers dipped a few years ago due to worries about the economy, the islanders were too busy to notice, welcoming waves of Eastern European, Russian and Chinese tourists. Cruise ships bring thousands to the alleyways of the Old Town.

There are several harbours in Rhodes town; this ferry docks at the commercial harbour, where the large ferries load and unload not only passengers but also trucks full of goods. It's still early as I walk away from the quay and stop to take a closer look at the crumbling, disused customs house that was built, I guess from its decorative flourishes, in the Ottoman era. Overgrown with ivy, it has an ornate, grand doorway, an archway with flower designs once white, now grey; windows with old wooden shutters covered in plastic sheeting and wooden pallets. A tower stands in the courtyard, its domed top covered in pigeons. On the gate is a familiar sign declaring an allocation of funds for a public works project, dated years ago. Through rusted ironwork in a window I see people in the courtyard sitting drinking coffee, others hanging washing; refugees from the Middle East.

Graffiti sprayed on the front of the building says: 'I see the executioners of Greece and the end of the Greek.' I wonder if it's racist or anti-government. I take photographs, notice a sign saying, 'No photography – no entry', and move on. A guy drives by in a BMW convertible. Across the wide road is the iconic abandoned ouzo factory, its stark lines against the cloudless blue somehow reminiscent of a grain silo in the American Midwest. Beyond are more empty warehouses and an old tax office block. The contemporary car showroom is empty. And beyond the black-painted 'gentlemen's club' and the restaurant by the exit to the harbour, both still functioning, I spot a derelict yard with iron rings fixed at regular intervals to the wall all around – for chaining animals? When I enter to explore, I see a sign on one of the empty office buildings: 'Farm Ministry – Agricultural Vet'.

Not all the deserted places of the Dodecanese are rural. In the same way that on the small islands once you start looking for old stone walls you see them everywhere, so in Rhodes town you see abandoned houses and public buildings at every turn. Corners I've walked past many times take on a different character when I'm thinking about abandonment. This island has all the history of the Dodecanese writ large.

On a February day, my friend and I walk the residential backstreets of Rhodes, finding amid new houses the crumbling plaster of a graceful period of the twentieth century, padlocks on faded grandeur, softened by years of decay.

At the southern edges of town, past graves cut into the rock more than two thousand years ago, we continue through a sports ground with fences around scrubland, an industrial estate with fences around rubble. Veering towards the sea we find an abandoned nightclub and a rubbish tip and Roma shanty houses with shiny new cars parked outside. Then we find the ghostly boatyard. The day is windy, the sky grey, the sea wild and rough, and these rusting craft haven't been on the water for a while. The sound from the boatyard is orchestral: a deep soughing, one sharp high note singing, and in between, a soft percussion tapping.

We turn back inland to what were once the outskirts of town. Near the road is a stone tower with a dilapidated wooden apparatus inside, maybe a pulley: a kind of windmill, it seems. Skirting around a big supermarket, we see an old villa with a high, square tower surrounded by fields. Further uphill are small farms: a cow and chickens, old homes with a view of the sea. The road winds through a valley full of flowers before reaching an ugly rash of contemporary apartment buildings of different architectural persuasions, and a highway. We re-enter the city on the busy Rhodes–Lindos Road, cross a stream near Rodini Park and spot a ruined shell of a square house with thick walls, once beautiful. Further on is a larger building, a row of arches with peeling plaster and an iron windmill; the garden is overgrown behind a locked gate, but there's an open doorway, a table and two mismatched chairs and a washing line. Someone is taking refuge there.

A year later I will walk by and find the ruined shell of the beautiful house demolished, the field cleared for construction.

Mandraki, the old harbour at the northern tip of Rhodes, is dominated by grand and ornate Italian architecture from the occupation of 1912 to 1943. Most of it adds greatly to the charm of the town: the gate to the Nea Agora or New Market; the Venetian-inspired governor's palace, built by order of the first governor, Mario Lago, around 1927; the art deco aquarium, with beach stretching to either side.

The austere National Theatre, however, has broken windows and patched-up doors, and is daubed with graffiti. Built during the Fascist period, it opened in 1937 as the Teatro Puccini for performances of Italian opera; its design is smooth and uncluttered, clean curving lines clad with *pietra finta* or faux stone. Within a decade, the Italian occupation was over and a photograph from 7th March 1948 shows the roof, ledges and every horizontal surface of the theatre's exterior covered with people standing, sitting or hanging off to witness the ceremony of the islands' liberation and unification with Greece. Now, only the trees and flowers are flourishing. A few years ago when the Greek government was struggling to pay off its debt, it launched an initiative to sell or lease some of the country's grander abandoned buildings, but there was an outcry against the sale of public property, including this. Across the street, attached to the door of a gorgeously renovated building is a sign for the 'Public Properties Company', surely a contradiction in terms, and a phone number.

Behind it is a mosque with ochre walls, a red dome and an exquisite white minaret. Built in 1524, it is named the Murad Reis Mosque after an Ottoman naval commander, born in Rhodes to Albanian parents and buried here. A few years ago it was possible to enter the Muslim cemetery that surrounds it, but currently the entrance is closed. Beyond the railings, in the overgrown old graveyard the tall, thin, grave markers lean at drunken angles, some with stylised flower patterns, some shaped like a policeman's truncheon, others ending in a point, all inscribed in Turkish. The sun is hot – a short visit from the gods of summer – and a tree casts shadows on faded ochre plaster. The garden is lush with grass, shrubs and flowers; a nice place to be buried. In the far corner is a little gatekeeper's lodge where Lawrence Durrell lived from 1945 to 1947, working for the British administration in the building next door, now the casino. In his writing he called this Muslim cemetery a place of beauty and silence, already then a 'forgotten graveyard' in a state of disrepair, being mostly the burial place of Turkish civil servants and political exiles.

Turning away from the sea, I enter the narrow alleys of the Neohori or 'New Town', the Greek quarter during Ottoman times, to find more dereliction: doorways with rusted metal openwork, rusted padlocks; weeds growing through cracked walls and paint peeling. A house with louvre shutters behind barbed wire, overshadowed by a modern apartment block. Beside a restored villa turned into a boutique hotel is an old stone house built over an archway, where bags of cement await use. I peer through the window at wreckage, plaster fallen to reveal stonework but the wooden staircase still in place, the back doorway open to an encroaching garden.

I emerge into another world of brash bars with English and German names, a tattooist and a sex shop. Gargantuan hotels dwarf old wooden windmills. I cross the busy road, find a footpath that winds around the rocks beside crashing blue sea, where the sound of waves drowns out the passing cars. In a crevice, steps lead up to a cave shrine dedicated to the Archangel Michael. The walls are covered in icons, swords and brooms, and I feel as though I've fallen through the looking glass.

Where the path joins the fast road out of town in the direction of the airport, a long row of cottages looks out to sea. With red-tiled rooftops against a backdrop of hillside covered in tangled trees and bushes, the small houses seem to belong to another era, sandwiched between mega-hotels. Known as the Kritika, they were purpose-built at the end of the nineteenth century for Muslims from Crete, and the neighbourhood is now half-abandoned.

From the start of the Ottoman occupation of the Aegean in 1522 there were Muslim Turkish communities on all the major islands, but gradually the Greek islanders started winning back territory and Crete, after an uprising in 1896, was declared a semi-independent state. This made it an unfriendly place for Muslims and in 1898, Cretan Muslims came and settled on Rhodes, which was still part of the Ottoman Empire. The administration set up new housing for them at Kritika, Sandy Cape and Hochlakas in the south, while some settled in the Old Town. More came in 1913, after the Italians had occupied the island but before it was formally annexed. The International Congress of Cretan Studies in 2016 reported that the communities at Kritika and Hochlakas are still populated by descendants of the original refugees: Greek citizens of Muslim faith preserving Cretan dialect, customs and traditions, integrated into local society.

The first house is missing, replaced by an apartment building, and its two neighbours have been replaced by small modern homes. But from there they continue in numbered, semi-detached pairs, some still cared for, others dangerously close to collapse. A modernised house uses next door's abandoned back yard to hang a washing line. Some have small fishing boats outside, one propped simply on a couple of old tyres. Alleys lead to other small houses and gardens up the hillside. Roofs in a desperate state are caving in, the terracotta tiles held down by rocks, occasionally painted over to seal them from rain. Sometimes fallen patches of plaster reveal the craftsmanship of stones fitted tightly together, wooden ceilings semi-intact; other walls have fallen in, revealing a tiled bathroom filled with rubble and fig trees.

I come across an arched shelter with stone benches and a tap. Maybe people used to collect water from here or do their washing. Now it's inhabited by cats. Up the hill are a simple minaret and a couple of buildings. I follow a path to a humble cemetery in a tree-shaded grassy plot looking down to the sea. These graves bear no relation to those in the old Muslim cemetery in Mandraki; they are basic, rectangular concrete outlines with the simplest of headstones, some carved in stone but others poignantly handwritten on wood. From the names and inscriptions, many of the people were born in the early 1920s and 1930s and died in the last twenty years, as recently as 2017. Most are inscribed with the words 'Ruhuna Fatiha', or some variation; the Fatiha is the prayer for the soul of the dead. Turkish Muslim names such as Mustafa and Mehmet are sometimes paired with a Greek-sounding surname, Rodanaki, spelled with Greek letters. Other graves have no inscription at all, just an ordinary household ceramic tile placed diagonally, some of them broken to stumps.

During the partitioning of the Ottoman Empire after World War I, the Greeks occupied Smyrna (now Izmir), setting off the Greco-Turkish War in 1919. The Greek campaign was defeated with the Turkish recapture of Smyrna in 1922 and a terrible fire. In the following months more than eight hundred thousand Greeks returned to their country in packed boats. In his classic 1939 spy novel *The Mask of Dimitrios*, Eric Ambler wrote: 'Many of them were naked and starving. Some still carried in their arms the dead children they had had no time to bury.'

There were still Orthodox Christian Greeks living in what we now consider Turkey – some families had lived there for four hundred years – and Muslim Turks living in what we now consider Greece. The 1923 Treaty of Lausanne attempted to resolve matters by defining the borders of the modern Turkish republic, and uprooted two million people in a population exchange. Families were forced to leave their homes and travelled on foot, by train and by sea, barred from returning to the places where they and their parents were born. Across the sea from Rhodes, just south of Fethiye in Muğla province in southwest

Turkey, is an abandoned village called Levissi by the Greeks and Kayaköy by the Turks. Its five hundred houses have stood empty since the Greek Christians were forced to leave in 1923. It inspired the Louis de Bernières book *Birds Without Wings*.

However, because the Dodecanese islands were under Italian rule from 1912 until World War II, the Muslim Turks living on Rhodes and Kos didn't have to leave and in 1948, when the Dodecanese united with Greece, they became Greek. While some elderly Cretan Muslims of the Sunni faith remain in these islands, speaking Cretan Greek, others settled in Ottoman-controlled parts of the eastern Mediterranean, especially Syria and Lebanon. In Al-Hamidiyah in Syria and Tripoli in Lebanon, many continue to speak Greek as their mother tongue.

My head hurts trying to disentangle the threads of history here. Through the last few thousand years in the Mediterranean, from Israel and Syria to Turkey and Greece to Italy and Spain and France, there has been so much complex movement of people and boundaries and interchange of cultures – the Mediterranean as a theatre of nations. When you look back in any history, victims become villains and vice versa. Territory has been won and lost back and forth over millennia.

Towards the end of the 105 Cretan houses is one with ornate railings, the paint peeling from the exterior plaster in layers of red and yellow. Inside, on solid tile floors are recently emptied boxes for electrical goods, an LG washing machine box amid the rubble. At the end of the row is a funeral director's and a nightclub, and then the big hotels and tourist shops begin again. I turn and walk back. Among the houses are a few businesses. The fish shop and bakery could well have served the original community; there's also now an ecumenical church, a diving shop and a café. Sitting watching the sea across the road, I eat tasty cheese bourekia and then get talking to Rena, the friendly woman who's been running the café for the last few years.

The original Cretan Turks at Kritika were fishermen, she says, that's why they were housed here. Half of today's residents are their descendants, and half are Greek; the oldest Turkish Muslim here is Sakkis, aged eighty-nine. The name sounds Greek, I say, and she explains it's a naturalised version of Yusufakis. She feels it's a shame some houses are left to rot because the owners are far away or there are too many descendants. People feed the cats – there are about fifty – to control the rats, snakes and cockroaches that can make their homes in abandoned places.

As we talk, she mentions that she prefers winter when the island is quieter; they have music at weekends and she loves to see the waves crashing in on a wild day. After homemade cake I say goodbye, cross the street and go down the steps to the beach. There's some plastic rubbish brought in by the strong winds, but no sunbeds, and I can throw sticks into the sea for Lisa, take her off the lead and let her race along the sand. Out to sea, a vast cruise ship is passing; further up the beach, some people are looking at a dead turtle washed into shore.

In the moat around the walls of Rhodes Old Town, big lizards sunning themselves on the stone scurry away. Dark doorways lead to mysterious tunnels. There are sections of stone vaulted ceilings, perhaps chapels or storerooms, among the masonry above. Some of it is Byzantine construction, some from the medieval Knights of St John of Jerusalem, while the minarets date from 1522 and beyond, during the Ottoman Empire. Rhodes Old Town is said to be one of the oldest continuously inhabited towns in Europe, though many of its houses are crumbling and empty. Many others have been restored and turned into tourist accommodation.

The eastern end of the Old Town was once the Juderia, a strong and prosperous Jewish community. Around the main squares were businesses and banks, while the narrow, serpentine cobbled streets covered by archways were full of houses. At the heart of it is the Rhodes Jewish Museum, which is also the only remaining synagogue on Rhodes, and where a couple of years ago I met a charming eighty-eight-years-old gentleman called Sami Modiano, who was born in the neighbourhood and now spends his summers volunteering here.

We laughed easily together after he found out that I spoke Greek and a bit of French (he spoke four languages, but English wasn't one of them). He offered advice on how to make the most of my visit and said he'd be happy to answer questions afterwards. Then he showed me the tattooed blue number on his inner forearm. He was thirteen when he and his family were sent to Auschwitz-Birkenau.

People of the Jewish faith lived in Rhodes as early as a few centuries BC thanks to trade between Rhodes and Jerusalem, where hundreds of Rhodian-stamped amphorae have been found. In the twelfth century AD, a rabbi from Spain visited the island and found a Jewish community numbering four to five hundred. When the Knights of St John arrived in 1309 and built the castle, the Juderia within its walls was home to Jewish Greeks, people with Greek names and culture who spoke mostly Greek but used Hebrew for worship.

This community fought alongside the Knights to resist the Ottomans; but when the Knights began to persecute them and oblige them to convert to Christianity, they welcomed the Turkish invaders. They enjoyed economic and political privileges and were again allowed to practise their own religion. Sephardic Jews from

Spain, expelled by the Catholic Queen Isabella, were encouraged to settle in large numbers and the main language of the Jews of Rhodes became Ladino. Over the next centuries, the community grew to four thousand people.

When Theodore and Mabel Bent visited Rhodes in the late 1880s, they noted that while the town as a whole was a mixed, multicultural society of peoples from around the Mediterranean, from Italy to Egypt to the Levant, the walled Old Town was inhabited only by Muslim Turks and Spanish Jews. The Turks tended to be fishermen, blacksmiths, tanners, painters and joiners, wrote the Bents, while the Spanish Jews 'managed to secure for themselves the best quarter of the walled town', their houses 'containing wood carving and decorations dating from the days of the Knights'. They spoke many languages and the children were intelligent, 'inquisitive'.

Living at close quarters in the Old Town probably contributed to the trust between Muslims and Jews; meanwhile, the fact that no Christian Greeks were allowed within the Old Town walls after sunset, but had to retreat to Neohori, led to resentment among some Greeks.

Around 1910, as economic crisis and political instability encouraged the islanders of the Dodecanese in general to emigrate, Jewish people also began to leave for professional and financial reasons, heading for the USA and Africa (Rhodesia, the Belgian Republic of Congo and South Africa). They still saw Rhodes as their ancestral home, and at first the men went for work with a plan to come back; but often they would only return to find a bride from the community and then start their family where business opportunities were better.

In 1936, the Italian General Cesare Maria De Vecchi, a fervent follower of Mussolini, took over as governor of Rhodes and, implementing the Anti-Jewish laws in 1938, ordered hundreds of

Jews to leave the island; they sought asylum in British-ruled Cyprus or French-ruled North Africa. Still, by the start of World War II, almost two thousand remained. Photographs from 1939 and 1940 show smart young people in modern fashions continuing to enjoy days at the beach, riding bikes or going for coffee. Few believed that the atrocities rumoured to be happening elsewhere in Europe could occur here.

Throughout the war, the British and Greek armies fought to defend the Dodecanese against the Nazis. The World War II cemetery, near the main cemetery of Rhodes town, includes graves for British servicemen. In late 1942, Winston Churchill planned a military intervention to recapture the Dodecanese, but the Americans assigned forces elsewhere. In September 1943, the Italians surrendered to the Allies and signed an armistice. The Allies feared too many casualties (says a sign in the cemetery) if they continued to defend Rhodes, Kos and Leros. Within a month, Nazi Germany had taken over Rhodes.

The British attempted to bomb German ships in the port, but according to Patricia Wilson's book *Villa of Secrets*, some bombs missed their mark and fell on the nearby Jewish quarter. Synagogues were hit, people tragically crushed in their houses or trapped in fires.

On 18th July 1944, male Jews aged sixteen and over were ordered by the Gestapo to report to a designated place and present their work permits – a ploy to give the impression they would be sent to work camps. Then their identity cards and permits were taken away. It was Sami's thirteenth birthday and I wonder if he knew, that day, why his father was missing. The next day, women and children were also ordered to appear, bringing their valuables, which were seized.

The community entrusted their precious Torah scroll to the Mufti of the Murad Reis mosque, where Suleyman Kasiloglou hid it under the pulpit. The Turkish Consul General, Selahattin Ülkümen, also intervened and managed to save 42 families by claiming the people had Turkish citizenship. The Nazis complied, but bombed the Consulate building, killing Ülkümen's pregnant wife, and he was sent to jail. He was one of a small number of Turkish diplomats who, at great risk to themselves, used Turkey's neutrality to save the lives of European Jews from the Nazi genocide.

On 23rd July, 1,673 Jewish people were marched to the port and put on to boats and, along with another hundred from Kos, landed at Piraeus where they were forced on to trains to Auschwitz-Birkenau. Almost all were murdered in Nazi death camps in the last year of the war. Sami's sister, mother and father did not survive. It was mere months before liberation the following winter.

Sami said: 'It was minus twenty-five when the Russians came. I was twenty-three kilos, closer to death than life. They thought I was dead and were going to put me in the pit with the other bodies, but then someone realised I was alive, and they asked the Russian doctor if they could do anything. I remember it like a dream. When I opened my eyes, the Russian doctor hugged me and I thought I was in paradise.

'Then came the pain. I never expected to survive. I felt guilty not to be with the dead. I *wanted* to be with the dead. Then I started to ask: why me? Over and over, why me, why me? Why not my father, who was forty-three, why not my sister? You continue life with this question. You close up. You don't want to talk about it because no-one will understand. But there's a wound inside. The things I've seen, you can't just take a sponge and wipe them away. I was a child.'

Only 163 survived from Jewish Rhodes, and of those, many did not come back. Sami did, and experienced great hardship on all levels. The houses of the Juderia had been plundered and officially taken over by Greeks. Eventually, Sami met the woman who was to become his wife. She had great patience, he said, because it's not easy to be with a death camp survivor. They'd now been married over sixty years and lived in Rome. Fifteen years ago, he decided to start talking about his experience.

'It's important to talk to young people, so they know what happened. So it doesn't happen again.' He showed me photographs of a talk he did recently for 1,500 high school students. He talked about all the innocent people who were killed, not just Jews but also homosexuals, people with disabilities, anyone who thought differently, anyone with different beliefs. He was interested in people, not religion; when someone from Israel started questioning him – using me to interpret – about the red colour of the mikveh, he switched off. But he was delighted to spend time with a German couple who had returned to see him with their eleven-year-old daughter; he insisted they take photographs together, so she could show them to her school.

The Torah, kept safe in the Murad Reis mosque, is now in the National Library of Israel. There are today about twenty or so Jewish people – five families – on Rhodes. My knowledge of the Old Town, and more than that, some part of me, was transformed by meeting Sami. The next morning, I returned to thank him, taking Lisa with me and, as I hoped, he was delighted by her. I asked Sami why he wrote his book, *Per Questo Ho Vissuto*, in Italian. He reminded me that Rhodes was Italian when he grew up, and Italian was the official language.

I later read that a few months after the Jewish community of Rhodes had been shipped away, the Italian ship *Donizetti* was packed to the gills with 1,500 Italian internees including troops and officers. It was spotted by British destroyers patrolling the strait between Rhodes and Karpathos, and being unarmed and unable to defend itself, was damaged by gunfire and sank with no survivors. The abandoned wreck of the *Donizetti* still lies off the west coast of Rhodes.

Along the coastal strip beyond the airport and the old power station, the land becomes agricultural, and buildings fewer. The bus stops at Kalavarda and since there are no more buses going further for a while, I walk for three hours along the northwest coast.

It feels as if the wind and waves have blown away all signs of mass-market tourism. The hills here look too friable for building, held together by mastic bushes and juniper, cistus and thyme, interspersed with wheat fields and bamboo. Goats wander nonchalantly. Caper bushes and dill, tangled grasses and vines spill into the road. Except for passing cars, the only sounds are birds and insects and the breeze through the Mediterranean pines. The stony contours of Mount Attavyros appear – at 1,228 metres, the highest mountain in the Dodecanese.

I rest at Kameiros Skala to pick up the keys for the house in Kritinia, the village up the hill. Emilia, who runs Makedonia taverna, grew up there and says that in the 1960s it still had a traditional, rural way of life, with only a dirt road and oil generators. Walking through a valley of fields, then up into pine forest, I find myself at the village's folk museum, filled with objects that were made and used here not so long ago. Villagers donated wool coats and carpets, saddlebags; clothing that was woven, stitched and embroidered by hand; sieves for sifting crops, strung by hand using natural materials. A plough that is simply a branch with three smaller branches growing from it, cut off at a sharp slant; shovels and spades delicately carved from a single tree trunk, with an ergonomic curve in the design that probably gave them leverage or strength. These everyday objects, crafted from wood, metal, earthenware and wool in the days when people had nothing, seem priceless.

Kritinia is now a quiet place. Wandering the alleys, I notice a dilapidated building and peer inside to find a vast room, the ceiling made of slim tree trunks held up by a massive carved beam supported by an equally massive wooden column, the whole thing dimly illuminated by the holes in the ceiling where the packed earth and grasses have given way. Plaster has fallen from stone walls. On a rough wooden platform of tree trunks sit a wooden cart and a vat for tipping contents into a large press below. I believe it was a flour mill. Nearby, I've read, there's an abandoned windmill that once was run by a man called Konstantis, born into the milling trade in Asia Minor but expelled in the events leading to the population exchanges of 1923. People from the surrounding villages brought wheat here by donkey until 1940, when use of the mill was prohibited. Konstantis was only able to run it secretly at night to keep his family alive.

The inhabitants of Embona, further up the mountain, remain proud producers of meat and wine and honey, their farming income supplemented by tourism in summer. The population has increased to about 1,500 in recent years. Locals have told me that the European Union, in order to limit European wine production, offered people on Mount Attavyros money some years back to tear up their old vines. Some did – it was during the economic crisis – but not all, and now those who kept their vines are doing well, including young people who committed to the family business and an agricultural way of life.

In March 2015 I spent a few days exploring the area. Pulling myself up a sheer gully to the summit, I wandered alone around the ruins of a temple of Zeus, with only sheep for company, and was mesmerised by the smooth grazing lands on the hilltops. When I passed some fields the next day, two farmers sitting under an olive tree invited me to sit and share a drink of souma, the strong local liquor made from grapes. We ate cheese and salted cucumber, and I learned they had both lived in northern Europe. When one of them arrived in Belgium in 1967 for work – many left Rhodes for Belgium in the 1960s to work in the mines – he was amazed to see electric lights, unheard of in Embona back then. 'Not just in the house, but on the road!'

After a few decades, though, he returned. 'They can't take this away from us,' he said, 'not even Merkel.'

During the later decades of their occupation of Rhodes, the Italians wanted to develop the island's farming and tourism to raise the standard of living.

They built bathing facilities at Kallithea Springs, and beyond, at what is now called Kolymbia, the orderly agricultural settlement of San Benedetto was purpose-built in 1935 in a fertile plain on land expropriated from the local inhabitants. By 1937 it had fifty houses and farms, granted to rural families from Tuscany and Sardinia and irrigated by systems bringing in mountain spring water. Both places, on the east coast, are now surrounded by big hotels. Another purpose-built Italian village was San Marco, near Katavia and Prasonisi in the south. The Nazis used it as an ammunition depot and turned what had been a silk factory into a brutal military prison, but its tall church tower and the remains of farmhouses are still standing. Perhaps the best known of the Italian villages, however, is Eleousa, which was then called Campochiaro. It is located on Profitis Ilias, the first of the big mountains south of Rhodes town, which at 798 metres is higher than any on the small surrounding islands. That is where I was heading on a hot morning in late summer.

My day had started in Tilos just after 4am. Walking in the night under many stars to get a ride to the port, I slept for a couple of hours on the boat, waking again as they announced our arrival in Rhodes. I'd left Lisa with a friend as it would be too hot for her. Having walked to the bus station near the Italian-built New Market I discovered the bus to Eleousa had left, so jumped on the next one going that way.

'Theologos?' asked the bus driver.

'I think so,' I said.

Soon after the airport, the bus disgorged most of the passengers and I started to see vegetables growing in fields. Eventually I was the last remaining passenger, and the driver gestured to me to come to the front so we could talk. Was there anywhere to find food in Theologos?, I asked. The taverna would be closed, he said, but I should ask the people in the shop to make me some cheese and ham sandwiches.

'I did that two days ago and when they sliced the ham and I smelled it… It reminded me of my childhood.'

Thanking him, I went straight to the mini-market where someone asked, 'Camping?' I had a camping mat strapped to my backpack. The man called someone, then handed the phone over to me. As I talked to the person on the other end of the line about camping on their land, I noticed a basket of fresh eggs on the counter, white and brown and pale blue. If Eleousa was too far, I thought, I would enjoy the walk and then turn back and stay here. The shop owner made my sandwiches and I bought an apple and muesli bars and a large bottle of water to decant into my bottles, leaving the plastic in the recycling bin.

Before setting out, I wandered back down the road to see the ruined temple of Apollo. Fig trees and capers had found their way up among the huge stones of the walls and the remains of massive columns. The temple, where Apollo was probably worshipped as a protector of agriculture, dates to 400BC, but excavations have revealed traces of much older civilisations, along with remains of an early Christian basilica. The site was probably abandoned after the Arab invasions of the seventh century AD.

Following the road up into the village, I found pretty alleys and simple whitewashed houses. There was such an aura of old-world tranquillity that I wondered how it had escaped development, so close to the resorts and the airport; then I looked towards the sea and glimpsed the old power station puffing out dark smoke. Still, when I continued to the end of the village and reached the road leading to the hills, it was lush and rural with pines and olives, sage and mastic and cistus bushes, birds and a breeze. A pristine white goat sat contentedly on the roof of an abandoned car. The narrow road was easy walking, although it was close to midday and hotter than I'd expected. Perhaps I should have waited a few weeks, and brought a hat. I found myself stopping from time to time in the shade, one of Lisa's habits. At a deserted house with a hefty crack down its brick-and-stone walls and the roof caving in, I lay on my camp mat in the cool shadow of a large eucalyptus and looked around me: acacia trees, wild fennel, stunted oaks, a dragonfly. The junction with the main road was nearby, where rental cars and tour buses passed on their way to 'butterfly valley'. Planes took off from time to time. But I was undisturbed on the grass listening to the wind in the trees.

As I approached the main road, tangles of blackberries were a surprise, tiny but sweet. I passed a winery and then a makeshift home of sorts, a caravan, a shed made up of old doors, a vine pergola and chickens wandering. According to the map, there should have been a village ahead, around the bend. But it transpired that the 'village' was in fact an army base. So instead I pressed on to the butterfly valley.

This nature park in the woods around a stream, a resting place for the Jersey tiger moth, has become a major attraction. Feeling a headache coming on, I rested on the shady restaurant terrace with a salad and a cold drink. The salad was meagre but the waitress agreed to charge my phone – I might need more battery. I realised I wouldn't make it to Eleousa that day, but decided I'd like to wild-camp in the forest, maybe continue tomorrow. The restaurant manager pointed out I had a good map, so I mentioned the disappointment of finding not a village but an army base.

'It used to be an Italian village,' he said. 'But now it has the name only.'

It turned out Upper (Epano) Kalamonas was part of the Italian settlement of Peveragno. It was purchased by an Italian company in 1931 from Turkish owners, and a new town was built complete with school, police station and mills, and the mosque turned into a church; the land was planted with vines and olives and fruit trees. Rural Italian settlers farmed the area until World War II, and then in 1947 the village was deserted. Now part of it is an army base. The winery is owned by the Kallas family who began their own olive production in 1959.

I mentioned to the restaurant manager that I'd like to walk towards Eleousa on the mountain tracks, and he cautioned me. 'The paths aren't easy to follow if you don't know the way. They aren't well marked. Better to go to Ayios Sylla and take the road.'

I made a deal with myself that if they had hats for sale at the shop next to the restaurant, even ones with butterflies on them, I'd buy one. And they did, so I put on my butterfly hat. After I passed two more car parks for the butterfly valley, as well as one of those little tourist 'trains' –

the butterflies must have been choking – the road wound steeply uphill, passing a lookout point staffed by bored-looking fire marshals. By the time I reached the monastery of Kalopetra, I was desperate to get off the tourist route. A softly spoken man sitting by a gift shop helped me with directions, mentioning that the path would pass through a section of forest that was destroyed by fire a few years ago, and suggesting I top up on water from the spring. As I filled my bottle, I noticed a pale green caterpillar as big as my index finger eating its way through leaves.

There had been several serious wildfires in Greece that summer, including on the large island of Samos just north of the Dodecanese. As I turned with relief off the tarmacked road and on to a forest track, I realised camping deep in the woods at the driest time of the year, when the summer had parched the land, was probably a stupid thing to do. But at the top of the track I found the red sign the man had told me about and a wide path, soft with pine needles and shady with the overhanging trees. It led me on. By my feet I spotted a couple of pink colchicums, crocus-like flowers. The path narrowed but red dots showed the way. I heard a loud noise and was thrilled to see a large deer, a stag, bounding away. Then, unable to find the path or red dots, I lay on the slope on the pine needles, and rested for a while.

Finding the red dots again, I followed them up to a track and a goat enclosure. The trail continued in glorious fashion through the forest, straight and easy, and I breathed in the fresh air. I reached a clearing with a single olive tree in the middle, a meeting of paths, none very distinct. I opted for the one that kept going in the direction I'd been walking, though it was faint and overgrown, keeping an eye on landmarks – wind turbines, a chapel. Maybe I'd go back to the olive tree clearing and camp. There were far more tracks than were shown on my map.

Perhaps it was stubbornness or over-confidence or curiosity, but I kept beating a path through scrub for maybe half an hour until there really wasn't a path at all, and I could no longer see landmarks. I kept going straight, thinking if I did that, I had to reach something. What I reached was a cliff edge into a deep ravine, with a sheer cliff on the other side of it where the forest continued.

I turned around and looked for the way I must have come, but the bush was thick and I was tired. I got scratched and bruised by branches and lost my sense of direction. I'd walked around in a circle and found no way down. I turned on my phone and tried GPS but all I saw was a green shape with a road along one side, and couldn't figure out how to reach it. The battery was going down, so I switched it off again.

There had to be a way across the ravine. I had got there somehow. I tried to calm my rising panic, as it wouldn't do me any good. With the setting sun in my eyes I searched for a route, stumbling through bushes and overgrown trees, cracking dry branches or sometimes just bashing into them, determined to find a way back. I had a day's water with me, at least. After perhaps a couple of hours, I saw what looked like a flat ledge on the hillside above me. Could it be a track?

I pulled myself up there with purpose and found to my relief that it was. It had to lead somewhere – it was suitable for vehicles, and the presence of sheep, the first I'd seen, meant someone might come by. The sun was close to the horizon so, feeling hopeful now, I could camp in a clearing nearby. My body was sweaty but the wind was cool. I ate something, drank a little water, laid out the camping mat on pine needles between bushes under a tall pine tree, removing pine cones. Wrapped up in warm clothes, I got in my sleeping bag and lay down, aching but no longer so scared. I turned on my phone to send a couple of innocuous messages giving a sense of where I was without worrying anyone, then turned off the phone again to preserve the battery, took a painkiller and tried to sleep. It was soon dark, bright stars appearing, and all I could hear was the wind in the trees and occasionally a sheep's bell. If I hadn't been lost, it would have felt like a beautiful adventure.

Although twisting and turning all night, when I woke at dawn to pale light in the dark pines I was optimistic and set off up the track in what I believed was the right direction. Sunlight soon glowed orange on the tree bark. I came across a sign, 'Psinthos–Archipoli', confirming I was heading back to familiar territory. But that road led around in a circle. I switched on GPS and this time it showed me the tracks and I realised the right way was something that didn't look like a path at all but a driveway to a barn, where cows shuffled in the dark. I continued down, because the blue Google dot told me to, and eventually came to another of those clear, wide, pine-needle-covered paths and followed it up a gentle slope until I came out at the goat farm from yesterday, and knew my way back to the road.

It was a relief to be alive, a relief not to be waiting for rescue. I'd proved to myself that alongside the tourist attractions, parts of Rhodes are still seriously wild. A pick-up truck appeared and the driver gave a cheery wave. I followed the same road as the previous day, ate blackberries, spotted an eagle gliding above the olive groves, and a few hours later reached the bus stop at Theologos just minutes before the bus. I was grateful that it wasn't the same friendly driver as the day before, because I had no energy to talk. As the bus filled with tourists on the way into town, I leaned my head against the window. The next day, I had to be elsewhere; visiting Eleousa would have to wait.

Five months later, in winter, I have rented a car and found a place to stay in Psinthos, a few kilometres from where I got lost. From here I will drive around the edge of the forest to Eleousa. It's an appropriate base, as Psinthos was the site of the battle in which the Italians defeated the Turks on 16th May 1912, marking the start of the Italian occupation. Psinthos seems to be one of those villages like Pyli in Kos that kept going strong because it had water to irrigate its fields via a network of canals – there's a small dam with turtles and gizani fish – and it had forest for timber. It's about twenty-five kilometres from Rhodes town, close enough but also far enough away.

On the road to Eleousa, at the small village of Archipoli, I spot ruins of maybe a dozen stone houses on the slopes above, the highest ones the most broken. Lower down, the front of one house has fallen away but a wooden shutter still hangs suspended in mid-air, and pieces of concrete roof dangle on steel rods. Wooden floorboards and furniture are rotting into the ground, and parked next to the house is a brown car with its wheels sunk into the road.

I continue driving for a few more kilometres until the rocky peak of the mountain rises ahead. The Italians built Eleousa – or Campochiaro, as it was called then – in 1935–36 for Italian settlers from Trentino-Alto Adige, South Tyrol, who each received a house and plot of land to cultivate. The village had a Roman Catholic church and a Fascist Party headquarters as well as a school, medical centre, cinema and a hydraulic system for irrigation and power. I aim for the centre and park on a long avenue lined by very tall, sturdy Mediterranean pines, near a house with washing hanging on a line, and a decrepit, arched structure with a long-abandoned Alfa Romeo inside. I notice a large yellow building above with distinctively rounded corners, and make my way uphill.

The square at the top of the village is wide and open with a promenade in the centre and large edifices all around. Though the trees and shrubbery are cared for, it's eerily empty; the only sound is that of a distant chainsaw in the woods. Spanning one side is what looks like a minor but elegant palace with a long, arched cloister, towers of varying heights, terraces and arched windows, red columns, fretwork for air circulation, and bulging wrought-iron balconies. Windows and doors gape open, yellow walls flaking away to grey concrete. Inside, tiled floors and garishly painted walls are dirty, exposed to the elements. The cloister is defaced by graffiti and patches of green mildew. Apparently built as a market in 1935, it was abandoned after the war.

Adjacent is a disused hospital, and it's with some trepidation that I pass through the open door into the crumbling building. The grim grey doors along the corridor give it the look of a prison. Some bear the remains of several hefty locks on the outside. But others stand ajar, giving on to large, airy rooms.

In 1947, after Campochiaro/Eleousa was deserted, an opportunity was seen to create a sanatorium for tuberculosis patients, who could be quarantined in this remote place. It opened with 54 staff and 80 beds, and the doctor Emmanuel G. Kostaridis – shown in photographs as a square-faced man, hair swept back from his high forehead, expression both studious and optimistic – became its scientific director. The mountain location was vulnerable to cold winds in the winter, and beset by difficulties relating to the supply of medication, recruitment of staff and transportation of patients to town for any complicated surgery. But the hospital treated patients with fresh air, rest and a good diet, while Kostaridis – often the only doctor on site – worked tirelessly. His approach was holistic and he began to monitor patients after their discharge to further the scientific knowledge about factors that contributed to the disease. Eventually, he would visit schools and educate the community about vaccination. When he retired in 1970, and the sanatorium closed, it had provided therapy to over 1,500 people and most likely prevented tuberculosis from affecting countless others across the Dodecanese.

I see a path down to a row of half a dozen strange houses set among fields. They have thick walls and capped chimneys, not dissimilar to Greek village houses, but also smooth, Italian-style columns outside which contrast weirdly with the camouflage colours painted on the outside walls. The windows, oddly set into the corners of the houses and still paned with glass, are protected by thick iron bars. Everything is faded, peeling, with no sign of life except for two goats tied to a tree, and the effect is decidedly creepy.

Past a corrugated iron shack in camouflage colours labelled 'Cookhouse', a path descends into the forest. Someone has seen this idyllic spot as a good place to dump rubbish. As the path narrows and the undergrowth becomes thicker, I see what seem to be concrete gateposts in the middle of nowhere and then, further on, the broken remains of a grave. Clearing fallen pine needles away from the white marble cross, I find an inscription to Zorzis (Georgie?) Kapetanakis, who left this life in June 1970. Is it a coincidence that this was the sanatorium's final year? Why was he buried here in the forest? I make out low walls surrounding this forgotten graveyard. Another grave, concrete, has a simple cross outlined by small pebbles, and initials. Were the rows of basic, unmarked squares, almost hidden in undergrowth, all graves? At first it seems sad, but perhaps it's not a bad place to crumble to dust.

I return to the car. The road continues along an avenue lined by tall, straight pines and soon the Eleousa fountain comes into view:

a huge circular pool of dazzling green water with an overflowing chalice in the centre. Swimming in it are rare gizani fish, found in fresh water in this region, and orange koi carp. I continue a couple of kilometres around the mountain past tunnels dug into the rock, undoubtedly military, and teams of spandex-clad cyclists competing in a race. When I park again and continue my walk, the only sound is birds among the rocks and trees. Two mysterious stone ruins loom up in the forest and shortly after I reach Elafos ('Deer') Hotel, built by the Italians in 1929 and named Albergo del Cervo for the rare *Dama dama* that roam the surrounding pine and cypress forest.

The large, alpine-looking structure with its odd gables, dormer windows and wooden balconies was intended to be reminiscent of Austro-Hungarian architecture. It was used during World War II first as quarters for Italian officers, and then as a military hospital for the Germans; later it became a hotel again. It's open but there is nobody around today except for the person in charge who, to add to the surreal feeling, is from Lahore, Pakistan. He says they get busy at the weekends, shows me photographs of the winter snow. The annexe, known as Elafina, is now empty.

But like many visitors, I've mainly come here to see the ruined villa across the road. The summer residence of the Fascist General Cesare Maria De Vecchi, Italian governor of Rhodes from 1936 to 1940, it was intended as a retirement home for Benito Mussolini. Although he never set foot in the place, here Italian generals dreamed and saw to fruition their grand schemes of developing these 'backward' islands of the Aegean, while building their own strategic power.

Set in the forest, it's less grand than I expected, less refined; an oddity more than anything else. The solid walls and fireplaces and hallways are intact but doors and windows are missing. I creep around to an entrance and then across a black-and-white tiled floor, hoping a ceiling isn't about to cave in, trying to avoid the worst of the broken glass amid the dust and rubble. An arched doorway and large windows give spectacular views to the coast and forest, but the frames are broken and some of the window panes smashed. Lisa races from room to room, peering from balconies bereft of balustrades or leaning precariously. The walls are completely covered in layers of graffiti in various languages.

The villa, abandoned for almost half a century, came to public attention in 2014 when a fifty-year lease was offered on the property by the Hellenic Republic Asset Development Fund, established to raise money to reduce government debt but sparking a public outcry at the selling off of Greek heritage. Looking at this wrecked building, I think it would take a gutsy investor.

In Psinthos, a man is selling almonds, beans, blue hen's eggs and fruit trees from his truck. I ask if the fat black home-cured olives are for sale but he says no and invites me to help myself.

He came to Rhodes to do his national service fifty years ago, he says, met his wife and settled in Archipoli. While twelve of his cousins left to find work in France and stayed there, he worked as a hotel cook in Rhodes for forty years and built five houses. He's now retired and a grandfather but keeps animals and plants trees because 'to keep working does you good'. I wonder if he knows anything about the cemetery in the forest at Eleousa. He doesn't, but it sets him on an interesting diatribe.

'The Italians built all those buildings – and the Palace of the Knights in the Old Town of Rhodes too, they rebuilt the entire palace from the ground up after it was destroyed in an explosion. The Turks had stored dynamite inside. But the Italians built things strong because they believed they were staying. You know the church of San Francisco?'

It's a Catholic church with a high campanile behind the Old Town; it's a landmark, but I've never paid it that much attention.

'There's a statue of St Francis holding a dove. The Italians said, "We will leave when the bird flies away." Of course, it was stone and would never fly away. The Italians used us for labour but it was their vision. Now, we only destroy things. We can't even look after them. You know the National Theatre in Mandraki? When the Italians built it, it had perfect sound. They've brought in good Greek architects but even they can't fix it. The government…' He rubs his fingers together and I interject, saying, 'they don't have the money'. He says no. 'They steal it.'

I buy an orange tree from him and he tells me what it needs, invites me to visit his home sometime for coffee. I thank him and say goodbye. What he said is an unmistakable echo of what the old man in Nisyros told me a few years back, 'Now we only break things.' But as I wander away from the village centre, I see that the Greek Neo-Nazi party, Golden Dawn, has left flyers on parked cars, campaigning for the upcoming elections; lest we forget, some of those things that lasted were built by Mussolini, dictator and ally of Hitler.

The next morning in Psinthos I look at a house with plaster clinging to half of its stone front, a stone doorway, a carving of a cross and the date 1895. The centre of the house is braced by the wide arch called a *kamara*, still holding up strong timber roof beams, although plants grow up through the door, several layers of blue, green and brown paint peeling away. Like many old houses built by Greek villagers, it has lasted through decades of abandonment.

A man is restoring a similar old house and invites me to look inside. He doesn't know exactly how old it is, he says; people built these stone houses in more or less the same style for hundreds of years, right up until maybe World War II. I ask him who it's for, assuming he's working on it for a foreigner.

'It's for my daughter. It was my wife's house, and now it's for our grandchildren.'

I am happy to see locals restoring houses for themselves.

I drive to a place near Archipoli and park where a track leads uphill. After rain overnight, mist hangs over the tops of trees. The birds are singing and all around is thick forest, droplets of rain sparkling at the end of green pine needles. All is green and lush, pure and lovely; the undergrowth is sage and cistus. Eventually I emerge into a high, flatter area of pasture, with two abandoned stone barns and the faint lines of terraces, a newer farm building and goats grazing. The sun wins over the clouds, leaving the sky blue, and an eagle takes off and wheels across the canopy.

A pick-up truck comes into view, the heads of an old couple poking over the dashboard. They look surprised, then wave. A stream babbles on the ridge as the track narrows to a rough stone road, then widens again on the other side and the view down is magnificent: streams glinting silver as they criss-cross a green hillside dotted with rocks, hazy in the sunlight which glows around grazing sheep; and a sea of olives all the way down through the valley.

BRIDGE OF LIGHT
KASTELLORIZO

After a languorous afternoon jumping into the sea off the rocks and then following a track along a tree-covered hillside, my friend and I find that the route back to the main harbour takes us through the army base. It's the only way, short of retracing our steps for several hours, and dusk is approaching. Thus we find ourselves, on our first day in Kastellorizo, with two machine guns pointing at us.

The soldiers watch us closely until their superior sternly allows us to proceed.

Most of the Dodecanese lie very close to Turkish shores and have Greek military tasked with defending this jagged border. There's no cause for concern when international relations are going well, but the countries went to war over Cyprus in the 1970s, and a dispute over Imia/Kardak brought them to the brink of war in the 1990s; regular territorial skirmishes keep everyone on their toes.

In many parts of Tilos, my phone welcomes me to Turkey, but there's something more extreme about Kastellorizo's position. A remote outpost of Greece, it sits two kilometres off the southern shores of mainland Turkey, and over one hundred and twenty-five kilometres (seventy-eight nautical miles) east of its nearest Greek neighbour, Rhodes. The proximity of Kastellorizo to Asia Minor has been, like Nisyros's volcano, both maker and breaker of fortunes.

And it is an extreme example of abandonment. These twelve square kilometres of rocky land once had a prosperous population of close to ten thousand. Today there are somewhere between 200 and 250 permanent residents, which seems more reasonable. How this drop in population happened is quite a story, as is that of its regeneration from literally ashes. 'Ah, everyone wants to go to Kastellorizo!' says a smiling shop assistant in Rhodes when I mention it. But everyone always has.

What we call Kastellorizo is a group of fourteen islands and islets. The main one is still properly referred to by its ancient name, Megisti – meaning 'Biggest'. The Greek government and Europe have an interest in keeping it both protected and populated, so there is an airport, and once or twice a week the big ferry from Piraeus that stops at Kalymnos, Kos, Nisyros, Tilos, Symi and Rhodes continues several hours east to Kastellorizo. It is a beautiful way to arrive.

The exquisite natural harbour is lined by neoclassical mansions painted blue, yellow and green with wooden balconies, standing out starkly against scrubbed, scratched, white karst hillsides and towered over by imposing limestone cliffs. Add sparkling blue water to the picture, the deep green of pine trees and a scattering of tiny islets – it seems you could swim or leap from one stepping stone to another – and the immediate impression is of an idyllically languid place to while away a couple of days, perhaps sipping at cocktails on the edge of the clear, blue-green bay. Taverna tables clustered on the waterfront offer fresh grilled fish while a turtle swims between painted wooden fishing boats, and water taxis flit about to swimming spots and the 'Blue Cave'. But at the mouth of the harbour, painted red and white, is the Old Mosque, now a museum telling the island's sad history.

In the pale dawn light, the bay is opaque, small ripples on its surface and houses casting shadows. Their colours muted, they face out of the harbour to mountains in Anatolia, named in Greek after the rising of the sun, a region where Greek and Persian empires took and ceded territory over the centuries. Near the harbour mouth, a Lycian tomb from the fourth century BC is cut into the rust-streaked cliff, looking across the water. The sun rises dazzling from the grey, uneven ridge and casts a solid gleam on the sea, a brilliant, sparkling line from here to there. The walls that face east receive the first warm glow of the sunlight that will soon burn them white.

From ancient times, the islanders produced wine and olive oil, but gifted with a deep, sheltered harbour they were always primarily merchants, sailors and fishermen. The Roman historian Livy wrote that Megisti's harbour was large enough to contain a fleet. After the Knights of St John were forced to give up their possessions in the Holy Land to the Saracens in 1309, the island provided a convenient stopover to regain forces on their way from Cyprus to take over Rhodes. They built a castle between the two harbours, which allowed them to control the main naval route to Jerusalem through the next hundred years.

When the Ottoman Empire conquered the Dodecanese, the little island surrendered in return for commercial privileges, paying only a light, fixed annual tax in return for a fairly independent existence with freedom of trade and religion. The Venetians, at war with Turkey, occupied Megisti briefly in 1570 and then again in 1659, but the Greek population remained and simply paid taxes to Venice instead. The 1700s brought repeated attacks by pirates, Greek and otherwise; there was even a brief Russian military occupation. (Ah, everyone wants to go to Kastellorizo…)

For several hundred years, the island was occupied by one so-called liberating force or another, the castle destroyed and rebuilt, but the Greek population flourished.

A great benefit of being so close to the Turkish mainland was the access to raw materials and markets. While under Turkish control,

Megisti established a colony on the nearby Turkish coast, at modern-day Kaş, at that time called Antifilo, bringing in a supply of fresh vegetables and wood, some of which was made into charcoal. The tiny island became, in the 1800s, one of the great shipping centres of the Mediterranean, wealthy through maritime trade with the East, with cargoes as various as Libyan sponges and pilgrims going to the Holy Land. Its tall ships employed 450 sailors.

The Greek War of Independence, which began in 1821, gave Megisti a few years of freedom, but it was returned to Turkey under the London Protocol of 1830, along with the rest of the Dodecanese; tolerant Ottoman rule and protection allowed the island to thrive again, however. In 1836 it was awarded self-government and its taxes reduced as the ship owners traded in charcoal, sponges, fruit, wine and oil with ports in the Middle East, North Africa, the Western Mediterranean and Black Sea. They sold goods to the large Greek Orthodox communities in the Turkish cities of Smyrna and Constantinople.

In March 1888, Theodore and Mabel Bent arrived on nearby Turkish shores in search of antiquities in the abandoned temples and rock-cut tombs; they lamented that the lucky Austrians had got there before them and taken all they liked, painting their flag on the rocks. The Bents travelled to Megisti only to register with its Greek consul that they had come from Turkey, so that on their return journey the Greeks elsewhere could not touch the items they had collected. It appeared to the couple 'a flourishing little town, divided by a point on which rise the ruins of a red castle'.

Already by the 1890s, some Kastellorizians had begun leaving for economic reasons, seeing the island's industries in decline. One was Peter Michelides, who told his story in the book *The Tobacco Pioneers*. He went to work in a Greek-owned tobacco business in Egypt, sending his earnings back home to support his family, then a decade later he took advantage of new opportunities for travel and set up his own business in Western Australia, a commercial success for the next half century.

Still, at the end of the nineteenth century the population of Kastellorizo was more than 8,500, with another few thousand living over on the Turkish mainland. Photographs from the time show the areas around the castle and harbour densely packed with houses. Benefactors built grand churches and schools, a nursery and even a girls' school. Large houses were ornately decorated, and the town burgeoned with craftspeople.

Then, around a hundred years ago, its fortunes changed.

After 1908, the political reforms and modernisation of the Young Turk movement swiftly led to a more oppressive regime in the Ottoman Empire. Taxation increased, Turkish became the official language and military conscription was made compulsory; trade and religious liberties were rescinded. In 1911 Italy declared war on Turkey and a year later liberated the rest of the Dodecanese, which declared itself the State of the Aegean, vying to become part of Greece. Megisti saw an opportunity and allowed its own ships to fly the flag of the State of the Aegean. In response the Turks broke off commercial relations with the island – and closed all Turkish ports to the ships.

Suddenly without work, the population was reduced by half in two years. The merchant fleet was stuck in the harbour, leading to food shortages, and there was mass emigration. The island invited in Cretan fighters and staged an uprising, but no support was forthcoming from the Greek government. In 1912, the Castellorizian Association of Western Australia was established, the oldest ethnic organisation in Australia.

Little Megisti had too strategic a position to be left alone for long.

In World War I, the French took over the island as a base of operations for submarines and a refuelling station for warplanes. In return they offered protection for the merchant ships, opened a free hospital, renovated the large public water cisterns and took on rubbish disposal. They built observation towers and paths, such as that to Navlakas, a deep fjord with a small mooring space where they unloaded armaments. But the French occupation also made the island a target, and it was bombarded by the Germans and Turks.

As the French prepared to leave after the war, in 1921 the Italians occupied Megisti, changing its name to Castello Rosso. But another political event hit the island's economy hard: the 1923 population exchanges between Greece and Turkey. The Greek populations of Smyrna and Constantinople, substantial markets, suddenly vanished. Adding to the island's woes, a severe earthquake caused destruction in 1926. More islanders followed their friends and relatives to Australia.

In the 1930s, with the rise of Fascism, the Italian regime dug in with heavy taxes and restrictions on trade and religion and language, with the usual negative effects on the economy. High duties imposed on basic foodstuffs led to social unrest. The Old Mosque, once a symbol of tolerant understanding between local Greeks and Turkish rulers, served as a weapons depot and a prison. People continued to leave. Presumably that suited the occupiers. By the start of World War II, around a thousand residents remained.

When Italy surrendered to the Allies in 1943, British troops were sent to take control of the island and prevent it falling into German hands like other islands in the chain. Despite repeated bombing, it remained under Allied control and therefore played a vital role. The stationing of more British troops here led to further bombardment and the Kastellorizians were evacuated by the British for their own protection to Cyprus, Palestine and Egypt along with thousands of other Greeks from elsewhere in the Dodecanese. They left their belongings and valuables in their homes. The island was bombed again, and a terrible fire consumed it in 1944, possibly started at the Allied fuel store. How could people have known the war and bombardment would end, when it had been going on for half their lifetime?

When the war did end, the British stayed to help bring the islanders home and supply rations as repairs and rebuilding began. In September 1945, the SS *Empire Patrol* left Port Said with almost five hundred refugees aboard, but caught fire and sank; thirty-three of them never made it back to their homeland.

Those who did limp home found their island in ruins, devastated by war, their livelihoods and everything they owned destroyed. We had nothing, says one old man. 'There wasn't earth to bury us in!'

This was the island that was finally returned to Greece in 1948, the unification they had so longed for. There were few opportunities to earn a living. 'Greek initiatives on the island were minimal,' writes the Kastellorizian Association of Victoria on their website. By then, almost all the islanders had sold whatever they could and were starting new lives elsewhere – some settled in the USA and others in Brazil, but most headed to Australia.

From summer 2014 to spring 2015, a few years after I moved to Tilos and just before my interest in the abandoned places of the Dodecanese began, I was in Australia. I wasn't there to look for the Greek diaspora, but I happened across it, homesick for Greece myself. I didn't meet anyone from Kastellorizo, but plenty of others who were wistful for the old country. The first was an old man I overheard saying '*Katse kato*' to his dog. He'd lived in New South Wales for decades, so I loved the fact that he was telling the dog to sit in Greek.

In Redfern, a district of Sydney, my friend and I stayed on a street called Kepos – Greek for garden. There was a Greek barber nearby, and a café with a Greek name, Metaxi Mas, meaning 'Between Us'. We sat at a pavement table under a plane tree and ordered Greek coffee. When my friend complimented the owner on it, his eyes lit up and he introduced himself as Panos, from the island of Lesvos, north of the Dodecanese. My friend said he'd visited the island and it was very green.

'You say green?' said Panos. 'I mean – walnut trees, olives, cherries…' Panos had lived in Australia for decades but still spoke with a Greek accent. He ran the busy café with his wife, son and daughter, and had moved on from the small flat upstairs to a big house. 'Greece – the land – is the best in the world. Sure, has problems with the money. But *the land* is the best. What you need? A few trees… Here I have the money but I don't have the lifestyle.' When we went back the next day, he knocked a few dollars off the bill and his wife gave us extra treats. We'd reminded them of home.

We found the ghosts of Greeks in another café, in Katoomba in the Blue Mountains. Zacharias Simos had arrived from the Greek island of Kythera at the age of fifteen and found work in fish restaurants and cafés in Sydney. Four years later, in 1916, he leased a shop in Katoomba and opened the art deco Paragon Café and Oyster Palace, delivering fish, oysters and lobsters across the Blue Mountains. Katoomba was then booming as a destination and he promoted extravagantly, developed sidelines in American-style refreshments. He went home to find a wife – a Kytheran from Maryland, USA –

and returned with her to Australia. When I visited the Paragon it was somewhat down-at-heel, no longer owned by the original family, and it closed in 2018 while I was writing this book.

Many Greeks moved to the other side of the world because life in the old country had been a bit too interesting, with occupation and war. People fled to a safe place, a refuge during tough times, where they could make money and build a stable life for themselves and their children; but they hung on to their culture, just as they did during centuries of foreign occupation. How much easier it is to live in a country where the systems function as they should and there are jobs – and yet even among the children born in Australia, often there is a longing to return to the rural life of Greece. In *The Good Greek Girl* (published as *The Mind Thief* in the UK) by Maria Katsonis, who grew up above her Greek parents' milk bar in Melbourne in the 1970s, there's an unforgettable detail of her father straining yoghurt to make tzatziki by hanging it in a singlet in the shower. She describes the oppression of the cloistered Greek community; but also the good character traits she inherited.

The Kastellorizian Association of Victoria, the province whose capital is Melbourne, has a database of some thirty thousand persons. Around a decade ago the Greek-Australian group Friends of Kastellorizo began donating money to set up new projects on the island, such as making olive oil, recycling waste and restoring an old windmill, to create jobs for its two to three hundred residents.

From the top of the castle, the scant remains of the Castello Rosso, I look down on the slope that was once densely packed with houses, still criss-crossed with their remains, now overgrown with wild shrubs, dry grasses and fig trees.

New houses are going up, windows waiting to be installed. Some 'Kazzies' as they call themselves have returned from Australia since the 1990s to claim their homes and rebuild; some have cisterns and are growing vines, olives and fruit trees. There are restored homes, freshly painted with neat, red-tiled roofs, some of them clearly only used occasionally, perhaps when people come back for the summer.

Other houses are in stages of disrepair, mansions barely standing, bare walls punctuated by holes for wooden beams that are gone. On ruined stone walls are handwritten signs with a name claiming ownership, sometimes just sprayed initials. Between two tall houses built into the hillside is a hollow space with the wooden floor-beams of the upper storey still clinging to stone and plaster walls – a wooden shelf and part of a wooden dresser, the window frame, the fireplace, a chimney above, a doorway – below, through half a floor, are bushes and rubble enclosed by wire fence. There's something beautiful about this genuine domestic scene preserved, decaying very slowly over the decades.

Perhaps the most famous Kastellorizian was Despina Achladioti. Born in 1890, she left busy Megisti with her husband in 1927 and sailed to the nearby islet of Ro. Ro had previously been occupied – it has the remains of a fortress with a rainwater cistern and a wine press – but had been deserted. There they lived self-sufficiently, growing vegetables and keeping goats and chickens. Despina stayed after her husband fell ill and died; she brought her blind mother to Ro and, after her mother passed away, single-handedly rowed her remains back to Kastellorizo. Meanwhile, she raised the Greek flag every day throughout World War II – presumably there was no need to evacuate her from Ro – and helped the Greek special forces, the Sacred Band. She continued to raise the Greek flag throughout the tensions with Turkey in the

1970s, and until her death in 1982, aged ninety-two. Pictures show her dressed according to the island's tradition with a shawl flowing from her headband, and shield-like buckles down her blouse.

The story of the 'Lady of Ro', as she is known, is always told as an example of great heroism. But I like to think she simply knew the value of quiet, empty, abandoned places. Maybe she got away from some annoying neighbours. Sensible Despina watched from afar, with the company of her animals, when Kastellorizo was repressed by the Fascists and bombed by the Nazis, and then when it went up in smoke under British control, and the residents lost their homes. Anyone who knows any Greek old ladies would not be surprised that she did what she damn well liked by raising that Greek flag.

The soldiers based on these islands now find it a lonely life; it's known as a hardship posting and an officer who puts in a few years here can expect to return to civilisation after. It's not a life most young men choose. But clearly it appealed to Despina.

It appeals also to the barefoot sculptor who came here years ago and stayed. His studio, slightly away from the village, has its feet in the sea, surrounded by olive trees. Now he works here, carving philosophical, abstract works from stone.

'I've drunk bottled water since the day I was born,' a thirty-something waiter tells me, laughing. All drinking water on Kastellorizo today is bottled.

The pretty buildings and churches have been restored, but there is no proper supply of drinking water. A desalination plant at Mandraki was faulty and its chemicals seeped into the shallow bay. Tap water for general use is brought in by ship from Rhodes, but during my visit the tap water stops running. With the economic crisis, the bills have gone unpaid and the army operates an emergency service every few days.

Long ago, people thrived on this island even though it had no fresh water, no springs. They built and maintained cisterns and gathered rainwater. At the oldest castle high on a hill, Paleokastro, where Byzantine chapels perch on ancient walls built from massive masonry blocks, and rectangular recesses once contained votive offerings, there are also hollows sunk in the ground, covered with old clay and lime plaster and still holding rainwater.

Nikos drives the water taxi my friend and I have hired to take us to swim at the cave and then to St George island. He also works as a fisherman, though not in the winter as there's not enough custom and the island can sometimes go fifteen days without a ferry for transport. Fish stocks are low, too, because water temperatures have risen, bringing in invasive species. He worked away on ships for a while and enjoyed ports like Southampton and Newcastle. ('I loved Poole!' he says. 'But it looked like it was about to rain all the time. Every country has good and bad.') He was born on Kastellorizo, his parents were born here, and he could never stay anywhere else for long.

'Why can't people use cisterns for water as they used to?' I ask.

'It's not enough,' he says.

'It was enough for a much bigger population a hundred years ago,' I reply.

'But they only had a shower once a week,' he quips.

There's a large, disused cistern just up the road from our hotel. I see them everywhere, in the fields and behind the town, neighbourhood ones, private ones. After World War II and the German occupation, Greeks were dying of hunger in the cities but on the small islands you could get by with a frugal existence, catching fish and growing beans, if you could access fresh water.

Modern attempts seem to have been abandoned, though. One thing you don't see if you come into Kastellorizo by ship, but which you do if you arrive at or walk past the airport, is a huge reservoir, enough to hold a year's supply of water, lying useless. Its lining has torn to pieces, flapping in the wind, swathes flying across the surrounding countryside. Like the one on Tilos, it hasn't worked since the day it was built.

Why do so many noble schemes fail on these islands? How does the money to get things working, to fix them, disappear? Greece has been self-governing for less than a century, and has a supremely challenging geography, a multitude of islands. Locals say political fighting and incompetence due to nepotism often prevail.

Association with Turkey mostly allowed this island to thrive, and at the time of my visit is helping it to survive again, with visitors arriving from the neighbouring country daily on small ferries and charter yachts. When relations are good, a blind eye can be turned to visa formalities for day trips, according to a local travel agent quoted in the newspaper *Kathimerini*. 'When we run out of everyday supplies we don't shop in Greece, we shop in Turkey.' Perhaps, he speculates, electricity and water could be procured from Turkey if it joined the EU.

But it's a precarious lifeline. Political incidents lead to restrictions being imposed again. And visitor numbers are affected by currency devaluation and the relatively high cost of visiting Greece for Turkish people.

At dawn on our last day, the bay is smooth as a mirror. I climb the steep cliffs behind the town and as the glowing sun lifts itself above the Turkish mountains a gleaming bridge of light appears, unbroken, linking the land across the strait in a bizarre illusion.

There are said to be antiquities on the plateau but the path is elusive. Impetuously finding a way over rocks streaked grey and rust-red, scrambling between thorny bushes, I reach the top and wander across fields. A stone farmhouse that once had a tiled roof; broken fences; red earth; a rectangular cistern half-full of water surrounded by a drystone wall. I walk over the upland towards the other side and come across a palm, more old enclosures and walls, another derelict little house of stone and wood with ceramic roof tiles, and a gently sloping field dotted with trees and carpeted with scrub, looking out to an islet and the open sea.

I could spend hours wandering here, but some missed calls come through from my friend, and a message: 'Which mountain are you on?' I must have lost phone signal.

When I walk back down, much easier on the stepped path although it's overgrown, the bridge of sunlight to the mainland has broken up again, shimmering silver.

CLOUDS OVER OLYMPOS
KARPATHOS

I am striding up the open road into the unknown on a sunny spring day with a backpack. I have a booking at a hotel in the mountain village of Olympos in the north of Karpathos, but also a tent which I'm secretly hoping to use. It's April 2016, I've escaped from the work project from hell and feel ready for adventure. Walking out in the wild, looking at the sky and at far horizons, thinking gives way to feeling.

The north of Karpathos – and especially its dependent neighbour to the north, the uninhabited island of Saria – are often visible on the horizon from Megalo Horio on Tilos. The journey to get there, however, requires a stopover elsewhere to connect with the *Prevelis*, a basic, old-fashioned ferry run by ANEK that meanders south from Rhodes to Halki, Karpathos, Kasos and Crete, then north through the Cyclades to Piraeus. When I try to book the ferry ticket, I discover that Diafani, the port in the north that serves Olympos, has been damaged by a winter storm and the ferry can only dock at the main port in the south. I don't want to rent a car, and taxis are close to 100 euros for the hour-long drive. I expect I'll find a way. Unsure of how difficult this journey will be, and keen to do some research, I've arranged a pet-sitter who is happy to stay in my house for a while and look after Lisa.

When the Bents travelled direct from Tilos to Karpathos in 1885 in their private boat, it took nine hours. They arrived in February, when rains had washed away the track to Olympos, and violent gusts of wind damaged the vessel. They wrote that both islands were 'very difficult of access and rarely visited by foreigners… consequently peculiarly retentive of customs and myths which bear the stamp of extreme antiquity', and both appeared to have had 'a much more considerable population in ancient times than they have now'. Theodore said Karpathos was 'one of the most lost islands of the Aegean Sea', with no steamer going there, yet it had nine thousand inhabitants living in villages amid sharp-peaked mountains and pine trees.

In the 1960s, people still travelled from the south of Karpathos to the north by boat and then mule. Olympos remains somewhat cut off by challenging geography; the rough road to the north was tarmacked only in the last decade, and in some ways the area is like another island, semi-deserted, retaining old customs. 'Ah, Olympos, beautiful!' they say in Rhodes, where I am making my ferry connection. Someone tells me a man there still makes leather boots. But no-one has been, although it's only a few hours away by boat. A woman in a shop tells me the people of Olympos are difficult customers. I'm intrigued and excited as I board the ferry in the early hours. I sleep for a while, and when I wake, the island seems to be one long, impenetrable mountain ridge; a single line of road up high, the white of a village here and there.

Few people disembark, the handful of early-season travellers continuing to Crete. The public bus runs to Olympos only once a week, and not for another three days. I accept a card from a taxi driver just in case. It's Sunday, so there are no shops open where I can buy a map, only a supermarket. I ask there about walking to Olympos and am told it's impossible. I copy a very basic map from the wall of a closed car rental shop (I forgot my licence anyway) and set off walking. A few days later, on a mountain trail I will encounter a Swiss German who says, 'I never do anything without a map.' But sometimes you have to, don't you?

After a stop for a swim, I happily make my way for a few hours up a steep, quiet road through green and brown hills to Aperi, an affluent-looking village with pretty domed chapels. At a taverna by a bridge, I order a gyros pita – meat, salad and fried potatoes wrapped in flatbread – and get another to take away. Having checked there are no rooms to rent and that camping on the beach at Ahata might be acceptable, I make my way downhill again, past the main road and through a steep-sided, wooded gorge for several kilometres. At last I reach a tranquil cove of white pebbles and turquoise water, which I have all to myself. I swim and set up my tent on the beach. With waves lapping, I fall asleep in the early evening, waking a couple of hours later to moonlight and stars and a fishing boat. I go back to sleep until extreme gusts of wind in the night threaten to blow the tent down. Shivering, I move to the shelter of the cliffs, put on more clothes.

Next morning, I hike back up the gorge while it's still cool, picking up a bag of things I left hanging in a pine tree. There are few cars on the main road north. The incline is challenging and I've put my backpack down and rested a couple of times when a pick-up truck stops. An old man gets out and moves a bag containing a recently slaughtered lamb or goat from the passenger seat into the back beside a pile of leafy branches. We soon crest the hill and descend past stupendous views of a sheer rock face dotted with pine trees falling away to deep blue sea.

The man tells me many of the islanders live in America and Australia, returning for summer. He turns off a dirt track into forest and tells me to stay in the car as he disappears with the branches. He returns after a while and puts a covered plastic tub by my feet, and I realise he's been milking the goats. We pause again for him to check his beehives and a few minutes later arrive in Spoa, built into the high hillside looking out to sea. I hope to buy him a drink at the café as a thank you, but he insists on buying one for me as a gesture of hospitality.

I continue walking and later accept another ride from a family in a packed pick-up truck, squeezing into the back seat with two young girls and a dog. They live on Rhodes and are going home to Olympos for Easter. I laugh with the girls who practise their English, telling me their village is around the next corner... Oh no, maybe the next corner... Oh, no, maybe the next... And then, suddenly, there it is, a dramatic jumble of tightly packed cube houses in faded colours on the ridge, with sheer, bare rock slopes rising on either side.

The hotel owner, Minas, speaks English with an American accent. He shoulders my bag and hurries along a narrow alleyway, up a flight of steps. We pass a church and then turn left down more steps. There's a strong wind blowing and a vista of open sea some two hundred metres below stretching to the western horizon. My room is in a restored stone house with painted wooden shutters; it was his grandfather's house, a ruin until he got an EU loan to rebuild it. The bed is a traditional *soufa*, a platform of elaborately carved wood with storage underneath. I ask if the water is OK to drink. 'More than OK,' he says, 'it comes from the mountain. If you want to turn on the air conditioning,' he begins, and I'm about to say I won't need it when he adds, 'just open the door.' He opens it and the wind surges in, and I laugh. Grinning, he says, 'Oh, and this is your television too,' pointing at the view, then he leaves; he has work to do.

I shower and change. The Wi-Fi isn't working, so I take my laptop and find out if I can get online somewhere because it's Monday and I should check with my client about the project from hell. I walk to the big church and along a little alley, and spot a short, stout older lady wearing a black dress with a colourful apron, knee-high leather boots and a black scarf tied around her head: the traditional dress of Olympos. She says hello. Through the doorway behind her I can see a perfect, old-fashioned café with simple wooden tables arranged around the sides of the room and framed photographs taking up most of the wall space. In Greek I explain apologetically that I need to find somewhere with internet.

'I won't lie – I don't have internet,' she says in a no-nonsense way. 'But you might be able to pick up the community one from the church. Go inside and try if you like.'

I sit down in the corner of the empty café, and it works. I order a beer and she brings green olives and orange kumquats to go with it. Archontoula, as she introduces herself, sits in the corner plaiting colourful cotton threads while I work. Her headscarf keeps slipping down and she has to retie it.

The next morning, I eat a breakfast of hard goat's cheese with bread and honey as Archontoula trims artichokes and talks with some workmen, every now and then erupting into laughter. Her voice seems built for shouting across mountains. A man arrives, tall and chestnut-skinned with a luxuriant moustache and twinkling eyes. Archontoula introduces him as her husband, Philippas. He sits straight-backed, a little bemused by everything going on around him, like a film star who stumbled on to the wrong set a long time ago and never found his way out.

His father opened this kafeneio around 1925. She was nineteen and Philippas was twenty-two, she tells me, when they had their first arranged meeting; his family asked for her three times, so they got married. Then he went away to work in America, in Crete and on ships, while she stayed with her family and worked in the fields in Avlona, and after he came back in 1970 they took over running the kafeneio. They haven't been closed a day since. In one of the many old photos on the wall, a younger Archontoula is sharply surveying a busy scene: a group of men wearing flat caps, playing music.

Most of the older women of Olympos wear the traditional village dress, called *kavai*, that women have worn here for generations: a black dress over a white dress, an embroidered apron, leather boots called *stivania*, and a black headscarf. All over Greece distinctive local costumes are worn for dance performances and special occasions; here these are simply their everyday clothes. None of the women wears make-up or jewellery. Yiannis the shoemaker, just along the alley, is the only person in the region who still makes the *stivania*, using a technique he learned from his father and grandfather. Men in Olympos wear modern clothes, probably because they have often worked abroad, but they retain the traditional skills of playing music, sometimes even making their own wooden instruments, and singing *mantinades*, improvised rhymes.

I walk to the edges of the village, moved by the severe beauty of the green and brown mountains, the pale houses and windmills clinging to slopes and ridges; the seventy-something windmills only fell out of use a few decades ago when electricity arrived. In terraces with olives and figs and vines, a boy leads a goat by a rope. It's so windy I can hardly stand, but a woman is hefting large loaves of bread out of a wood-fired oven built into the hillside. I buy *hortopita*, or spinach pie, and take the well-marked footpath up the valley, over the ridge and down past flowing springs towards Diafani. The hills are covered with *phrygana*, rockrose and prickly shrubby burnet. Reaching the sea I swim, then walk uphill a different way through pine forest, past square shepherds' huts built from dark stone into the slope, deserted but still solid. I emerge on to a flat plateau divided by drystone walls into fields of different colours. This is Avlona, where the people of Olympos have had fields for generations. There are small flat-roofed cottages or *stavli* huddled together on the side of a hill, and the only sounds are the wind and the animals' bells. An older couple are butchering a slaughtered goat. I greet them before continuing past fields and threshing circles, a mule or sheep tied here and there, prickly pear, vines and figs glowing in late afternoon light. During World War II, food supplies from other islands were stopped when boats were targeted by enemy fire so people had to live from their own produce, and Olympos fed the whole island.

In the evening, back in Olympos, the church bell rings; inside are old frescoes and gilded wood and huge, brilliant chandeliers, the sound of chanting and the smell of incense. It's dark beyond the soft lights of the village, and stars are coming out. Cut off from modern convenience, with scant public transport and one little shop (closed if the owner isn't there), no permanent doctor or proper post office, bank or petrol station, intermittent phone signal… This area could so easily have been abandoned but it kept going, and some of the old culture I've been tracking through deserted places is still here.

I enter a café on the tiny square. Men sit around the edges of the room and at first it seems they all stare at me, but they're watching the football on the television above the door. A loud bang makes me jump – but it's just from the card game in the corner. I find a seat, order a small glass of wine. The ceiling is wooden, the shelves behind the bar filled with Cutty Sark bottles and hung with embroidery, the walls decorated with wooden musical instruments, gleaming trophies, a framed poem, a sheaf of public announcements with a pair of reading glasses hanging from the nail, and photos, groups of mostly men from decades ago; there's a sense of being surrounded by the past, a nostalgia and pride in what came before.

I get talking to the owner, Nikos, who's around my age and, like Minas, speaks English with an American accent. He tells me the café was built by his great-grandfather a hundred years ago, and was run by his grandfather and his father. Like many families from Olympos, they left for the States in the 1970s. Most went to Baltimore or New York, set up businesses and sent money back. It's one reason the village survived. When Nikos returned in 1987, there were still eight or nine hundred people in Olympos. Now there are only two hundred, while thousands from here live on Rhodes and elsewhere. Few young people want to continue the family business or work their land.

One of the older people who died that year was well known and loved as a skilled player of the traditional *tsambouna*, a bagpipe made from a goatskin (the Bents found one of these 150 years ago on Tilos and took it back to the Pitt Rivers Museum in Oxford). He and his wife Kalliopi ran another tiny kafeneio squeezed between two alleys on the square. Kalliopi, dressed in black, at first looks severe but when I overcome my nervousness and go in, I find her warm and welcoming. She often sits alone with her needlework. There are too many cafés for a village that now has so few inhabitants, but she stays open to have something to do every day and for company. While she makes me coffee, I look at the photographs from decades past on the walls, and comment on how lively it was.

She murmurs something and points to a photo. 'See this?' She indicates the blue formica-topped table in front of me, the same one in the photo. 'And these people?' She points out the group of men sitting around the table, enjoying themselves; then makes a cutting gesture with her hand, and says, 'No-one.' There's no-one left.

I find myself sitting at a bar drinking raki with Minas. His uncle asks my name, then says: 'OK, we call you Evgenia – that's Greek for Jennifer.'

He gives me olives from Avlona. Every family here has a windmill, fields and olive trees. That contributes to a sense of heritage, I'm sure. If you come from one of these islands, you are likely to own part of it, even just a scrap of land high up a mountain or a pile of fallen stones. Ownership ties you to the place, for better or worse.

I walk the footpath through Avlona, where a man sits in his courtyard carving a musical instrument from wood. A little beyond the fields, the island drops dramatically away before levelling out near the coast where, on a promontory, a village stood in ancient times, the precursor to Olympos. Vroukounta was abandoned around the sixth century after Christ, its inhabitants driven into the more defensible mountains after attacks by Syrian pirates. But Minas told me, 'If you looked at our DNA, I bet you'd find we're descended from the Syrian pirates.'

It takes another hour to walk down to Vroukounta. The only remains are sections of wall and a mysterious multitude of tombs cut into the rock, square entrances opening into multiple chambers with stone platforms. There is nobody here, and not a glimpse of modern life in this vast landscape except for a church bell. Two mules wander on the beach. As I start to walk back up the hill, a man loads bags on to their wooden saddles and walks them up the path.

As Archontoula tops up my glass of water filtered through the mountain, I tell her about my walk to Vroukounta, but she's unimpressed that I didn't visit 'the saint', the church in the cave.

'You went to the spring and you didn't drink,' says a man with a beard, smiling.

Looking out of the window, I think maybe I love Olympos because it's the last of something. It's hanging on, with difficulty; it's changing but there are still vestiges here of an older world. People still speak an old dialect, having been isolated so long; when they talk among themselves, it's hard for me to understand.

'You never stop working,' I say to Archontoula as she hauls a sack of walnuts up the stairs.

'Thank God that I'm well and can still work! Because if I get sick and I can't...' People here are used to relying on themselves as they haven't had a lot of support. The TV is on, showing politicians with pious expressions attending a church service in Athens, and she looks up and laughs. 'There they are, all the dogs!'

Towards the end of Easter week, the bell tolls off-key in mourning as people bring wreaths with photos of their loved ones who have passed on in the last year and place them on Christ's funeral bier. Girls stand outside the church wearing leather boots and long, trailing headscarves, stiff skirts colourful with embroidery and gold thread sparkling in the sun that sets off their dark eyebrows, strong features and olive skin. Most are visiting from Rhodes. Although the village looks impressively large, flowing around the side of the mountain, many houses are only used during holidays like this and remain empty the rest of the time.

I walk a path along a sheer grey rock slope then down amid herbs and mastic and pine to Evgonimos Bay where the sea glitters sapphire. Stone walls support the path held in place by heavy slabs of stone, and I imagine donkeys carrying loads up and down. The west-facing bay is sadly marred by rubbish washed in by the sea – plastic children's toys, engine oil containers, spray foam and synthetic sponges – so I continue up the steep hill to a deserted stone farmhouse with a wood-and-earth roof surrounded by grey drystone walls and abandoned olive trees. From a little chapel incorporating early Christian marble columns, in silence I look back to Olympos and the peaked dome of

Koryfi mountain. Nearby, there's a single stone beehive. I lose the path a couple of times crossing hills and streams, but keep ascending to the high point at Ayia Marina. White rock rises in improbable shapes from green forest, and the land drops sheer into the sea, and at the edge of a mountain there are a dozen threshing circles all together. Sheep emerge from a stone barn.

I return along the side of the mountain, Profitis Ilias, as clouds sweep across and cover everything with a chill damp, birds shrieking their high whistles, goat bells clanging.

Yiannis, the former school headmaster, says, 'I like winter, when I can sit with my olive trees.' Many Olympos people have olive trees at Ayios Minas.

I follow the road along the spine of the island, with mountains and sea to either side, turning on to a twisting dirt track cut into the hillside with steep drops to the side, descending into a valley. I reach the white church on a clifftop and look down to a curving, unspoiled beach around a bay with impossibly clear sea. Continuing down to a scattering of little houses, at the one closest to the sea I find Minas dressed in old jeans and a sweatshirt from Maryland, still fixing up his taverna for the season. It was originally a farm building, like all those in this valley.

As I swim, a wooden fishing boat glides in and Minas appears to help it moor. He beckons me over and we climb aboard using a wooden ladder; he introduces me to the fisherman, his friend. That evening, the fisherman returns with heaps of *menoula*, a smallish black fish with blue stripes, and we pour ouzo and water and have a simple feast, the three of us alone in this wild valley. We sleep outside under the stars.

In the morning, the valley is silent and the sea sparkles through a gap in a wall built from smoothly rounded stones. Barely noticeable in the grey cliffs below the church are the mysterious ruins of old buildings, straight stone walls stuck into the crumbling earth, and the plastered hollows of stone cisterns like broken pale pink eggshells. The stones and plaster are gradually falling away and tumbling into the riverbed.

A pick-up truck arrives: Minas's cousin Evgenia is rounding up her goats. She gives us bread and *dhrilla*, the strong sour cream her mother makes from the milk. After she leaves, Minas reiterates an invitation he gave me a few nights ago: to come back, live and work here for the summer, helping with his rooms in Olympos and the taverna at Ayios Minas.

At first I laughed it off, although I was tempted, saying I had my own work to do, and my dog and my rented house on Tilos. Minas said I could bring Lisa, and still do my work. Then I received the news that a friend on Tilos had died, reminding me that life was too short not to challenge myself with new experience. I decide to sublet my house for the summer to reduce the risk and come back in a few weeks. I don't want a job or payment, but I will be happy to help with cleaning and laundry in return for the opportunity to stay here longer. Olympos seems to be a link to skills and knowledge lost in other places. If I have come to the spring, I should drink.

'Welcome back, Evgenia,' says Nikos at Parthenon café when I return a few weeks later, offering me home-cured sardines. I ask if I missed anything and he says, 'Just a funeral. An old lady, ninety-nine years old. My arms are hurting. There weren't enough guys to lift the coffin.'

Maroukla in her black dress and headscarf is grinning as she leans on the rock outside my door. 'When did you arrive?' she asks, as if she didn't know. I often hear a shout and see her waving to me from her yard around the curve of the steep mountain. People live cheek by jowl here. 'Can you go down to get my bread?' she asks. 'My legs are hurting.'

When I return with her bread, she thrusts out her hand so I can help her up. It makes me happy. There's a closeness, a lack of inhibition, among the hard-working women of Olympos. Helping one another was once a necessity. I'm glad to have a physical job to do, to show I'm not afraid to get my hands dirty, to feel I'm pulling my weight. I've never felt so accepted as part of a community.

Another day Maroukla asks, 'Can you do me a favour? And give me a kiss first.' She calls out to me to come and eat with her, and if I'm not hungry then at least sit and chat. Archontoula calls out as I pass: 'Come in and keep us company! Can't you sit here and work?' Sometimes she'll ask me to keep an eye on the café while she does chores. She tells me, 'Don't know why, but when I first met you, for some reason I just liked you. And when I like someone, I love them.'

As summer begins, the entrance to the village starts to be jammed with rental cars and tour buses and the alleys fill with day trippers, and locals with restaurants and gift shops compete to sell things – some made in Olympos, some made in China. But without tourism, would Olympos have been abandoned? As on most islands, the money they make in summer helps them through winter. Those who stay year-round keep the village alive.

Even in summer, I find, Olympos can be cool and damp and fiercely windy; I struggle to hang up the sheets and then I find the washing line is covered in strange dust and I have to wash them again, carrying them up and down several flights of steps. I clean dust off the shutters and doors, lugging buckets of water. By the time I'm hauling rubbish to the bins at the edge of the village, I'm ready to drop. But my friends are always feeding me: rosemary or cistus tea, fava and fried courgette, light doughnuts called *loukoumades* covered in honey and sesame seeds.

And by evening, the village is quiet again. The setting sun casts a soft yellow light on the white, ochre and blue houses, cloud covering the grey slopes and ruined windmills. Sheep roam through the village. The blue sea sweeps in far below, waves smashing white on the rugged coast. The wind howls, shaking a fig tree that grows out of the broken roof of a stone mill.

Sophia, who has a café at the entrance to the village, sometimes does her weaving on the loom in the courtyard. She tells me her daughter knows how to use the loom but her granddaughter doesn't learn because there's no market for such things. Her husband can make brooms and cheese holders out of strong reeds gathered from a wetland – but it takes a whole day, and who will buy them?

The last woman in the village who knew how to weave cloth for the *kavai* dresses died recently. Rigopoula, who sits sewing in a tiny shop, tells me young women now go to university and most don't learn how to sew and embroider the traditional clothes.

A man laments that no-one builds in the old way now, making things instead with breeze blocks. 'How many beautiful old stone buildings are left?' Our builder friend Pavlos tells me that the old buildings mortared together with earth withstood earthquakes better than concrete made with cement.

One day, after a walk up the mountain, I wonder what they used for carrying water in the old days. Yiannis the bootmaker might know. He's carving the leather heel of a shoe as we talk, and his eyes light up as he tells me about it. It was called an *askouli*: a goatskin coated in pine resin, which made it waterproof. Only one man still makes the resin, collecting and then boiling it, and he has less inclination to do it these days. The skin would be from a young goat – more supple and likely to be free of holes and blemishes from ticks – so they'd make them when the kids were slaughtered for Easter. It was the same system used when making the *tsambouna*, the bagpipe. They'd fill out the skin with dry lentils or peas to give it shape. It was carried with a plaited cord, and held about three litres of water, keeping it cool even on hot days if you hung it on a branch or a rock in the shade. His grandfather could take one of those and work out in the field all day with just a pocketful of raisins and dried figs. 'Ah, the smell of the pine resin…' he says, reminiscing.

We talk about what happens when the old ways are lost. He says it's not just knowledge but experience – you learn from years of doing something to know when something is right or not, whether it's building a wall or making a shoe. It's not something we can easily get back.

Someone has been clearing out a house and I see two mattresses being thrown away. One is a modern sprung mattress, but the other is simply a sheet knotted in the corners and stuffed with sheeps' wool. It was made with what materials people had, and eventually will leave no trace on the landscape. Perhaps birds will recycle it to build nests.

At Ayios Minas at the end of the afternoon, the sun shines into the sea making it crystal clear so you see every pebble on the seabed.

When the sun goes behind the hills there's a soft dusky light, and a wind blowing through the olives and pines. Except for a few goats clambering over the cliffs, there's no-one else to be seen, nothing on the horizon. It is true wild beauty: *agria omorphia* as the Greeks call it.

After helping at Minas's taverna in the afternoon, I sit alone to watch the colours in the bay, metallic blue and silver-green water and the orange-pink of the sunset, and the wind spreading ripples out to sea. The beach is so often my own, I develop a strong connection with it. A swim at dusk: deep blue sea, grey pebbles and the golden glow of my skin. I get accustomed to swimming when everyone has gone, when the bay is empty and grey and pink; sometimes close to midnight, when the moon is casting its brilliant light over black water.

As the summer has progressed, I've been sleeping in a tent in a field at Ayios Minas. Beyond the lights of the taverna, the Milky Way is a stripe across the starry sky. I sometimes take my sleeping bag and pillow and head down to the beach. The sound of the waves is mesmerising, hypnotic, the lapping and slapping of sea against the rocks. I look up to see a shooting star, then close my eyes and let deep sleep take over. I wake at dawn to a pink-tinged sky, the cliffs orange, the sea still and smooth, and swim just as the sunlight starts to warm the beach.

One night in late summer, there's a wedding at the church on the cliff. It's midnight by the time I am free, but I decide to go, expecting to see dancing outside in the courtyard. But everyone is sitting on benches inside the hot, stuffy hall. On the long tables are baskets of sweets, large bottles of Coca-Cola, and half-empty retsina bottles. I find a space to sit and watch from underneath a wooden platform covered in mattresses. The top table is occupied only by men, mostly older men including the priest, and two are playing the traditional *lyra* and *laouto*. A slight woman stands near them in a shiny dress in pink and gold, heavily ornate, constricted from its tight sleeves and bodice. Her eyes seem so big and striking in her pale face under hooded lids, her hair hidden under her headscarf. She holds a carafe of wine in formal fashion and walks around the room. When she stops and pours for one of the men he sings a *mantinada*, an improvised song about her that makes her cry. Then she moves on to the next, and the same happens. A younger man sings a *mantinada* that makes everyone laugh. Then it's back to sorrow.

There's a little house near the taverna at Ayios Minas that was built, like most of those in the valley, for people to stay in while working on the olive harvest. Owned by one of the ladies of Olympos, it's been abandoned for years and was loaned to Minas for storage. I've sat outside it to work in the evenings and gradually as I have more free time, as the season draws to a close, I start to clear it out and work inside in the daytime, not too worried about mice or spiders. A wooden platform bed makes a comfortable couch, with a view of olive trees, the church on the cliffs and a sliver of blue sea. There's a solid wooden door and shutter; a window with iron bars and a mesh screen tacked into place; and a fireplace because the harvest happens in November or December when nights are cool. The cement for the roof is flecked with smooth, rounded pebbles from the beach and the iron frame used to hold the cement is now rusting so that small pieces of rust and tiny pebbles occasionally fall. I try not to think about that. It has survived plenty of earth tremors.

As I walk down to the sea, I look around at the rugged, untouched hills. The wind is blowing on the gunmetal-grey bay, the light turning pink. All I can hear is the wind in the trees, and the gentle lapping of the water. Minas says he could build wooden walls around the taverna's courtyard for the winter, put in a wood-burning fire, stay open for friends. Lisa enjoys the daily ritual of barking at goats to chase them away from the olive trees.

The first rain comes, starting softly at dawn, bringing the rich, intense smell of spices and wood as it darkens the dusty ground. The horizon is clear but there's a thick bank of cloud above and gauzy curtains out to sea. The rain, heavier elsewhere, has taken out the power, and without refrigerators running at the taverna, it's even quieter. There's no water in the taps – the pump is electric – and no lights or internet. I take Lisa to the beach and go for a long swim with raindrops falling on calm water. Then the sun comes out and a light wind makes the sea sparkle. I head to the little house; if it didn't rain through the ceiling, it would be perfect.

We have goat's cheese and honey made at the top of the valley, olive-wood charcoal made by a man from another village. In November, we gather olives and preserve them using herbs. Sophia and Evgenia, when they come to round up the goats, show me the *skinokarpo*, the tiny red berries of the mastic bushes that look like peppercorns and are ready to pick when they turn black; they make biscuits with them. Minas gathers olive wood for the fire and brings me myrtle berries.

The full winter rains happen in January and February and we take refuge in the hotel rooms in Olympos. The roads are full of fallen rocks and there's an astonishing noise as water runs down the mountains, washing earth into the sea and changing its colour. Waterfalls appear. When the sun comes out again, the air is clear and the light intense. At Ayios Minas, the riverbed that is a road to the beach in summer turns into a raging river, the banks thick with flowers, bordered by fragrant pine trees. Abundant flowers take over the lush green fields: pink campanula, poppies, Bermuda buttercups, orchids. We see hoopoes and Bonelli's eagles and a heron. Then the trees overhanging the riverbed shed their yellow pom-poms, leaving the ground dusted with gold, and the lemon-yellow broom flowers smell sweet. There are still small waterfalls and rock pools up the stream beds in grey gorges, carved by years of gushing water, swallows flitting.

One morning I set off with Lisa up the hill, the sea glassy calm and misty-blue far in the distance. We follow a track around the back of the mountain to the mostly abandoned settlement of Asya. At the end of the road, amid old stone houses and threshing circles, an old lady in a white dress and black headscarf is waving her arms and shouting at the goats.

Minas helps his uncle trim the vines in Avlona and takes me to see wild peonies. Back in Olympos I hear a shout and see Maroukla sitting in her courtyard. '*Ela!*' Come. I find her down some winding steps, and she tells me to sit down with her in the sun. 'Where've you been? When are we going to eat together again?' she asks. There are *makarounes*, the local pasta, laid out to dry.

I stand in the square with Anezoula, watching a wedding party pass through the village. This is the first village wedding in Olympos for years, she says, holding her aching back and retying her long grey plaits around her head. She has a few teeth missing but a great natural smile.

'Are the couple from Olympos?' I ask.

'Yes,' she says, but when I ask if they live here she says, 'No, no, in Athens.'

When the next generation get married here, will the village houses be mostly deserted? The young women walk up the steps carrying baskets of gifts, stiff in their ornamental dresses, almost hobbled by their shoes – for a moment I think how restrictive the traditions can be (although I suppose it's not that unusual for women to wear uncomfortable shoes at weddings). People are still strongly encouraged to marry someone from the village, and family feuds can still arise when someone marries a person from elsewhere, even another village.

I'm sad because after a serene winter and spring, my second summer on Karpathos has been hard; it might be time for me to leave. I am too caught up in the stress of the bills and bureaucracy; part of it is personal, but I am also being reminded of what people do to survive here, how tough it is to run a business all summer, as so many do on these islands to get by. Like them, I've also been caught up in a war between rival businesses, aggression and bad feeling. Ayios Minas is somewhat changed for me when the owners of the other taverna that opens in the valley in the summer bring a white shipping container to the beach to use as an outlet for serving drinks. A bulldozer arrives and a team of men stick two rows of metal poles in cement by the sea for umbrellas. I cry when I see what they have done. They erect more signs, and I realise how it feels for the people I've spoken to on other islands who have lost their beach.

When I talk to my friends in Olympos, it transpires that every sweet old lady and hardy, self-sufficient man I know has stories of lawsuits or stone-throwing, of jealous neighbours wanting to shut them down or steal their land. A friend who wears traditional village dress but speaks English with a New York drawl, says, 'We lived in America for forty years. When my husband say he want to come back here I say he's crazy. Olympos people are always fighting.'

One villager after another says, 'They are bad people here!'

But they are all kind to me, and say, 'We want you here.'

I sit with Kalliopi at her café. The church bells clang. While she makes me a coffee, I notice a head of garlic hanging from a hook behind the door. I ask why it's there.

'It burns, doesn't it, garlic? If someone says bad words, it burns their tongue. Other people use the eye, you know…' She means one of those round blue symbols that are used to deflect the evil eye, when someone is jealous. 'But the eye does nothing.'

I've stayed overnight in a room at Sophia's because a friend is visiting Olympos and our own hotel rooms are full. I go to pay.

'I don't want money,' she says.

'I'm going to leave it somewhere,' I say.

'Don't make me chase you.'

There is something special here. It's the experience of being in the café with Archontoula while she trims artichokes that Philippas has just picked, and shouts at the TV: 'See! The Turks are going to kill us!' Sitting under the stars with Vasilis at a church on the ridge of the island, enjoying his homemade wine and cheese. Sophia and Mike quietly weaving rushes into crosses for church. It is like nowhere else. I can understand why people cling to this difficult place and won't abandon it.

I came for just three days; stayed to learn; ended up with a second home, people I love. I have to get out of my element sometimes to learn and to grow, challenge myself with new experience – otherwise what is life? Yiannis, the former headmaster, one day gives me a painting he has done of Odysseus, with a quotation adapted from the poet Cavafy: hope that the road is long and filled with adventure and the widest knowledge.

The village of Olympos looks stunning that September as I prepare to leave, standing out in high definition against the dark mountain behind, wisps of cloud sweeping across the bright rocks. Rigopoula is struggling with a crate of grapes and asks me to help her carry it up the steps, saying, 'See that's what happens if God loves you. When you need someone...' At night, Nikos sits and plays his *lyra*, lost in its soft, haunting sounds. He learned to play, he says, from listening to Antonis Zografidis in the square. Zografidis was getting depressed in the last years, he thinks, as all the old men of the village were dying.

Down at Ayios Minas, the sea is clear, the waves gently carving the smooth curve of the bay with every stroke. Its colours are navy and grey mixed with luminous white, the wind blowing the rippled surface, the sky mauve and orange-pink fading to pale blue. I listen to the deep living sound of the sea slapping into the caves.

Over a few days, I start swimming beyond the bay's limits. First to the cave, where a cormorant skims close by me. In rougher waves, I swim further and catch the bright blue-green flashes of a kingfisher. Another time a heron flaps its way smoothly up to the clifftop where it perches. On a completely still day, I swim to the other headland, much further, but it feels easy once I hit my stride; I'm heading back when an eagle or a buzzard flies a few metres over my head, close enough for me to see the markings of its white and brown breast and wings.

In the boat of captain Vasilis from the port of Diafani I visit Saria, the rocky, mountainous, uninhabited island separated from the northern point of Karpathos by a narrow channel. It was an important place in ancient times; its ships sailed around the world, says captain Vasilis, some of the old buildings are Middle Eastern, and there are the remains of four large churches.

Until recently, the people would row their goats in wooden boats across the 120-metre strait, pulling their cows behind them through the water. They used half the island for grazing and half for growing crops, and would switch over from year to year so the farms were fertilised naturally. Running water traces can be seen in old riverbeds, but some say an earthquake around 1950 stopped the spring water flowing. The houses had rainwater cisterns after that (before, they only had storage for oil and wine), and for the animals they had cisterns for brackish water, where fresh water still flows just under the sea.

People stopped living on Saria in the late 1970s, but still go there to gather the olives. The captain remembers the island from when he was young; at fourteen he went to work in Hamburg, the Caribbean and finally New York, before retiring and moving back to Diafani.

'When people come to Saria for the festivals of Saint Zacharia and Saint Sophia,' he says, 'they play the old music and sing, and they cry for their memories.'

I visit Olympos briefly several months later that winter, arriving at Diafani on a calm, blue day. My friend Georgia meets me and we sit down outside the kafeneio. It's almost silent. Then a man starts playing the *lyra*, and another sings *mantinades*.

That afternoon I find my Olympos muscles again, and wild blue irises in the valley. There's a sound of water trickling, and I pick a pocketful of dark myrtle berries in the riverbed. I'd forgotten the spicy, citrusy taste. By nightfall, the village seems empty but a light is on outside Archontoula's café, and as I open the door I realise everyone is in there. I surprise Archontoula, busy in the kitchen, and ask how she is.

'Here,' she says. 'The same as when you left us.'

'Good,' I say, 'I'm glad.'

I sit down to chat and eavesdrop; I'm only able to do this as an outsider – local women aren't supposed to go to a kafeneio alone. With my wine I'm offered a little plate of seaweed-like *yialohorto*, 'shore-grass', with olives and fresh broad beans. The leather boots I ordered from Yiannis have been delayed, because he needs an eye operation. I think about how tenuous it is, this last link to Olympos tradition. He buys me a drink instead and tells me not to worry, he'll be able to work again soon.

The next morning, I listen to the sea far below, the wings of a bird, sheep's bells as they scrabble across the scree. Despite the crowds of tourists in summer, the strife that arises from rivalry for business in that season especially, and the families who live on Rhodes, Olympos remains cut off in some ways from modern life and in return has nature, silence, solitude, emptiness. It's still a refuge.

During breakfast at Archontoula's, I overhear Manolis, the man who looks after the footpaths, saying stone paths are better because water can seep through; when paths are made with cement, they eventually wash away in a rainstorm. I've read in the news that they are putting in a road to the abandoned settlement at Tristomo. He confirms they are, but it won't be near the footpath. I want to come back and walk there. He pulls six mandarins out of his pack and insists on giving them to me.

Sophia is picking the thorns off wild greens, painstaking work. An older woman is carrying two bags on a stick – I say they look heavy but she laughs; another is loading cement into sacks; another planting rows of onions in her garden, down at the bottom of the valley. The strong women, always working.

Early on my last morning, the paths are slippery-wet from rain and I see salamanders in the grass. An old woman is walking her goats on a rope in the fields as I board the small winter bus with just a handful of passengers for Pigadia, the port in the south. Mike, the driver, plays traditional Olympos music as we set off into dark clouds.

We arrive and I spot Maroukla walking up the road. She recognises me and we embrace.

'You live here in Pigadia now, with your daughter?' I ask.

'What am I going to do in Olympos? There's no-one there.'

I take the ferry back to Rhodes, where I'm staying at Domus Studios, run by my friend Stergos. He and his wife have restored several houses in the Old Town. He tells me that when people from Karpathos moved to Rhodes to find work in the decades after World War II, those from Olympos mostly settled in the Old Town because they were poor and it had the cheapest properties. Stergos also introduces me to one of his closest friends, whose family came from a small mountain village called Othos in the south of Karpathos. The man speaks to me in English and I try to place his accent. His grandfather went to Rhodesia, he says, which is where he was born. He brings me a booklet published by the Society of Othitans of Rhodesia, established in 1937 with Yiannis Antoniadis as its honorary president.

Antoniadis left Karpathos in 1897, first for Port Said in Egypt to join his brother, then on to Beira in Mozambique, and finally by ox-cart to the small city of Gwelo in the centre of Rhodesia. He intended to continue to South Africa to work in the mines, but without a permit or experience he was persuaded to stay in Gwelo. Having opened a general goods store opposite the railway station, which became a success, in 1902 he brought over another man from Othos who opened a store elsewhere, and started inviting relatives to work with him. More and more arrived, opening their own businesses and sending money back to their village to help with schooling during the Italian occupation. When Greece was invaded by Germany in 1941, they gave financial help for the resistance. They funded roads, churches, a water system.

During the Turkish occupation, men from the Dodecanese had often worked in Asia Minor. But the removal of privileges in the late nineteenth century, and the Greek defeat in Asia Minor in 1922, cut them off from working there. The demand elsewhere for skilled labour led people to seek work further afield. Many went to America, Asia and Africa; a piece in the *Journal of the Hellenic Diaspora* tells of masons, builders and carpenters from villages in the south of Karpathos who went to work in Sudan. Greek communities grew, with churches and schools. There were eight hundred Karpathians working in Sudan between 1900 and 1920.

On a hot, sunny May afternoon three years after my first sight of Karpathos, my friend and I survey the seemingly impassable, sheer and rugged cliffs from the ferry and wonder where the path can be. The mountain above rises to seven hundred metres, though the footpath runs much closer to sea level. The next day we plan to walk it and camp at the deserted settlement of Tristomo.

Our ferry docks at Diafani and the pale buildings contrast starkly with the backdrop of mountain and forest. I notice a useful new ATM and mini-market. The river is still flowing from the winter, but locals confirm the path is in good condition.

Close to the narrow Steno strait that separates the very north of Karpathos from Saria, Tristomo is a natural harbour almost cut off from the sea by two islets, lending it the name 'three mouths'. It was always an important place – antiquities have been found showing that it was likely inhabited for thousands of years – but it was mostly abandoned around 1950 along with the nearby agricultural settlement of Kilios. People continued to stay at Tristomo from time to time, fishermen and sponge divers, and just one old couple lived there alone, self-sufficiently, until recently. The inhabitants of Olympos and Diafani still head to Tristomo by boat to fish, and a few houses around the bay have been restored by the owners.

Michalis, the owner of Corali taverna, says a few families still lived at Tristomo when he was growing up. We fortify ourselves for next day's walk with a hearty dinner. I choose *makarounes* with butter and cheese, and a salad, and drink generous amounts from the jugs of cold tap water. Lisa gorges on the remains of lamb chops. Then big pieces of cake arrive – and several shots of raki, which we are assured will aid a good night's sleep.

In the morning, on the track leading north, an old lady in grey dress and black headscarf appears in a cloud of smoke, burning old branches in an olive grove surrounded by skilfully built drystone walls. It's warm when we reach the cove at Vananda, and Lisa and I gratefully dive into the cool, clear water. Water is gushing from the spring. From there, the track gradually ascends. We pass a beekeeper making smoke at the roadside. The green slopes to our left are dotted with the pink of oleander, cistus and mallow, with bare rock high above, the pale shimmer of olive trees. To our right, through dark green Mediterranean pines bent by the wind and giving off heady scent, is deep blue glittering sea and, faint on the horizon, the peak of Mount Attavyros on Rhodes rising from the mist.

At a little house, the track turns into a path clearly marked by painted red dots on rocks. We pass among boulders from a rockfall, abundant sage and thyme and deep red poppies, stopping from time to time in the shade of a thick-trunked pine or juniper. The top of Xiloskala, the rock steps that negotiate a narrow gorge, seems a good place to pause and appreciate the expanse of blue sea and sky. Diafani seems very far below at the foot of the slopes, the sea is deep blue-green glass under chocolate-brown cliffs. Despite the heat there are clouds over Profitis Ilias, making water for Olympos. I am grateful for the breeze whistling through the trees.

The landscape is painted yellow by the flowers of Jerusalem sage, and martens flit about. After a few hours of steady, slow walking, rugged rock gives way to straight stone terraces covered in shrub. To the right the pines grow horizontal, flattened by the wind. We turn a corner to see a sweeping valley with an amphitheatre of old terraces and field walls, golden with broom. Beyond a ridge and another amphitheatre of terraces, the track showing evidence that donkeys have passed through, a long valley appears far below. Square green fields descend in shallow steps, scattered with olive trees, the solid high mass of Orkili mountain and its secondary peak of Malo looming above. The deserted settlement of Kilios looks magical, lost, beautifully shaped by man then left to nature.

We will return that way tomorrow, but for now we continue along the ridge. At a few stone cottages abandoned to the elements, the path divides, one branch heading to Steno, the other to Tristomo. The way down is a little overgrown, then a few buildings appear and the topaz blue of the bay. As we descend, I am surprised to see a neat, white-painted house on the bay's edge with an open back door and washing on a line. A young man in a red T-shirt appears. I wave, and he waves back. When we reach the shore, Lisa pulls on the lead to get in the water and I'm heading that way myself when the man shouts,

'Come inside to eat fresh calamari with us! Tie the dog under the tree, because we have cats.'

I look around for a place to tie Lisa that isn't strewn with fish bones or goat bones or cats. She seems reasonably content to sit in the shade and not walk any further.

Andreas looks to be in his early thirties with a tanned face and short, curly black hair, wearing baggy track pants and flip-flops. His wife Marina is fresh-faced with a soft voice and a big smile that lights up her eyes. She's also wearing T-shirt and leggings and flip-flops. The house comprises one large room containing a *soufa* bed, a fireplace and a kitchen and eating area, with a few small outbuildings.

'You live here?' I ask Marina.

'Yes, it's like a country house. We just arrived four days ago. Please, eat! We have already eaten, this is for you.'

It's surreal to have hiked in the wilderness for hours and then be invited in as if we'd been expected for lunch. But I'm not complaining. As we eat fresh fried calamari, we learn that Marina is from Olympos and Andreas is from Diafani. He works as a ship's captain, his dream job, although it's hard and monotonous work. When he returns after months on the ships they come here as soon as possible, catch fish to eat, work hard from morning to night but enjoy life with no-one else around, no need for entertainment. The drinking water is pumped from a tank, and they have brackish water for washing and a petrol-powered generator if they need electricity for refrigeration. I ask about the old couple who used to live at Tristomo.

'My grandparents,' says Andreas. 'This was their house. My grandmother died three years ago and my grandfather couldn't stay without her, after so many years together.' They lived here alone for sixty years, keeping sheep. By the time Andreas was growing up, his grandparents were the only inhabitants of Tristomo; he would come to stay in the summer and remembers the houses all ruined, before the people came back from America with money and restored them.

They encourage us to eat cheese preserved in salt and olive oil made by his mother, cabbage salad and homemade sourdough bread.

'We like to be able to offer something, at least water, to people who come all the way here on foot. Sometimes people come by boat and I offer them fish if I have extra, and they are suspicious and ask me how much. They don't understand when I say it's for free.'

Marina laughs. 'What was it you said to them? *Your money has no value here.*'

They excuse themselves as they must clean the fishing nets outside. I watch as Marina pulls the net from a heap and passes it over a wooden rod to Andreas. They shake out the net and he winds it into a neat pile on a tarpaulin, a cigarette hanging from his lips. They were married a couple of years ago, after meeting then losing touch for a decade. Marina had moved away and was working for a mobile phone company and as a waitress in Athens. When he first told her about this place, he was nervous as there wasn't even a bathroom, and to get a phone signal they must walk to the top of the hill. But they have both clearly embraced this life, which is their heritage, laughing when they talk about all the things they have to do to make it work.

'The biggest problem here at Tristomo is the rubbish,' says Andreas. It washes from the sea on to shore and is blown into the fields behind. It's the usual bottle tops and fishing nets and yoghurt buckets with Turkish writing. 'Me and my wife tried collecting it, but in one month it fills up again.'

If the rubbish didn't gather here, it would be idyllic – but maybe it wouldn't be so tranquil. I ask what they feel about the new road being built.

'Me and Marina don't want it. People will come and destroy our quiet. Then maybe people will start businesses, and it won't be the same, it will change here.'

They say we are welcome to stay the night. In the meantime, they must go and work on the boat, his grandfather's old wooden boat, which needs cleaning and painting. It's their main source of fresh food and their way in and out of Tristomo. We ask if there's anything we can do to help and Andreas winks and jokes, 'In the morning – I'll give you the bill.' So we go to explore.

A dozen houses are hunkered around the water's edge, some restored but closed-up, others abandoned with dark grey stone walls showing through the plaster. There's a rectangular pool and cistern with brackish water for animals. Behind the bay are broken stone walls, broken buildings, fields full of rocks and thorns, trees turning wild. A long building with no roof was the Italian barracks or *kazarma* in the first half of the twentieth century. Nearby are what seem to be the rusted inner workings of a windmill. One house has been converted into an 'eco-lodge' with recycling bins separated into six different categories standing defiantly among the blown-in detritus. I take a swim, carefully picking my way around fishing hooks and fish bones on the steps, and dry off in the sun, listening to the water lapping, the birds and insects. Across the inlet, the bright yellow-green slopes are etched with the horizontal lines of very old terraces, here and there a ruined stone hut.

I follow a path up and around a hillside until the strait of Steno appears. I stop at a stone house with a wooden door and lintel. The branches of the roof are still in place and there's a wooden *soufa* inside, disintegrating. A channel curved into the plaster wall directs rainwater into a covered cistern. The house looks across to a stunning blue bay with a white beach and bare mountains of Saria soaring behind. I find my friend and we continue down to the mole; the currents are dangerous, but we swim close to the black rocks. A memorial is inscribed with poetic words in honour of the oarsmen who rowed people across to Saria.

Back at Tristomo, the sunset bathes the craggy hills and stone terrace walls in rosy tangerine light, as a bright white moon rises almost full. In the evening over dinner, we talk with Andreas and Marina and listen to their stories, then sleep in an adjacent room with fishing nets in bundles outside, and water lapping and slapping all around.

They insist we stay for a breakfast of bread rusks with olive oil, herbs and cheese. Afterwards we set out again, following the path above the shoreline in the direction of the open sea. Looking back, Tristomo is soon just a small huddle of low houses with their feet in the sea, the remains of terraces all around, overgrown and softened by scrub. Crossing over the first hill, we see another cascading amphitheatre of squat old terrace walls ending at a few deserted stone houses just before a shallow wetland of pinkish-brown mud edged with clumps of green reeds.

Most of the houses here still have straight, strong walls, and are divided down the middle; they have heavy beams across the roofs, though nettles grow inside. Some walls are fallen into piles of rocks and sometimes just a door still stands. There are enclosures for animals with branches held in place over the stones. Someone keeps blue beehives here and has painted their initials on a ramshackle chapel using the same paint. A rough, windblown, stony white beach separates the brilliant turquoise sea from flat fields completely overgrown with thorn bushes.

This was where villagers from Olympos grew wheat and barley. The life here was good, I've been told, when people cultivated their fields and kept animals. But after World War II, they had little left and one by one, they went away. These spare dwellings buffeted by sea winds belonged to families who went to New York and Baltimore. There had been anti-Greek race riots in the USA in the early twentieth century when the first waves of emigrants arrived. In the 1960s and 1970s life was still challenging. They lived downtown among gangs and guns. Many of those who left were skilled craftsmen, stonemasons, but found it was easier to flip burgers than work with rocks. The skills were lost, but they learned others. At least one of those families, as Andreas said, 'left with a penny and became millionaires'.

We follow the path to the ghost village of Kilios, mountains protecting it from the winds. The riverbed is lined with pale stone houses standing empty with dark open doorways; there are leafy fig trees, red and yellow euphorbia and fields of olives, still green and healthy. We continue to another level of the valley and meet another riverbed street of two-room, windowless square houses, sometimes with fireplaces, each with a threshing circle. A few donkeys are grazing.

We have a steep climb up the mountain for five hundred metres or so, but it is a joy because of the views and because of the path, made from heavy slabs of rock. Strong enough to be a donkey track, it is easy on the feet. Clouds are blowing over the peaks of Saria, giving us occasional shade. I see from above how the green fields stretch back to two valleys, one cultivated for olives and one for grain. The houses with their threshing circles and the square fields form a glorious artwork on the empty landscape. The only sound is of waves far below and wandering sheep.

After the last two days of living in a landscape virtually unchanged for a hundred years, as we reach the plateau we are suddenly confronted by a horrendous gash slashed across the hill opposite – the most recent extension to the new road – and two bulldozers. Plodding onwards, I try to make myself feel better by imagining it is to help people access their properties (though later I will hear that it's the military building it, and 'even they don't know what they're going to do…'). My friend, saddened, tramps on ahead. Where the rocks are covered in a bright orange lichen, I sit for a while and listen to the whirrs and squeaks of birds, hidden in the thick bushes covering the old stone terraces; I hope one day the wild will cover the new road too. If they do extend it to Tristomo, perhaps build a car park and a shop, something important will be lost forever.

As we continue, the road disappears from view and we enter a long valley overlooked by the rocky peaks of Malo and Orkili and Ardha. There's a cistern and fields filled with wildflowers and dry fig trees. I never realised how much of the north of Karpathos was abandoned. Yet there's also a field of pruned vines, well protected from wild goats. We descend to Ahordeia, a beautiful, flat valley of green meadows with figs and vines and a couple of sheep and donkeys. On the other side, we regain the old path paved with slabs of stone that winds down a steep-sided gorge, red with euphorbia, mist eerily blowing over the slopes towards Avlona.

NO MORE THAN STORIES

KASOS

Rounding the south of Karpathos, the ferry leans into whitecaps as it veers west. It's a bright day, the sea is deep blue and I get that glorious feeling of adventure, heading for a new island. Soon I see the sharp edge of Kasos: severe grey cliffs, islets broken away. As we continue, the peak slowly transforms itself into a humped back and falls away in smooth curves with the faint lines of long, straight terraces. The hills have turned brown after the dry summer, a stark contrast to the brilliant platinum gleam of the sea on a windy day.

The harbour appears and while my friend gazes at the view, I hurry to disembark because after here the ferry continues to Crete. Kasos is the southernmost of the Dodecanese, the southernmost island in the Aegean (though Crete is further south, it and its outlying islands are in the Sea of Crete), and the closest island of this group to Africa. It's the end of September and there are no other travellers walking off the ramp; even Lisa has been left at home on Tilos. Locals load and unload items, greet or say goodbye to loved ones. The small crowd disperses quickly. People drive up and ask in a relaxed way if we need a room.

The harbour village of Fri (pronounced 'Free') feels peaceful with its understated blue-trimmed white buildings, dominated by a large multi-arched church and blue-and-white belfry, against a backdrop of mountains. Nets are wound into neat loops on the wide empty quay. Fishermen sit in their boats. An old man is carrying a large fish by its tail. He sits on a bench with a younger man, slaps the fish down a couple of times and the younger man hands over a note.

There are no large signs to spoil the scene; the only one I notice is for Alpha Bank. Kasos, along with Tilos and Lipsi, almost lost its bank recently. In the end, public protest saved these outlying branches.

Kasos, at sixty-nine square kilometres including its uninhabited islets, is roughly the same size as Tilos. Its slightly higher population, between seven hundred and one thousand residents, lives in a few villages around the port, which faces north towards the rest of the Dodecanese. Like most islands, its population swells in summer when many Kasiots living in Australia and the United States return for family holidays. Some are moving back and restoring their houses, and many studios to rent are listed as 'condominiums'.

A local woman meets us at the harbour to take us to the studio my friend has rented. On the way, I mention the bank and ask if life on Kasos is difficult. The bigger island of Karpathos is just an hour away, served by a small ferry in the summer; but in winter their only ferry service is on the big boat that passes through a couple of times a week, though they do have an airport.

'It's not difficult for us who've learned to live here. I never want to leave. We have good people, no crime, clean air.'

When we arrive, I'm slightly disappointed that our home on Kasos for the next few days feels more like a city condominium than an island studio, the clean air overpowered by air freshener. She offers a bottle of water.

'Can I drink the tap water?' I ask.

'Well, we don't. It's salty. But they recently switched it over to another well, so it should be better.'

I thank her, and we set out for a walk.

At a small enclosed harbour with wandering geese, a pocket-sized terrace with four taverna tables overlooks the wooden fishing boats with carpets on their decks. A little further along, sheltered by the long arm of the breakwater protecting the main harbour, is the tiniest patch of golden sand shelving into turquoise sea.

A woman with olive skin and long, dark hair is swimming to shore. Seeing us as she gets out, she waves hello, then welcomes us to Kasos with a dazzling smile and an Australian accent. She has an Australian flag on her towel. We get chatting and she tells me her parents left Kasos for Australia and ran a takeaway shop in Canberra, then started coming back for visits after they had children. As a little girl she loved the island but lost interest as she grew up. Then she fell in love with a man from Kasos and moved here at the age of thirty, falling in love with life here too. She inherited a house from her aunt, gradually restored it, and now has a busy life as a mother. 'This beach is my escape,' she says, tying the laces of her running shoes and getting dressed. Her baseball cap says 'Kasos', her shorts say 'Australia', and the T-shirt she ties into a knot over her trim waist says 'Love'. She says goodbye and bounds energetically away.

Rusted iron workings stick out of the stone windmill and some of the struts of the sails are still holding on. Soon we come to the tiny airport, a ten-minute walk from town. The small island of Armathia appears offshore, abandoned in the middle of the twentieth century. In summer, excursion boats take people to its beautiful beach.

The coast becomes more windswept. From rugged mountains, the island tapers away to rocks and crashing sea, waves surging in from the northwest. Beyond Ayios Georgos Vrisis, St George of the Spring, are a few tiny beaches dotted with bottle tops washed in from the sea. Sheep are grazing, and fishermen casting off from the rocks. We swim, dry off in the cool wind as the orange sun sinks into the Aegean, then turn to see the moon rising large and bright white over the hill.

The village above here is Ayia Marina, the biggest on Kasos. Its lanes are surprisingly quiet. A café-bar appears, lit up and full of men. Half of them rise from their chairs to vacate a table – they're just sitting there for company. The waiter shyly asks if we'd like food, but it's pizza only so we hold out and order drinks. I listen to a man saying that if you feed a cat but don't overfeed it, it will catch rats and snakes. Then conversation turns to the winds forecast this week, whether the storm will bring rain.

'If it doesn't rain, forget about olive oil this year!'

Someone asks his dog, 'D'you want to go home?' and the dog seems excited.

Gradually one by one the men leave as dusk turns to darkness, bidding the company goodnight. The night is still and quiet again.

We go in search of a taverna, and find a lively restaurant, again full of men. I see a familiar dog and realise that all those men who said they were going home were actually coming here to eat and watch the football on TV. The owner at first says he only has souvlaki but, when pressed, turns out to have also tiny stuffed vine leaves, wild greens and cuttlefish cooked in a wine sauce. A big wood-burner sits in the corner, ready for winter.

After a feast, we look for the owner outside but a couple sitting with a dog say he's gone and will be back soon. We learn the couple are from Kasos and live in New York, though she is from Canberra. I tell her about the woman I met from Canberra and she says, 'That's my cousin.' They each have houses on this road. She misses Canberra and wants to teach the owner of the restaurant to cook chicken wings.

Her husband speaks with a thick New York accent and works as a painter on big buildings. The day the World Trade Centre towers went down, he should have been painting them but happened to have a day off. What brings tears to his eyes, though, is the idea that they must leave Kasos in a few days. 'Just one more year,' he says, before he can retire and move back here.

The tiny settlement of Panayia, above Fri and with an official population of thirty-four, is home to the 'Six Churches': tiny whitewashed Byzantine chapels with red painted roofs joined shoulder to shoulder down the slope of the hill. All around are the broken stone walls of abandoned dwellings, and I find what I believe were the houses of ships' captains. Through the large back windows is a view of sweeping mountains, a ridge rising over five hundred metres; the front windows look to the sea. Tall ceilings are still intact with herringboned wooden rafters, as are delicately carved cupboards and plastered walls with decorative panels hand-painted in ochre and red and pale blue.

Kasos, like Kastellorizo, was once wealthy from merchant shipping. In the first decades of the nineteenth century, the island had a population nearing thirteen thousand and a large fleet, and built freight sailing ships for other islands in the region.

During the Greek War of Independence, as the uprising against the Ottoman overlords spread from the Greek mainland, the Dodecanese were soon on the front line. Kasos converted its merchant fleet for use as a navy and aligned itself with its much larger and more powerful neighbour, Crete, sheltering Cretan freedom fighters. Its ships made raids on Asia Minor and the Levantine coast.

The Ottoman sultan asked his Egyptian allies to get rid of the problem. In May 1824, the Egyptian navy under Ibrahim Pasha besieged Kasos. In June, they massacred all the men they could find of fighting age, took the women and children to sell into slavery in Alexandria, and set fire to the island.

By 1830, the War of Independence was over, but along with the rest of the Dodecanese, Kasos was excluded from the new Greek state and remained part of the Ottoman Empire. The Kasiots who had escaped by boat to other islands returned and began to rebuild, continuing their nautical traditions; soon, however, the introduction of steam ships decimated the economy and people began to leave. Amazingly, after the massacre enacted by the Egyptian navy, many Kasiots went to work in Egypt on the Suez Canal from 1869. Some ship owners made the transition from sail to steam and continued to be successful. Many shipping companies set up offices in London.

Elias Kulukundis came from a family who had contributed ships to the War of Independence; his grandfather had been captured and forced to work in Egyptian warships but escaped and settled in Syros. From 1881 to 1898, Elias revitalised the family fortunes, shipping grain from Black Sea ports and coal from Wales. His son Manolis was born in Kasos and planned to study at the University of the Bosphorus, but in 1914 Turkey entered World War I so he moved instead to London. With his friend Minas Rethymnis, Manolis Kulukundis set up R&K, the biggest Greek shipping company of the time.

I walk back down to the sea and wander the backstreets of Fri. I peek into deserted houses to find decoratively hand-painted walls, picture rails and beautifully crafted wooden ceilings. One home has a pebble mosaic in the courtyard, but the garden is filled with fallen wooden doors, discarded Coke cans and the packaging of a set of

H&M 'short trunks cotton stretch'. Gateways are often rather grand, two columns supporting a triangle.

Among the deserted houses is a large mansion with a red gable, falling into disrepair with a handwritten 'For Sale' sign. A plaque tells me the 'poet of the sea' D. I. Antoniou (1906–94) 'lived and was inspired' here. Later, I find out that Antoniou was born to a great Kasiot shipping family in Mozambique and spent part of his early life in Suez. He joined the navy and reached the rank of commander. Concurrent with his naval career he was a renowned poet, keeping company with some of the most famous in Greece, including George Seferis and Odysseus Elytis.

Roderick Beaton's biography of Seferis tells of how the twenty-five-year-old Dimitris Antoniou, then serving as navigation officer on a long-distance cargo ship, visited Seferis in his office in Gower Street, London, and impressed him as a real seafarer. He also impressed Henry Miller, who wrote that he envied him his life, forever stopping off at islands and battling the elements: 'In Antoniou's countenance there were always traces of the weather.' Antoniou's cabin aboard ship was filled with books, empty cigarette packets and manuscripts. I find one of his poems from 1939, 'Obstacle to What?' translated by Edmund Keeley. It tells of a ship returning after many years of exile in distant places, bringing 'no more than stories'.

We walk up the road alongside a steep canyon. Seemingly in the middle of nowhere, someone has tilled the earth and carefully cultivated olive trees.

There's little agriculture to be seen, though a few small fields have been ploughed ready for the rain. Produce comes by ship from Rhodes and Crete. Kasos focuses its farming efforts on sheep, making dairy products in stone huts, called *mitata*, in the hills, while a modern creamery with a shop in Fri produces various cheeses and local types of savoury cream and butter. I notice a distinctive breed of sheep with a soft, gingery fleece.

In the south the road divides, each way leading to a different church and then meeting again for the descent to Helatros bay, where signs of Minoan settlement around 1450bc have been found. Here, where the Aegean Sea meets the Libyan Sea, Helatros is naturally enclosed and protected by cliffs but too shallow for modern ships, no longer used. The water is clear, the beach a mix of bright white pebbles and golden sand with a few fishermen's trucks and some persistent flies. I put on mask and snorkel and glide over pebbles that give way to sand covered in miniature sand-volcanoes, cones with blowholes in the top. I watch a flounder tapping the sandy seabed with its tail. When I come up, eagles are crying in the clifftops. I rest on the beach, the sea and sky a deep blue and nothing on the southern horizon.

On the walk back, soft pink light picks out the old terraces and rocks in between dark green thorny bushes. Goats watch from above. A red moon rises from behind the empty hills. A truck with two fishermen on their way back from Helatros stops to offer us a ride.

The young man says they didn't catch much. 'Kasos has many fish. But they are clever! They know to hide in the rocks.'

My friend asks about a good place to eat fish, and on their recommendation we go to Emborio, the little bay below Panayia, and eat grilled red snapper and tiny local shrimp, and salad made with the family's juicy little olives. When we go to pay, we get talking to the owner, Kikis, who has a bushy moustache and a New York accent. Born in Kasos, he was working on a ship when he jumped off in America. He ended up simultaneously running two restaurants in New York and working on ships until he got his pension, then came back here and opened this taverna. But he tells another story, even more interesting.

In the last years of the Italian occupation of the Dodecanese, an Italian soldier was stationed first in Rhodes and then in Kasos, where he fell in love with a young Kasiot woman. When Italy surrendered to the Allies in 1943, Italian soldiers were to be sent back to Italy (many on the *Donizetti*, which was attacked and sunk), but this man escaped on a little fishing boat, returned to Kasos and hid in a cave, kept alive by a shepherd. The shepherd couldn't risk telling anyone, not even the young woman. The couple were only united after the war ended and it was safe for the soldier to come out.

They started to raise a family but after 1948, when the British administration handed the Dodecanese back to Greece, all Italians were expelled. The family packed up what belongings they could take with them, ready to leave, giving away their animals to friends. On arriving in Rhodes, they pleaded with a sympathetic official to be allowed to stay on Kasos. He ordered that the islanders should decide. They voted for him to stay, so the family returned home. The Italian man was Kikis's father.

Next day, we walk to Emborio again, stopping to watch two women and a young man in wetsuits cleaning parrotfish on the shore. They insist on giving us a bag of fish.

Emborio was the old port, built by the ship owners along with the roads, the library, the wells. Fifteen years ago, when the new dock was built at Fri to accommodate the big ferry, Emborio was abandoned as a port. Now, behind the pretty beach, a vast church is being gutted and restored. The man working on it says it's being done with private money – one man from Kasos, who's getting older and has no children, is financing it together with a man from Athens. Nothing from the government.

We swim in the big swell of the waves. Underwater there are shipping remnants – machinery, cables – covered in the accretions of the sea. Kikis fries our parrotfish, and we try his octopus cooked with onions and olives, with wild greens and oven potatoes. My friend asks him if he misses New York.

'I miss my friends,' he says – meaning Kasiot friends. 'There are more people from Kasos there than here.'

Men are hauling a small boat out of the sea. A gale is predicted, a *fortuna*. The ferry from Piraeus has been cancelled due to weather, but there are seats available on a flight to Rhodes tomorrow. While arranging tickets at the travel agency, we meet a couple of American Kasiots; they describe themselves as 'empty-nesters' who rebuilt his family house and spend more and more time here.

There's a mix of blue sky and puffy clouds, a feeling of a change in the season. With an extra day on the island we walk to Arvanitohori, the furthest of the settlements from the harbour, where another vast church is being restored. At the delightfully minuscule café, the young man says he has no food but we order drinks and talk to another customer, an older man who, after a career on the ships, was deputy mayor of the island in the 1980s. He talks about the work they did on the port and airport, the roads and the wells, bringing in outside expertise. I tell him I've been admiring the colourful rows of recycling bins but he says the recycling doesn't work. He keeps asking the young man if he can't make us something to eat. 'If you just had some stuffed vine leaves ready…' We try the mini-market where a man sits watching a fifty-year-old television with a fuzzy screen. He tells us the bakery van will arrive at quarter to twelve. It does.

It's warm but so windy as we walk south that I wrap my sarong around my hair to stop it flying in all directions, thinking of my women friends in Olympos and their headscarves. The air is clear and bright, and I take in all the details of the landscape: stone huts; olive trees in red earth; sand-coloured hillsides; dusty-green scrub in the valley. The sea is jewel blue at Helatros but grey and whitecapped beyond the bay. We sit for a while in a monastery. Trucks are parked nearby and figures stalk the horizon: it's too windy for fishing, so men are out hunting. We continue to where the land drops away down a sheer mountain, falling steeply then splitting off, waves smashing against headlands at the wild southern point of the Dodecanese.

ROADS TO NOWHERE

HALKI

The two-storey Venetian-style houses, painted in an array of vibrant colours with pitched ceramic-tile roofs, are jumbled on low hills around the bay in Imborio, little Halki's gorgeous port. The quay is lined with café terraces and shops, sailboats neatly tethered, fishing boats bobbing in water so clear you see starfish and sea urchins below. It's all postcard-perfect, set off by the grey mountain behind.

The port of Imborio, a variation of Emborio, is the island's only village. From the Pano Meri or 'High Places' of Tilos, and from the ferry, I've looked across at Halki and seen nothing but steep and rugged cliffs all along the back of the island. But I first became intrigued by the hinterland by chance on a flight to Rhodes. The pilot, awaiting permission to land, gave us an aerial tour of Halki and I was amazed to see extensive swathes of grazing lands high on the plateau.

In ancient times around seven thousand people lived on Halki's twenty-eight square kilometres. By the nineteenth century, the island still had three thousand inhabitants, and despite having no natural water it was self-sufficient, growing wheat and, like Kalymnos and nearby Symi, prospering from sponge diving. The architecture was influenced by towns the divers saw while travelling around the Mediterranean. The exodus from the Dodecanese left houses empty, and the sharing of property among siblings often led to disagreement. Most of the prettily painted, immaculately restored seafront houses have steps into the deep blue sea, a 'Villa' name and a label of a tour operator. They are used only in summer, and in between are places still in disrepair, faded doors and crumbling walls.

Ferries go back and forth to Kameiros Skala on Rhodes daily; the *Prevelis* ferry stops here between Rhodes and Karpathos/Kasos; and the *Dodecanese Express* catamaran calls on its way between Rhodes and Tilos. But despite its location – just six kilometres west of Rhodes, with easy access to its conveniences and airport – and a functioning desalination plant, Halki (also spelled Chalki) has a population of only about 250 permanent residents, the number dropping even lower in winter. When I passed through on my way from Tilos to Karpathos one time, a friendly couple sitting outside a mini-market say, 'Stay here, we need people!'

A straight new road funded by the Halki population of Tarpon Springs, Florida, connects Imborio with its past, the old village of Horio. The road passes through a valley of barking dogs and scruffy fenced fields, then sweeps up beside old field terraces, a dark green cascade of trees, to a high col.

After an hour's strenuous walk my friend and I are at the foot of the old village, which faces the interior of the island, hidden from the sea. It was once the main settlement, inhabited since the sixth century BC or earlier, and the remains of walls from different eras are scattered around the steep slope – rectangular blocks of ancient masonry, smaller polygonal stones, chapels. We wander the paths; it feels similar to Megalo Horio and Mikro Horio on neighbouring Tilos. The castle at the top of the hill was built by the Knights of St John, incorporating elements from an ancient temple in its doorways, and had rock-cut cisterns for collecting rainwater. The fortification eventually proved indefensible against artillery and fell out of use, though people continued to live on the slopes below. The village was abandoned in the mid-twentieth century, when people either emigrated or moved down to the port. Near the road, some old houses are spray-painted with initials asserting ownership, a few are being renovated, and there's a 'For Sale' sign.

Viewed from up here, the port already appears small. We follow the road further uphill, the only traffic a man riding a donkey with a wooden saddle. We pass several of Halki's traditional shepherd's huts called *kyfes*, round structures with very thick walls made roughly from field stones, tapering towards a stone roof, with an open doorway. Then there's a cluster of churches high on the mountain, one built in the nineteenth century by sponge divers, some older chapels. They would not have been so remote in centuries past when people stayed on the high lands to look after their animals, before the days of roads and pick-up trucks and the move to the coast.

We veer off the road to the church of Stavros stin Plekti, but the footpath to the other churches seems blocked by fences and we can't find a way through. Turning back, I notice a rusted old trunk with addresses handwritten on the side: from the Republic of Zaire to Rhodes, the same Greek name on both. It lies next to a squat, misshapen chapel built of grey field stones, where even the cross above the doorway is askew. I follow Lisa inside to see large blocks making up a simple altar. Plaster has fallen to reveal the neat, small masonry blocks of the vaulted roof, and the walls show, in faded reds and blues, images of saints, defaced by Ottomans.

The light is very clear, the old terraces and squiggly lines of field walls well defined. It's a steep, long climb as we continue up the road, Lisa pulling to rest in any available shade. We stop near the remains of a windmill. At the edge of the barren, harsh plateau, the rock is almost white in the bright sun. There are broken field walls all around, stones tumbling into the land. The road beyond leads only to a monastery, Ai Yianni Alarga, 'St John the

Far-Away', and abandoned rural settlements on the far side of the island. We'd need more time and more water to reach them.

Halki is one of the smallest inhabited islands in Greece. Yet because it is mostly deserted and empty, when I start to explore it feels vast and wild, and most traces of the old way of life remain as they were, untouched. The place names on the map tell stories: Dry Fields; Cliff; Hell; Capers; Barley; Narrow Point; Wide Point; Two Beaches; Wild Sea.

We pass a rusting, abandoned taxi and walk a rough track fringed with masses of wild oregano, descending towards what is marked on the map as a beach although we see no sign of it. Jagged cliffs rise on either side, and all over the slopes are drystone walls around small circular enclosures, now empty. We continue on the road to nowhere and gradually see curly-horned sheep and goats, a rusted Lamborghini tractor, fenced fields of prickly pears, vines and hives. As we keep going down, there's a coil of old ship's rope, a mass of sheep's wool, a satellite dish, a wind turbine, a water butt, a caravan, and finally a couch on a ledge of rock over the sea.

A couple of fishing boats are pulled up on a tiny cove of smooth white pebbles worn to sand in patches, turning the sea a pale turquoise. As we strip off sweaty clothes and prepare to plunge in, a man appears and starts nailing a roof in place. We swim, looking below the surface at crabs clinging to rocks, while someone builds a life on this remote outpost. The island beyond here is all sheer, stark grey mountains stretching off into the distance.

I arrive on the catamaran, alone with Lisa one late afternoon in autumn, pleased to have made it as strong winds and big seas were forecast. As I celebrate with a beer at a waterfront café, I get talking to someone before suddenly I realise night will be falling in an hour. I say goodbye, buy a few tins for dinner and set off hastily up the road. We're going to sleep in the hills.

Dusk is gathering as we turn off up a dirt track that's a dead end according to the map – likely to be deserted. We pass through a gate cobbled together with the usual bits of rope and reused wood and fencing. A dog barks below; we need to get off its radar before settling down for the night. I follow the rock-strewn track, hoping to find a suitable spot before dark. The arches of a large chapel appear in silhouette and I head for that, although the wind picks up as we go further towards the sea.

The church, when we get to it, seems to have been abandoned halfway through being built or rebuilt, and the area where I'd hoped to find shelter is scattered with rocks and bricks. From what I can see in the gloom, the doorways have been blocked up with wooden gates to stop goats getting in. The wind is lively so I find a site next to a drystone wall, clear the ground a little and get the tent up and everything inside to hold it down. Every few minutes a gust threatens to blow it over. I take a swig from a little bottle of ouzo, happy to be on a mountain for the night. The sky is soon a magnificent canopy of stars with only a sliver of bright crescent moon. Over the wall I see the lights of the harbour below.

Lisa is distracted by wandering sheep and I drag her into the tent and zip up. She spends the night making her way from one end of the tent to the other and crouching to see out. The tent leans and flaps in the wind, and I twist and turn to give my body a break from the stony ground. Somewhere in the early hours, the wind drops and we fall asleep for a longer stretch.

As dawn begins to light the sky, I wake feeling surprisingly good, and emerge from the tent to note that the field is covered with some of the sharpest rocks I've ever seen. Just over the wall there is, strangely, a patch of sand which would have made a far more comfortable mattress. Maybe they used it for making cement when working on the church. The shell of the church has a smooth concrete floor, and its walls would have saved me from the battering of the wind if only I'd clambered over the makeshift gates.

Below, the houses of the harbour have their faces lit by the rising sun. Above, to the other side, the bare grey mountaintops are bathed rose pink against a blue sky. Out to sea, the island of Alimnia and other tiny islets lie still. Alimnia (or Alimia) always had a small population but because of its natural harbour it played an important role in World War II, when the Italians used it as a base. It was abandoned after the war.

I hear wings flapping overhead and look up to see an eagle, my good omen. While it's still cool, I decide to explore what look like old fields on a plateau marked on the map as 'Pefkia' (pine trees). A footpath follows a drystone wall gradually uphill, and half an hour later we're at a circular stone hut, or *kyfi*, with thick, inward-sloping walls and a roof made of seriously hefty rocks with earth packed on top. They must hold everything in place with their weight; I wouldn't want to be inside if they fell. Looking down, I can clearly make out the curved terrace walls of old farms. The smooth, pale headland is spotted with dark bushes, resembling the pelt of a cheetah.

We emerge on to a flat upland dotted with pines and juniper bushes. A well with an old piece of marble in its rim has water inside, though it hasn't rained for half a year. There are drinking troughs carved out of rock. The pale grey stones underfoot are mixed with terracotta shards of broken pottery. I leave Lisa in the shade as I pick my way around ruined houses and enclosures of rough stones, and sections of smooth, carved white marble column – the remains of three ancient temples dedicated to the god Apollo. Temples and then churches were built on the high ground where there was water for crops and animals, for life. My ears ring with stillness, silence.

In spring, I arrive again in the late afternoon with a plan to camp at Pefkia with my friend, then the next day to continue around the coast to Kelia, a cave where hermits painted frescoes in the ninth and tenth centuries. Then I'd like to follow the rugged coastline to a chapel and up to the plateau. The map warns of indistinct paths but we'll have all day.

Dogs bark, cocks crow, bells clank and shepherds shout as they round up their animals for the night. The path feels rougher and more overgrown, probably not much used since the previous year. There's a cool wind and it's rockier than I remember at Pefkia; we clear the biggest stones from a patch under a wind-bent Mediterranean pine, its needles softening the ground, and the drystone walls around offer a touch of shelter. To save on weight for hiking, I've left the tent behind and have just a mat and sleeping bag. Mount Attavyros on Rhodes is grey, the sea pale blue, the sky changing to mauve with a streak of white cloud.

We drink raki and eat graviera cheese while it gets dark, listening to the scops owls' reedy high-pitched call, like a short note played over and over on a wooden recorder or a whistle. Meanwhile the wind drops and the mosquitoes move in. Because of the wind we hadn't bothered to rig up the net and although I throw a rope over a branch above to hang it from, the positioning isn't ideal. My new sleeping bag is too hot on this balmy night for me to retreat into it entirely and the mosquito repellent makes me feel sticky but doesn't deter them. I long for my tent, and eventually move off to sleep fitfully on a sloping, smooth rock which catches a bit of breeze.

The morning is serene, however, with a golden light on the grey walls and pines, the only sounds a few goat bells and the distant engine of a boat. We set off a little later than I'd hoped and follow traces of a path along a hillside of rocks and scrub, with deep blue sea far below, and faint old stone terraces, signs that this steep, deserted land was once cultivated. As it levels out a little there are more field walls, a threshing circle here and there, a tiny, broken *kyfi* with a low door and thick walls. I hear waves far below and birds around us. The shape of Tilos is visible in the distance.

Lisa is already panting in the shade. She needs water but I have to ration our limited supply to see us through. She pulls one way or the other to avoid the thorniest bushes. Round stone huts on the hillside above blend into their surroundings, the solid black of an empty doorway often the only way to make them out.

A flat coastal strip gradually comes into view, with lines of threshing circles and walls, maybe a church. We find no waymarkers but negotiate our way around an enclosure with thorn bushes and broken rusted fencing, then what seems to be the path begins to drop, crossing a gully with oregano, butterflies and euphorbia dried to vivid red. A covered cistern is built into the ground. According to the map, there are cisterns all over the island – though since the paths seem neglected, there's no guarantee that they still function. I hope we are descending to Kelia, but instead I recognise the stupendous sheer cliffs of the canyon at Areta, further along the coast. The spirits of the hermits didn't want to be disturbed.

The sticky ropes of large grey spiders are suspended across the trail down. Areta cove is alluring with its tiny pale pebble beach, still in shadow. Behind a wall at one end, according to a local elderly gentleman, there was once a brackish well for animals, now filled with rocks. Just as I'm about to cool off in the pale aquamarine water, I notice something rare in these islands: jellyfish, transparent but for a ribbon of purple running from the bell to the thick tentacles and thin trailing strings. I try a quick swim but bump into one (it's surprisingly hard), catching a frisson of sting.

I get out and sit on the beach, watching one come to the surface then propel itself through the water, the tentacles twisting to shift course. A bird sings up in the clifftops while a raven caws. Green shrubs and flowers grow from the vertical sides of the ravine over blue-green shallows. Sea flows in and fills the caves, softly gurgling, and sunlight reflected on the water flickers fast on the dark rocks above like flames or the northern lights.

Loaded up again, less refreshed than we'd hoped in the hot midday sun, we pass a deserted stone barn and a couple of threshing floors, with wheat growing wild in one, and for a while are blessed by a wide, clear path along the coast. At one point it's possible to descend into the deep, open sea and, with no sign of jellyfish, I swim with Lisa off the sharp rocks in wonderful cool water. As the map warned, the path pretty much disappears thereafter but I am confident we can find a way along the steep hillside to the oasis of green in the distance, from where a distinct trail ascends.

We scramble up cliffs, across scree and down rocky outcrops. My friend and I opt for different routes but focus on the target, the monastery of Ai Yianni tou Riakiou. I sit for a while in the shadow of a boulder and share with Lisa a little of what remains of my water before pulling myself up the hill, then collapse under a tree and remove my boots and lie on my mat for a while.

I continue to the church, hoping to find a cistern or spring; a water supply is marked on the map and the greenery suggests one, but we see nothing. I realise my mouth is too dry for me to speak properly and it's still a long way up an uncertain route, the afternoon sun still beating down. My friend discovers only a bucket of rank-looking rainwater and Lisa gulps from it. He thinks we should rest but, scared by the dehydration and still hoping to find water, I suggest we keep going.

Within minutes we see the cover of a cistern, and a rope tied to a stone weight and half a plastic bottle for a cup. We let it down hopefully, and bring it up full of clear water. There are a couple of flies but it's cold and smells fine. Gradually we bring up cup after cup which we guzzle down, feeling immediately better, and fill our bottles. People relied on these cisterns once, built them well and sank them all over the island so they could use the land. I'm massively grateful.

Up the mountain all we can see is thick scrub and rugged rocks, but after one wrong turn we eventually find the start of a solid, stone-built donkey track that zigzags up a narrow gully. We finally spot the railing of a road and keep going up until we emerge at the open plateau.

This is the place I wanted to see. I gaze at the expanse of faded land, yellow from dry grasses, pale grey rocks scattered all around. Slowly shapes emerge, broken field walls, stone huts visible only by the blackness of their doorways. The sides of the island were steep and rocky but people farmed these hidden uplands. Unseen from the sea four hundred metres below, it's so empty and mysterious now.

We cross to the old windmill. The tarmacked road descends above another flat swathe of abandoned fields in a strange patchwork of rounded shapes in varying sizes, with one single well-kept olive grove at the top and a farm with goats and chickens at the bottom. Behind and below the next ridge is Horio. We continue down until we see a person on a motorbike, then a truck. At the very end of the island there is a little line of colour that's Imborio, and all the way down there at the waterfront, a cold beer awaits.

ENOUGH

ARKI

I thought the journey was over, but there's one last place calling me. The northernmost island in the Dodecanese is Agathonisi, but I'm more intrigued to go to Arki (also spelled Arkioi), just below it, the smallest inhabited island in the north of the Dodecanese that can be reached on a regular ferry route. I've been told that Arki has just one teacher and one pupil in the school. In Greek, it sounds like the word *arkei* that means 'it's enough'.

I haven't covered everywhere on this journey, by any means. I would love to explore the little uninhabited islands of Alimnia off Halki, and Ro off Kastellorizo, but they can only be reached by private boat or on a day trip. The same is true of Levitha in the municipality of Leros, inhabited by one family; the father used to take his daughter to school by boat, and they support their farm by running a taverna and charging mooring fees. There are many stories to be told on the island of Symi, another shipbuilding and sponge-diving island whose population is now a tenth of what it was a century ago, its emigrants contributing to the Greek community of Tarpon Springs. I've stayed on Symi in a house at the very top of the old Horio with no phone signal, no traffic, no neighbours, yet noisy with the surrounding chickens and church bells; there's an abandoned village above Pedi bay and old wine presses on the top of the island. One day and night spent on Patmos were enough to reveal the surprisingly empty, wild back of the island, with old stone barns and field walls. This journey could go on and on. But for now, *arkei*, it's enough.

On Kalymnos to connect with the ferry north, I'm at a bay full of fishing boats and local families on this Saturday lunchtime in the Greek summer holidays; a place that is far from deserted.

On the beach, old ladies bob in the clear water wearing flowery housedresses and hats, then walk home in wet dresses carrying plastic bags of bread. Young children play. Older children swim with spear guns. I continue to a place where someone has painted on the road, 'Stop Road', and it turns to gravel. The taverna at the end of the road is a good place for me and Lisa to eat lunch but, when I go to swim, a super-yacht has come in with American and Greek flags, and a speedboat full of young people is soon doing the equivalent of wheelies and skidding, last-minute turns across the bay. Back at the beach, crowds of people stand in the shallows. It's too hot to walk back yet and one of the beach bars is playing loud music so I sit at the next, which is quieter. A girl asks her dad if she can have an ice cream. A little kid spins in an inflatable ring. The tamarisks and palm fronds blow in the wind. Children talk and shout, a mother shouts, '*Ochi, ochi!* ' – 'No, no!' – and another woman talks on her phone. There's laughter and a motorbike and cicadas and splashing.

In the early evening, I'm back in town and setting out to withdraw some money for the days ahead, a precaution given that small islands don't always have working bank machines. Suddenly there is an ear-splitting explosion. Just when you thought Kalymnos in summer couldn't get any louder, it surprises you. Lisa runs from side to side, whimpering, tail between her legs. There are a few minutes of quiet and then *boom! Boom!* again. Someone explains there's a wedding, and people are celebrating by throwing dynamite. This tradition was originally begun by Kalymnians as a show of resistance against control by outsiders, it's said; they recovered mines and torpedoes left behind from the battles of two world wars, scraped out the dynamite and made bombs out of old cans or cigarette packets.

It sounds like a war zone. Lisa makes terrified squeaks as she paces and pants frantically. Hoping the wedding is reaching its finale, I continue with her straining at the lead to reach what she imagines is safety. At one point I pick up my 25-kilo dog to get her away from traffic. A local man tells me his own dogs are terrified of the dynamite – all animals are. It stops at last and I head for the fishermen's tavern.

I order a bottle of retsina, and it's soothing to sit and listen to the guys talk about fishing. One of them comes over and puts a grilled bream on my plate, taken from their heaped platter. They are soon telling me about the Kalymnos boats that will be near my home on Tilos over the coming weeks, and that I am to tell so-and-so to give me fresh fish. They ask if I like Kalymnos.

'I love Kalymnos! Except for one thing.'

They know what I'm talking about. Someone says, 'There are idiots here who throw dynamite for any reason, a cat giving birth. We don't all do it.' They tell me stories and show me videos on a phone; it's clearly a controversial topic. In 1980, fifty sticks of dynamite stored in a church killed four children. 'If all three thousand pieces had exploded, it would have destroyed the island. What kind of custom is that?' I ask if it's true that fishermen use it. 'Some do. The police do nothing.'

They offer me more retsina and ask where I'm going. Arki, I say, with a tent as I'm not sure about finding dog-friendly accommodation, especially in summer when it's busy. A man with long, wild hair calls a friend on Arki and tells him to look after me. After five hours of sleep and snoozing my alarm, I dash across town to buy a ticket for the 6am ferry that will drop me there close to midday.

It's windy and there are big waves out to sea as the crew of the *Nissos Kalymnos* go back and forth preparing to leave. The only other passenger on deck is a woman in a pink T-shirt, tight jeans, pink-and-white trainers and white nails, her curly black hair clipped back, and her lipstick the same pink as her sunglasses, smoking long thin cigarettes. As we set off, she pets Lisa and I find out she's Maria from Kalymnos and works as an agent registering boats that arrive from Turkey.

She seems pleased to have someone to chat with as her husband, a ship's captain, has just left to work for a few months on a tanker between the UK and France. Her three boys and little dog – also a Lisa – are staying with her mother. The family home is in Masouri, on the west coast; when her parents grew up, the road only went that far. Now it's packed in summer with holidaymakers; from May to October she works every day, sometimes until after midnight, too busy to go anywhere. 'Winter is much better!' Today it's too windy for boats – it was a close call as to whether this ferry would run – so she's visiting her colleagues on Leros.

The almost-empty ferry passes Kalymnos's sheer, bare cliffs. The sun is bright but the fierce wind still cool so I'm wearing light jeans, two T-shirts and a jacket. A northerly wind can feel like a blessing in summer. I keep Lisa tied to the bench. The northern point of Kalymnos almost touches the southern point of Leros, and Maria says goodbye as we enter the bay of Lakki, surrounded by low hills and trees.

Although Lakki is one of southern Europe's largest natural harbours there was little here until the 1920s, when Mussolini created a base for the Royal Italian Navy, naming the new town Portolago. It was mostly built in the Rationalist style during the 1930s, and many of the striking buildings still exist, though it was bombarded and invaded by Germany in 1943 after Italy's surrender to the Allies. There are abandoned Italian military installations across Leros, the remains of landing craft, planes and anti-submarine nets on the seabed, and a Greek warship, the *Vasilissa Olga*, sunk in Lakki's deep harbour.

One large, pale building stands out on the shoreline, somewhat sinister, with dark, empty windows four storeys high. Built as barracks during the Italian occupation, this place was used to detain prisoners during the Greek Civil War (1946–49). In 1958, it became the 'Leros Colony of the Mentally Ill' with long-term patients brought here from cities all over Greece; in the 1970s, it housed over three thousand patients. Later, as people with chronic mental health problems were being deinstitutionalised, many were relocated closer to their families, and the hospital closed in the 1990s. The buildings were left to fall into disrepair. Now, they have been taken over by refugees camping in its grounds, designated a 'hotspot'.

'Leave the lady and her dog alone,' says a mother in black jacket and jeans and sunglasses to her young daughter as the ferry sets off again, but I say it's OK. Lisa often does a public service by entertaining children on long ferry journeys. Enthusiastic Emmanuela spends the next hour lavishing so much attention on Lisa that she tries to hide under the bench. Meanwhile, I chat with her mother, who's from Lipsi, our next stop. She says that on Lipsi, people shout at them if they take their dog to the beach (something I experience there too, which prevents me from being able to explore in the summer); they've left their dog at home this time.

'I'm going to do some work on my mother's house. She lives with us on Leros but likes to go home from time to time. She's seventy-five, but one of the old-style women who used to work in the fields

– you'd think she was a hundred. She has an old-fashioned mentality, compared to my daughter, so there are non-stop battles.' She chain-smokes as she tells me all this. She asks if I have kids and I say no. 'Lucky you,' she says, grinning.

The islands and islets around here all seem to merge into one another, with no long stretches of water in between, unlike further south. Distracted by chat, we're soon approaching Lipsi's low, green hills, blue-domed churches and signs for accommodation, and I say goodbye to our new friends. Tourists board the boat and I lie down on the bench and sleep, waking when the short man wearing lots of cologne walks around saying, '*Yia Patmo?*' 'Anyone for Patmos?' More tourists with suitcases board, and two well-dressed ladies sit pouring rosé into glasses for their lunch.

I like this boat with its shaded benches, close enough to the water that I can watch the birds gliding across the waves, but I'm excited as we approach tiny Arki. Part of the municipality of Patmos, it has a land mass of 6.7 square kilometres and a permanent population of around forty. It looks to be all gently undulating hills with yellowing grass and low shrub and scattered limestone. I shoulder my backpack and make my way down the steps with Lisa. The ferry passes a white pebble beach with tamarisk trees then backs towards a small concrete dock.

Someone has spray-painted on to a boulder, 'No Camping', followed underneath by 'Sorry'. I walk away into the quiet of Arki, hoping to be able to stay. Lisa sniffs the new territory. A narrow concrete track leads along a low hill towards the old harbour, an inlet with the remains of stone cottages scattered around. There's a tree-shaded square and a couple of tavernas. Manolis, known by his nickname Trypas, is the friend of the Kalymnos fisherman; his cousin Niki brings me an iced coffee, and I ask if there's any chance of a room. She points up the hill. 'With the pink flowers.' After finishing my coffee, I walk the few minutes up the road and open the door to a simple room with a cool stone floor and a bathroom. Perfect. *Arkei*, it's enough.

The harbour has space for half a dozen or so boats but there are hardly any cars on the island and just a few motorbikes, no roads more than a single lane and no road signs. After coming from one of the noisiest islands, it feels incredibly peaceful. I look forward to staying for a couple of days, though the price of the room makes it possible to stay longer if I decide to.

I return to the taverna and Lisa stretches out in the shade with a gentle breeze while I eat a salad with *paximadia*, capers and goat's cheese. Trypas says they are open in winter but only about twenty people stay on the island over Christmas. The population is decreasing because there are no young couples having families here. I ask about boat schedules, and scribble down the routes and days he reels off. There's a surprising range and most run year-round, weather permitting. The boats provide a lifeline, access to medical facilities, and there's a helicopter pad for emergencies.

An area of thick woods and parkland leads down to a couple of empty huts at the water's edge. Curious, I follow a path that leads to a closed door in a stone wall topped with rusted, twisted barbed wire. I continue to the other side of the headland to see a two-storey grey house half-hidden in tall Mediterranean pines and cypress, abandoned in this overgrown oasis. I descend to a jetty of weather-worn, hand-cut timber planks nailed together loosely over a shallow bay; then cross a spit of land with pink salt-marsh plants and brown sand, goats fenced into grazing land covered in golden grass. I swim in cool, deep water as the sun goes down. The only people around are in boats. At the shallow end of the bay are old stone goat pens. Seagrass grows close to shore.

Up the hill, the limestone used for the drystone field walls is cut into shapes so it slots together without concrete. Sharp dry branches are held on top by more rocks and an angled row of bamboo stakes provides a further layer of defence against goats. A footpath winds among mastic and thyme to pale blue sea, a view to uninhabited islets.

In the evening there's the sound of goat bells, and sunset lights up what look like ruined farmhouses under the church on the hilltop.

A slim teenage boy with caramel skin is slapping octopus down on the quay beside the slipway in the morning. Fishermen sit on upturned paint buckets at the water's edge in a stone hut, cleaning fish. A cock crows. Another fisherman sits in his boat with two boys, picking debris out of nets. I hear tinkling goat bells, a cooing pigeon and twittering birds. The boy carries four limp octopus to the taverna and hangs them in a net-covered box to dry.

I walk the concrete track straight up the hill, opening a substantial gate and closing it behind me. A long fence divides the lower part of the hill from the upper, where the goats are kept, distinctly greyer and browner where the vegetation is grazed away. At the top, the hill flattens out and is criss-crossed with walls. I turn right to the church of Panayia Pantanassa and the ruined farms around it, possibly the island's oldest settlement. The ground is littered with bits of old pottery, terracotta handles, shells. A weathered wooden gate still hangs from a wooden pole across an entrance.

A little down the hill is a more recently abandoned house. Timber beams are slowly falling to rot in the earth, surrounded by a stand of old trees, carob, pine and olive; there's a threshing circle but also broken glass, concrete and tiles. I look down at the village of a dozen or so houses; one of them, with a slide and swings in the garden, is the school.

In the cool of early evening, I cross a field to a stone cottage a few minutes' walk from the harbour. Low, long and flat like the island itself, it is made of field stones locked together, a neat bamboo ceiling held in place by timber beams. Through the open doorway I find snow-white plaster has half-fallen from walls, revealing stones held in place by rich brown earth. Shutters are closed on a wooden window frame still nailed deep into an opening in the wall, like a cupboard; the same design as those in the house that Trypas's taverna is built on to, from 1956.

On my second night on Arki, the square on the harbour is busy. There's a big boat and a lot of foreigners at the taverna tables. The Dodecanese have always been a meeting point of cultures, but now people come for tourism rather than trade. I drink an ouzo by the water's edge at the other taverna, eat grilled local cheese and baked aubergines in tomato sauce. When people start to drift away later, I talk to Nicolas, who looks to be in his fifties and runs this taverna with his mother.

There was no electricity here until 1989, he says, when photovoltaic panels were installed on the hillside. Residents were given special energy-friendly lights and fuses, a free TV and a fridge. But the solar panels weren't maintained properly, and soon people wanted bigger fridges and microwaves and more lights and the renewable energy wasn't enough, so generators were brought and now the panels just sit on the hillside and don't do anything.

It's a good community, he says, everyone related somehow and they try to get along, even the competing businesses. As for the school, he adds, there's one family with five boys who have kept it going, one student at a time. The current student is seven or eight years old; after he finishes, perhaps the school will close. It's hard to have a family here. And it's hard to be the only student.

Fresh fruits and vegetables and olive oil must be brought by boat, but the family who live on the hill have a thousand goats and make four kinds of cheese: hard feta, xinomizithra, mizithra and the hard mizithra for grating on spaghetti. Another family, he says, have three hundred and fifty goats. They send cheese to other islands, including Kalymnos; it's amazing for such a small place.

Thinking about the island that produces goats but not children, I walk back to my room, looking up to see stars and a ribbon of Milky Way, and decide to stay another day or two.

I'm lying on smooth rocks above a blue-and-bottle-green sea. The curving layers of grey rock are split and streaked by white, spotted with seagull muck and dried pools of salt. Just above are the remains of an old circular lime kiln. In a fold in the cliff, the grey rock meets porous white limestone with lines of ink and rust.

I jump into the water, swim and pull myself back out where sea plants grow over the sharp rocks, with limpets and barnacles clinging to them. I sit mesmerised in this peaceful place, with a cool breeze from the north blowing over me, nothing but hillsides and cliffs and sea and islets, all empty except for the white of the Hora on the highest point of Patmos in the distance. There's the sound of bells from the hillside and up on the cliffs stands a goat with long, twisted horns. I watch the sea crashing and worrying at inlets, filling the gaps, rising and falling. A brown bird of prey with white tail feathers flaps up from its nest, making a high-pitched call.

I'm sleeping a lot on Arki. Is that what happens in a sleepy place? I sleep until the light comes through the window and a motorbike passes or the mosquitoes wake up and I plug in the mosquito repellent, and then I go back to sleep. I walk and swim, but in the middle of the day in the summer heat with a dog, there's nothing to do but retreat to a quiet, dark room and sleep.

Goats have taken over the stone barns, lying in the shade and on the rooftops. The whole area is grey where they have eaten the new shrubs and grass. The concrete path turns to a gravel track heading along the back of the island. Lisa and I follow it to find more stone barns and gangs of goats under trees and squatting in the old buildings.

Drystone walls stand straight and thick with branches and bamboo spikes. Within them are sweeping fields in terraces cut into the curve of the valley, and straw bales piled under a tree. Walking downhill, we startle dozens of partridges. From a stand of trees comes the throbbing noise of cicadas. Eventually, passing a few houses, we arrive at the edge of a small natural harbour, with an old stone sea wall and shelters for animals and fishing.

It's north-facing so there is the usual stuff washed in on the shoreline, and I sit and take an inventory: polystyrene; part of a glass bottle; plastic bags; fishing nets; plastic bottles once filled with washing-up liquid, soft drinks, lemon juice and engine oil; the float from a boat; a plastic tahini tub labelled 'Made in Lebanon'; a plastic cup from a Greek coffee-shop chain; the sole of a shoe; a Fanta bottle; a tyre; a spray can; a child's toy; a plant pot; a lifejacket; some piping; a crate; a water bottle; the plastic wrapping for water bottles; a tobacco packet. The stuff of our lives today. Some things float in the sea, some are caught in overhanging branches, blown by the wind. It remains a beautiful place.

Walking back around the headland, I find another lime kiln in a narrow gully and then a rocky little bay with clear, deep, blue-green water, and another large boulder just right for lying on next to the sea, enjoying the breeze. I'm reading Roger Deakin's *Wildwood: A Journey Through Trees*, a section about people who find a use for every growing thing, and of how decay in the wild leads to growth. It seems to fit with the things I'm thinking about.

There's no noise but the sea hitting the rocks with a gentle rhythm. Lisa has found something under the next boulder and sticks her nose and paws further and further down. It turns out to be a tiny rabbit. She stands patiently waiting for it to come out. On the walk back, a brown owl flies up and then sits on a rock close by. A goat jumps out of a tree.

Beyond the power plant with the redundant solar panels is a track to the helicopter pad and the desalination facility and the rubbish dump. But I notice a pile of stones poking up on top of the hill and find remains of an ancient fortification in a strategic position looking west. The rough boulders give little away but the lines where they meet were cut very straight; maybe it's fanciful but I see a connection with the way they build the walls here today. Seagulls sit on them, facing out to sea.

I scramble down to a beach with rich red, orange and pink rocks, and broken glass. I examine translucent white pebbles and tiny shells. The sun will soon go behind the hill, and the rippling sea is dark blue, the islands across the way mostly in shadow, boats coming and going.

We're hidden in this cove listening to waves. Every day I think I could leave, and at a moment like this I decide to stay.

The mini-market was closed the first time I came, but I realise now that the family live in a house to the rear and they only open when they have a customer. They don't have dog food so we discuss alternatives; then I mention the lime kiln I found. The man says, 'Once all the bays here had a kiln, and the wooden caiques would come by and take the lime to sell. It's the same on all the islands.'

The young teenage girl sitting in front of the shop, playing with her phone, asks why I like living in Greece. I mention liking nature and not too many houses and cars, the opportunity to live by the sea.

'You see?' her mother tells her. 'There's nowhere better than this. Here we have the oxygen from the sea…'

'But I've never been anywhere,' says, the girl, smiling wistfully, sensing already the freedom that may be hers in a few years. 'I want to see other places.'

That evening I meet Stephanos, who has a white beard and peaked cap and gold chains around his neck and wrists and is usually pottering around the small boats in the harbour. He confirms there are ten lime kilns around the island – he counts them on his fingers. He grew up on Arki, left at fifteen for Athens and then worked on ships and went around the world. He moved back in the mid-1980s and has been here ever since. Life was difficult here in the 1980s, he says, with no electricity or drinking water. It's better now.

Stephanos says most people don't drink the desalinated water from the tap here but it has been tested and is fine – though he'd recommend boiling it. I explain why I avoid buying plastic bottles of water and he says on Lipsi they have a proper, functioning recycling plant. He invites me to come and drink homemade tsipouro with him one day.

'If you need something, just ask. We are Greeks here. Real Greeks.'

On a foray to Lipsi for cash and dog food, I walk around the harbour to the petrol station that sells local cheese and I meet a skinny, grey-bearded man who calls himself Moon. He's painting a fishing boat and tells me he lived for twenty years in America. He says he used to drive fresh fish from Florida to Ohio – Greek types of fish and lobster from Key West, that they'd put in saltwater, to taste more 'Greek', then sell to the Greek community. He got used to making the drive in eighteen hours, the speeding tickets eating into his profits, until they took his licence away in the late eighties. 'I was coming back to Greece anyway.' Now, he does repairs and sleeps on the boat, listening to the sound of sea on wood.

Another day, I go to Agathonisi. The little port seems very organised with its solar-powered streetlights and big road signs. A woman tells me she grew up in Athens but her family gradually moved back to the island, and now her husband runs a taverna and they have rooms and a shop. There are barely 180 inhabitants in winter but she says life is good here. Up the hill, I find a vegetable garden with oars and pipes used as fence posts, the rural cobbling together of crates and goat skulls, make-do-and-mend farming. It gives these islands their character; just as the old houses, when the plaster falls off, reveal the spirit of the place in their stones.

The stocky fair-haired boy who I've seen mending nets on a fishing boat delivers a bag of fish to the skinny, caramel-skinned teenager with the shy hazel eyes at the taverna and, in a serious voice, tells him to weigh them. It's a lovely moment, the new generation practising their roles.

An English couple on a boat have kindly offered to look after Lisa today while I walk to the old Italian jail in the north of the island. I walk up the hill, passing through the goat-fence, and look down at the undulating hills with the humps of green mastic bushes and the soft, feathery golden grasses. There are dogs barking, wind blowing from the northwest, and the bells of goats all around.

I pass through a gate to an area of bare rocks, goat dung and bright yellow thistles. Soon I can see much of the archipelago. I come to a large stand of olive trees, close-cropped spiky bushes giving way to leaves and fruits higher up. The other day I found something similar on the hillside over Tiganakia and was told they were wild olive, *agrielia*. Sometimes fruit-bearing varieties are grafted on to the rootstock of the wild olive, in order to be hardier. The olive trees here are said to be very old, the remains of what were once significant groves – perhaps the most important crop once on this waterless island. Though as on other waterless islands, cisterns were used until recently for collecting rainwater, if it rained.

Further away from the goat farm, the hill becomes greener. There's an enclosure surrounded by a stone wall with a stone trough, the remains of stone barn walls and wooden beams, then a huge threshing circle, ten paces across, with a floor of flat rocks.

Ahead, at the tip of the island, the old Italian building is surrounded by mastic, thyme and sage, cistus and wild olive, with blue-green juniper down towards the coast. It stands tall but collapsing and melancholy. There were once decorative touches around the door and the roof. To the front, a spiral staircase winds up inside a cylindrical tower, suggesting a lookout post with views out to sea to the west, north and south. The red brick frames around the large windows and doors are now empty. In the half-dozen narrow rooms on the ground floor, the walls are painted and covered with graffiti, names and dates. Some of it is scratched into the plaster from as recently as 2018, while more elegant handwriting dates back to 1951. There are no bars on the windows, but strange iron hooks in the walls, plastic sacks stuffed into holes. Concrete sinks have fallen to expose stone walls. Ceilings reveal rusted iron bars. The floors are soft with goat dung.

I make my way down the hillside to a narrow scrap of beach on a little turquoise bay, then back to the farm where the female goats are heavy with milk. A cockerel crows and two pigs lie contentedly in the shade.

At dusk, a few children play football in the square by the harbour. Lisa lies stretched out, an eye open for cats. I drink my ouzo and write notes before ordering dinner. I draw out my final evening as long as possible. By the time I eat, it's dark and the tables are busy. Suddenly the lights flicker and go out and the music cuts out too. There's laughter as everyone realises it's a power failure.

The women from the taverna come out a few minutes later with lanterns – they used to have blackouts every other day when the island had only one generator – but everyone declines. Conversation turns to quiet murmuring as we look up at the stars.

REFUGE

TILOS

It is summer on Tilos, and afternoon has turned the abandoned wheat fields golden. There's the breathy whistle of bee-eaters as I pick my way down the path, Lisa eagerly pulling on the lead. A harmless black whip snake disappears into the rocks. I let Lisa cool off in the water first, then from the grey pebble beach I swim with a mask, seeing a painted comber – a zebra-striped fish with yellow fan-tail and a blush of blue underneath – and armoured grey parrotfish.

If winter is a time for long walks, summer is for long swims. When the sun is baking hot, it's essential to dive into the sea's soothing, silky coolness. The summer months warm the water, making it easier to keep going until my muscles ache, explore around the headlands, scare myself looking down to rocks dropping away into the depths. I also love the pure pleasure of lying on an empty beach and listening to the waves, drowsy from swimming, falling asleep. There's something sensual about lying on warm sand, like being pressed against a body.

Gliding into shore, I notice an old stone structure, circular with tall walls, rocks loosely fitted together, some of them scattered. Barefoot, I carefully clamber over to look inside: washed-in rubbish, a firm base and cracked mud. So many beaches have ruins from earlier times. At dusk I prepare to camp, alone with the drystone walls of goat pens, sunset light on the headland softening its rugged rock and garrigue. The sky turns yellow-pink and pale blue, the air cooler. There's the occasional butterfly, the smell of wet dog (mine), and the sound of the sea. Gradually the moonlight becomes more intense, casting shadows, infusing the night sky. I'm in a deep sleep when Lisa howls at a goat approaching. She's not always a great camping companion but she does keep guard. I see brilliant star-like phosphorescence when I run my hands through the waves.

This beach is warmed early by the sun – enough for a swim. There's soon a heat and humidity haze, a flicker of birds taking off in the distance. It's utterly peaceful but the flies are biting. After packing up, I follow a narrow path around the rocks to a sheltered cove with shallow water and pink-and-white pebbles, beautiful despite the plastic rubbish that has washed in and accumulated, untouched, over who knows how many winters. Here too are bleached driftwood and seagrass, dragonflies flitting and fish jumping from the still water. A series of short high whistles comes from a bird up above somewhere, the buzz of a hornet, the chug of a fishing boat.

Heading up the hillside, Lisa veers off the path to bury a bit of long-dead goat she's found, and thanks to the detour I discover a stone wall with two intact doorways leading to animal pens in deep caves.

When my three days in Olympos turned into a year and a half, I gave up the house I had been renting for three years in Megalo Horio on Tilos. When I returned, it had been promised to someone else. For a few days I stayed there again, felt the old wooden floorboards beneath my feet, and realised that I'd lost something by giving it up. I had made the most of my freedom, but I'd also learned something about abandoning a place that felt like home.

I rented a temporary place by the sea in the newer village of Livadia. At first, after the apotheosis of wild abandon in north Karpathos, it felt strangely tame and almost urban. But Tilos accepted me back gently. I fell asleep to the sound of the waves and woke to the sunrise. Greek and Syrian children would ride their bikes up and down the seafront.

While so many places closed their doors to refugees, Tilos had welcomed them since 2014 (and earlier) and finally invited them to stay more permanently. Tilos, like several islands, didn't even have its own doctor, but in 2017 the island offered fifty Syrian refugees the opportunity to live here and find work, even if the homes were only Portakabins in an abandoned army camp. In the long term, Tilos is not a place where they can build a new life and people were gradually finding a way to move on. But at least it was a refuge for a while.

This small community on the edge of Europe includes people from more than twenty countries. Some came for work, some for an escape from work. A quarter of the children in the school are not Greek by birth. Without foreigners settling, the population would dwindle dangerously low, and there wouldn't be enough of a market for the farmers to keep working the land. Perhaps the future lies in embracing outsiders and melding the old culture with the new. The local people may have given up many of the old ways, but they welcome all to join in the traditional dances that go on and on into the night.

In the height of summer, even remote beaches can be invaded by a jet-ski or kite-surfer, toys and noise. Some of the visitors are the children and grandchildren of those who grew up here, staying in family property, coming back for the festivals. High on a dark hillside, people gather on a religious feast day to eat and drink and dance to traditional songs. The food is goat in tomato sauce, served with potatoes and cooked in great vats over olive-wood fire. The first dance often begins with an elderly man, red headscarf in hand, leading a few ladies in a circle around the dance floor. As the evening progresses, the line of dancers includes people of all ages from young children to those in their eighties and nineties, who know the often complex, subtle steps, exactly which way to hold your hand and foot and who is allowed to lead a certain dance. The folk songs tell of a way of life almost gone, but the dancing is a skill that has not been lost.

Though so much land on the hills has been abandoned, there are still people growing crops and keeping animals on Tilos. The farmers from the Eristos valley sell their produce from the backs of trucks in Livadia square. Michalis, in his eighties, is out in the fields every day. Dina, who has run a taverna in Megalo Horio since the 1990s, is up at six to look after her goats, sheep and chickens, and at the field with her husband in the evening. Hippocrates is in his nineties and still zealously planting olive trees.

Rena runs the shop in Megalo Horio but is often at her smallholding at sundown. She says the old people in the village are still sharp-witted because they grew up eating well. 'People would eat a small amount of meat and keep the rest preserved cold in a well. For sweets they had dried figs with an almond inside and sesame on top, or raisins with cinnamon. They'd dry tomatoes by slicing them and sprinkling sea salt on them and leaving them in the sun, to make sauce in the winter.'

We're talking in her shop, and when someone comes up to the cash register with a bag of crisps and a couple of packaged crème-filled factory croissants, she grasps the money without flinching. Business is business.

Before air conditioning and electric fans, Tilos islanders slept on their roofs in the hottest months. Ever since I moved here I've spent some of the summer sleeping outside in the natural cool of the night. It got me used to waking with the sunrise.

In summer, the village is noisy until late at night with children and cats and television, everyone living outside, but it's an easy walk over the mountain with my friend. My body and mind relax as I swim then doze, put up the tent, have a last cooling swim as the sun goes down. It's a perfect evening to lie on the fine pebbles, drink a little red wine and make gentle inroads into the picnic, talking quietly.

The feeling of lying on a wild beach, looking and listening to earth and sea and sky, is completely different from being on a developed beach with buildings and people and roads. I'm so grateful to be able to find places like this, even in summer. We feel alone, cut off from the world – the faint shape of an island on the horizon but few ships passing. Birds flit from one cliff to the other. I contemplate the rocks: wrinkled red, copper green and smoky blue, flesh-coloured cliffs mottled and pricked with caves.

It seems hours before dusk begins to fall – a slow, lingering evening. The stars appear, brighten and multiply. When I wade into the sea, it's as if there are fireflies caught in the waves. I hear a strange noise in the tent; a big mouse has got itself trapped and we help it find its way out. I go to bed and zip up, keeping Lisa inside to stop her barking at goats, and sleep deeply, waking to calm and clouds of mist. In the early morning, goats come down to the rocks by the water's edge to drink. Later, I take my mask and snorkel and dive into the sea.

There's something a little zen about snorkelling. You swim with no expectations. Sometimes all I see are different patterns in the sand on the seabed, long lines created by currents, or the shapes of the rocks. You need patience. If you get into the habit of looking, sometimes you see things.

A long, thin fish with a tail like an electric-blue needle stares up at me with round eyes as it hangs, alert; pale blue, it changes colour to camouflage itself, and kinks its body to dart away. The lionfish – an invasive species that entered the Mediterranean via the Suez Canal or in ships' ballast – spreads its heavily ornate, venomous spines around its body like a show of feathers. A cuttlefish watches me warily with huge eyes, using tentacles to adjust its position, both of us treading water until it billows its diaphanous silvery wings like a cloak and shoots away.

A moray eel, its beautiful, mottled, yellow and brown body flowing ribbon-like in and out of the rocks, freezes in an S-shape when it sees me, points its narrow grey snout towards me and shows its teeth, then ripples away, slinking under a rock. A mullet with its long white moustache-like barbs rummages messily in the sand, and a mottled grey flat fish follows it – a flounder, here called glossa or tongue. Sea anemones wave their soft orange hair. Dark brown crabs with yellow spots on the joints of their legs lie flat on the rocks.

When I first started to watch the wildlife underwater it was with a friend who dived down to put a starfish or an octopus in my hands so I could feel them. Now, I've learned to spot an octopus nest myself. I find an octopus clinging to a rock, puffing itself up when I dive too close, curling and unfurling tentacles to move from rock to rock before turning into a two-pronged torpedo and shooting away.

In a fold of a hillside above Eristos bay, an old chapel is hidden, hunkered to the ground and falling apart, so the subtle artwork just surviving inside is a surprise. An arch is painted with black and red triangles enclosing flower-like swirls. The alcove has bearded saints in chequered robes and golden sashes, reading from scrolls. The eyes have been scratched out, most likely during the Ottoman rule by Muslims who opposed religious icons. Around it stand three houses built later, in the early twentieth century. They appear to have been flimsily constructed using cheap materials, the roofs fallen in.

In the late 1880s, the Bents were told that Tilos was full of lepers. The disease had spread from the East and Egypt to the Dodecanese – though people would always deny that it was present in their own village. The 'decayed men' hid in dark corners of their houses so they wouldn't be taken away from their families, as the bishop of Rhodes and the government wanted to remove them to hospitals. Eventually, the people with leprosy were isolated in these buildings. There was no doctor, but the families helped as much as they could.

During World War II, according to one account, German troops were threatening to kill the remaining inhabitants of Megalo Horio in retaliation for their harbouring a Cretan commando who had attacked German soldiers. An Italian officer called Luca Dogliani, who had escaped from Rhodes and was being hidden and fed at Ayios Antonis, pretended to be Greek and told the commander that it was dangerous to search Megalo Horio because the leprosy patients had escaped to find refuge with relatives. The Germans left, and the village was saved.

Another story recounts an incident when some lepers, poor and without shoes, took the boots from the feet of dead German soldiers. When the rest of the German troops discovered what had happened, they came to these buildings at Eristos, and shot and killed the guilty. By the time the war ended, there were no more leprosy patients here, and the place was abandoned.

On Pserimos, one of the smallest inhabited islands in the Dodecanese, half a church stands on a cliff above sand scattered with seagrass.

I found it one day when evading the day trippers that pour into the little island's main harbour from neighbouring Kos and Kalymnos.

I followed an indistinct path over the hills of thyme bushes, until a shallow bay appeared: blue sea with glittering ripples, a thin strip of pale beach, low red cliffs and half a whitewashed church, the remainder having fallen into the sea years ago. Its roof was bare, the tiles lost. The empty windows were frames for the sea. Looking up from the sand where only birds had left their prints, I saw broken plaster, a wooden screen with faded paint and a framed notice that no-one could read any more. Nearby was an old stone cistern, and carved old marble column bases, maybe early Christian. The church from just a few decades ago was now gradually being broken and reclaimed by nature. Yet fresh goatskins hung to dry on a fence.

I'm reminded of it when I read Geoff Dyer's description of a work of art on the landscape in *White Sands*: 'it was lovely in a subdued and desolate way. It felt abandoned but it was not a place of abandoned meaning'.

My reaction to these deserted places is emotional; I am moved by their beauty. But is there also a meaning, a message?

One thing is certain: I long for things to be left this way.

The Meteora, on the Greek mainland, are monasteries built on the tops of huge rocks, once places of refuge where monks sought to escape the world and be closer to God. In those days they were reached by arduous and dangerous methods. Now they are accessed by tarmacked roads with coach parks for the tourists. The experience has been packaged, tidied up and commodified, and the sense of refuge from the world has been destroyed. I've heard rumours that Eleousa will be made into a museum, and maybe it should be; but I'm glad I experienced the village the way I did. I hope they never finish that road to Tristomo.

Things will continue to evolve, and maybe we're at a turning point. On a later trip to Nisyros, I found that cement had been laid around the abandoned harbour, and a handful of people were making the most of the tranquillity; I also learned that since I last visited, the permanent population of Emborio was down to ten, as some inhabitants had died and others moved away. I learned of more abandoned places to be explored, including an Italian factory that once made matches with the volcanic sulphur. More cave-houses had been restored, part of what was once a dirt track had been paved, and an old man was repairing a cistern to provide water for his crops.

What's important is that we need quiet, untamed places away from the modern world, places free of greedy commercial impulse, deserted places; places that allow for a break in the cycle, a hiatus, breathing space, solitude, quiet, calm, escape. Wildlife also needs them. When one day I am swimming at a hidden cove and a cormorant flies out of the sea, I feel slightly guilty for invading its place.

And people need to be able to find refuge.

Of course, I'm in favour of freedom of movement. That's been my life so far, learning from living in different places. When I lived in Canada, there was some fuss about there being too many immigrants from Jamaica. Meanwhile, most Canadians wanted a holiday in Jamaica to escape the winter. I thought we should all be allowed to swap countries for several years, so that Jamaicans could have steady, well-paying jobs and no crime, and Canadians could live somewhere warm and colourful and learn to dance in a really sexy way.

And it's a bit like that with the Greek Australians and Greek Americans I've met on this journey. People need different kinds of sanctuary and opportunity at different times. Those who left have also kept the spirit of the Dodecanese alive. Every March the Federation of Dodecanese Societies USA celebrates the islands' unification with Greece. In Astoria, New York, in a Greek Orthodox church they remember those who fought for the islands' freedom. These families proudly continue their Dodecanese cultural heritage through dance, language and food, generations after they left.

Tranquillity is priceless. When I'm in busy parts of the world, the roar of traffic is overpowering to me and I yearn for deserted places. I'm horrified when I see a village in the south of England with no fields left around it – they are all being filled in with new houses. The only place people can still walk their dogs is the abandoned railway embankment. Something left behind has become a refuge there, too. Don't let everywhere become the same, so there's nowhere to escape.

While I'm musing over the down-to-earth place names of the Dodecanese – 'Fields', 'Upper Places', 'Big Village', 'Wells' – I recall that in the village where I grew up, no-one called the pubs by their names. They were the Top House and the Bottom House, and the open hillside accessed from the bottom of the garden was Down the Back. Do the high grazing lands on these islands remind me of the hills on the edge of the moor in the South Pennines where I grew up, with its drystone walls, stone cottages, animals? Saddleworth had once thrived on cotton-weaving, an industry abandoned. Summer was punctuated by local cultural festivals. When I lived there, the area was already becoming a place to visit, the canals being revived, some of the mills turned into craft centres. But in *The Moor* by William Atkins, his chapter on Saddleworth Moor tells of farmhouses where 'the yards were scattered with building waste and rusting JCBs, the concrete driveways cracked, the gardens overgrown…' He writes of flagstones prised from the floors of derelict mills to form a path across wet terrain, a ruined inn's cellar being used for sheep. It sounds familiar. Maybe this quest for abandoned places has its roots partly in the home we had to leave when I was seventeen. My dad's job moved to the south of England and so, like the islanders, our family moved with the work. I'm now back in the wild, with hills on my doorstep.

Away from the islands, my body becomes impatient to swim after just a few weeks. I like to feel strong, the ache of muscles after a long hike. When I walk out the door and into nature, thoughts can play or settle in my mind because there is no modern stimulus, no advertising or entertainment, no-one telling or selling me anything. Just space, and the poetry of the landscape: the ruined farm buildings that are like old friends, the light on a cliff, the shades of sea and sky.

In the year after returning to Tilos, I decide it's time to have a home here. I sell my flat in England and find a house for myself in one of the quietest parts of the island.

It was empty for five years after the elderly owners moved closer to their children and hospitals. It's near the sea in a quiet place, with a garden overgrown with fig trees and vines, where Lisa can run free. At one point during the purchase process, I cannot get a large bank draft without a signed contract for the property, and yet I cannot have a signed contract without that bank draft. It's perplexing and I say to my lawyer Maria that this rule makes no sense, it's impossible… She gives me a wry smile and says, 'Why do you think all these places got abandoned?'

But she finds a way around it, and I move in to my island house. The owner has agreed to leave everything in it, so I have an abundance of things from decades past, as well as pots that might have been made a hundred years ago, and a large piece of ancient masonry. The intense heat of summer has passed and the tall white sea squills are in blossom.

By late October, most hotels and restaurants are closed. The island is semi-deserted again. One grey morning, prompted by an infestation of fat flies, I am cutting back an overgrown vine on my terrace when the first drops of rain begin to fall. The sea is glassy calm, the only sounds the birds and the occasional fishing boat or a farmer calling out to his goats. The next day, the rain falls properly, with dark clouds and thunder, water gushing off the roof and the leaves. With the rain comes the incense smell of herbs on the hillside – oregano, sage and thyme – and the spicy smell of grasses. In late afternoon it stops for a while and Lisa and I walk up the footpath to the monastery. The wet has deepened all the colours, and the sea is pale and gleaming. The day after that, an eight-Beaufort wind has blown away the clouds, the sky is bright and the waves loudly crashing into shore. It's going to be a wild winter.

DODECANESE HISTORY:
SOME KEY DATES

395AD   The Roman Empire splits; the islands become part of the Byzantine Empire

1309   The Knights Hospitaller, or Knights of St John, capture Rhodes and take over most of the Dodecanese

1522   The Ottoman Turks, under Suleiman the Magnificent, oust the Knights; under Turkish rule most of the Dodecanese become 'Privileged Islands'

1822   Most of the islands join the Greek War of Independence

1830   Under the London Protocol the Dodecanese are excluded from the new Greek state, and remain part of the Ottoman Empire

1860s   A wave of emigration from the Dodecanese

1865   The diving suit is introduced to the sponge islands, leading to widespread disability and death among the diving communities

1908   The 'Young Turk' revolution; removal of the islands' privileges

1911   Italy declares war on Turkey

1912   Italy defeats Turkey on Rhodes and takes over the islands (except Kastellorizo). The islands declare autonomy as 'State of the Aegean'

1919–22   Greco-Turkish War

1921   Italy occupies Kastellorizo

1922   Greek defeat in Asia Minor with Turkish occupation of Smyrna; Mussolini comes to power in Italy

1923	The Treaty of Lausanne, ending the Greco-Turkish War, consolidates Italian presence in the Dodecanese and leads to a population exchange between Greece and Turkey – 1.6 million people are made refugees
1923–36	'Italianisation' leads to 16,700 Italians being resettled in the Dodecanese, mostly on Rhodes and Leros
1940	Italy invades Greece
1941	Germany invades Greece
1943	Italy surrenders to the Allies; Germany assumes control of Greece
1944	The Jewish population is forced to leave Rhodes and Kos
1945	Germany surrenders the Dodecanese to the British
1946–49	Greek Civil War
1947–48	The Dodecanese are liberated and reunited with Greece
1967–74	Greek military Junta, or Regime of the Colonels
1970s	Tourists begin to arrive
2009	The Greek government-debt crisis begins
2011	The Syrian civil war begins, leading to refugees arriving in the Dodecanese

RESOURCES AND
FURTHER READING

I'd like to acknowledge with thanks the following sources, which I found useful during my research.

BOOKS

The Dodecanese: Further Travels Among the Insular Greeks – Selected Writings of J. Theodore & Mabel V.A. Bent, 1885–1888 edited by Gerald Brisch, Oxford 2015
Tales from a Greek Island Roger Jinkinson
Ta Paidia tou Patriarchi Iakovos Kypriotis
Martoni's Pilgrimage 1394 translated by John Mole
Tilos in the Past Vangelis Papadopoulos
Villa of Secrets Patricia Wilson

WEBSITES/BLOGS

w amandasettle.com
w archipelago.gr
w astypalaia.com
w barrysramblings.com
w discoveringkos.com
w secretrhodes.gr

ARTICLES

Brian Kaller, 'Burning the Bones of the Earth: Lime Kilns' in **w** solar.lowtechmagazine.com (September 2013)

David Sutton, 'Explosive Debates: Dynamite, Tradition, and the State', *Anthropological Quarterly* Vol. 69, No. 2 (April 1996)

M. Zotos, 'The red castle of Castellorizo', *WIT Transactions on The Built Environment*, Vol. 143 (2014, **w** witpress.com)

WHAT WE LEAVE BEHIND

While much of the plastic detritus that washes up on Dodecanese beaches does not come from the islands themselves, the quality of what we leave behind on the landscape changed dramatically in the last few decades and there have been few regulations or resources to deal with it. Waste disposal, along with water and healthcare, are some of the biggest challenges facing these islands, but this is beginning to change. Tilos was designated a 'green island' for having introduced solar and wind power and, at time of this book going to press, recycling bins have been installed on the island, with a system in place to transport recyclable waste to a mainland facility.

Living on a small island makes me careful about what I buy. Cafés and restaurants on some islands are happy to provide carafes of water. We can also buy local, seasonal food and natural products with as little plastic packaging as possible, or reuseable packaging, and bring reusable bags when shopping. I have found local natural sponges an effective alternative to synthetic ones, and they last longer; I also like the local skincare products made from olive oil, beeswax and herbs, sold in glass jars. I order bamboo toothbrushes, wooden hair combs and natural brushes for household cleaning from British website &Keep (w andkeep.com), which delivers in eco-friendly packaging. Let's keep the islands beautiful.

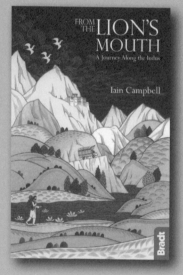

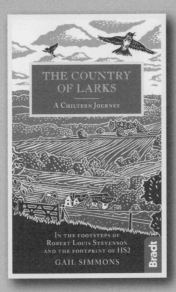